Best Dog Hikes
Southern California

Best Dog Hikes
Southern California

Linda B. Mullally
and
David S. Mullally

FALCONGUIDES

GUILFORD, CONNECTICUT
HELENA, MONTANA

FALCONGUIDES®

An imprint of Rowman & Littlefield

Falcon, FalconGuides, and Make Adventure Your Story are registered trademarks of Rowman & Littlefield.

Distributed by NATIONAL BOOK NETWORK
Copyright © 2016 by Rowman & Littlefield

All photos by David S. Mullally

Maps: Alena Pearce © Rowman & Littlefield

British Library Cataloguing-in-Publication Information available

Library of Congress Cataloging-in-Publication Data
Names: Mullally, Linda B. | Mullally, David S.
Title: Best dog hikes Southern California / Linda S. Mullally and David B. Mullally.
Description: Guilford, Connecticut : FalconGuides, 2016. | Includes index.
Identifiers: LCCN 2016023562 (print) | LCCN 2016031004 (ebook) | ISBN 9781493017942 (pbk.) | ISBN 9781493017959 ()
Subjects: LCSH: Hiking with dogs—California, Southern—Guidebooks. | Trails—California, Southern—Guidebooks. | California, Southern—Guidebooks.
Classification: LCC SF427.455 M834 2016 (print) | LCC SF427.455 (ebook) | DDC 796.5109794/9—dc23
LC record available at https://lccn.loc.gov/2016023562

∞™ The paper used in this publication meets the minimum requirements of American National Standard for Information Sciences—Permanence of Paper for Printed Library Materials, ANSI/NISO Z39.48-1992.

Dedicated to Gem, our sweet, enthusiastic Siberian husky, who joined our pack in time for the last of the Southern California adventures. Her youthful, bouncy nature has given Gypsy renewed spark in his senior years and added bushels of joy to our life at home and on the trail.

Another perfect pooch day at Long Lake

Contents

The Hikes

Big Sur Coast

San Luis Obispo County

Santa Barbara County

Ventura County

Overview

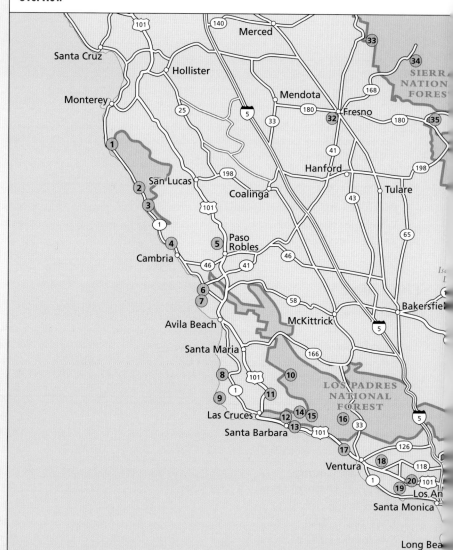

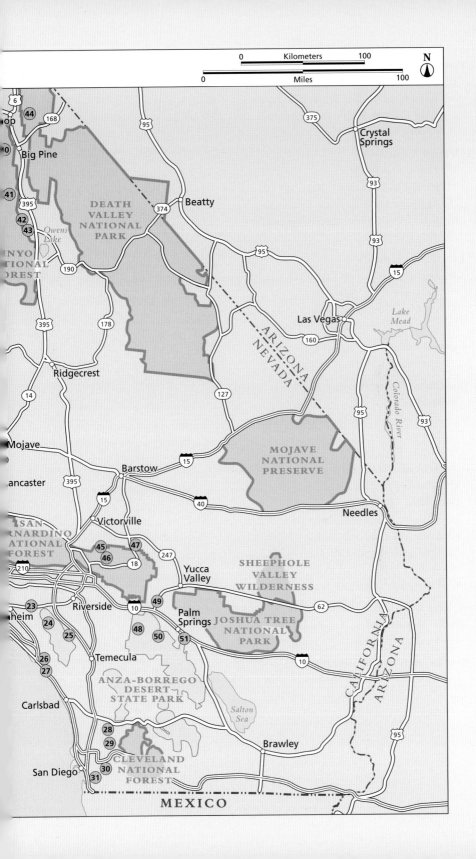

Los Angeles County

Orange County

San Diego County

Central Valley

Southern Sierra Nevada
West Side

East Side

White Mountains

San Bernardino Mountains

Riverside County

Map Legend

Municipal

≡⟨5⟩≡ Interstate Highway

≡⟨101⟩≡ US Highway

≡⟨126⟩≡ State Road

═══ Local/County Road

══ ══ Unpaved Road

⊢──⊣ Tunnel

⊢─┼─⊣ Railroad

━ ·· ━ ·· Country Border

━ ── ━ State Border

Trails

------ Featured Trail

- - - - - - Trail

────── Paved Trail/Bike Path

↗ Trail Direction Arrows

Water Features

⬭ Body of Water

∿ River/Creek

≋ Waterfall

Land Management

National Park/Forest

State/County Park

Sand

Symbols

▲ Backcountry Campground

▬ Bench

◣ Boat Ramp

⌣⌢ Bridge

■ Building/Point of Interest

⩍ Campground

━ Dam

🗑 Garbage

❗ Gate

⚲ Lighthouse

🅿 Parking

⌣⌢ Pass

▲ Peak/Mountain

🛆 Picnic Area

🛈 Ranger Station

♻ Recycling

🚻 Restroom

◀ Scenic View/Lookout

‖‖‖ Steps/Boardwalk

☎ Telephone

🗼 Tower

○ Town

⟨20⟩ Trailhead

❓ Visitor/Information Center

🚰 Water

Acknowledgments

It may not have taken a village to put together the best dog hikes of Southern California, but it would not have been as pleasurable an adventure without the enthusiastic support and responsiveness of all the public land employees and volunteers we approached for input during the course of the year we spent exploring Southern California trails. It's an understatement to call road traffic in Southern California a frustrating experience. But the warm reception we received, from rangers and park administrators to business owners and local residents, when we approached them to talk about all that is canine including hiking, lodging, eating, and playing was friendlier and more open than we could have imagined.

Several public land agency representatives shared their expertise and answered our questions about the local ecology as well as future plans for expanding trails.

Thank you to Ranger Jamie Neville and Ranger Pattie in the Sierra National Forest, as well as silviculturist Dave Smith in the Bass Lake District. Carlos Mendoza and Elise McMillen helped us discover Fiscalini Ranch's amazing open space in Cambria. Shawn Cooper, senior planner with the San Luis Obispo County Parks and Bob Jones Trail project manager, was eager to answer our questions about the future of the trail expansion. Ranger Larry at the Monterey District for Los Padres National Forest personally researched additional resources on dog policy for Sand Dollar and Pfeiffer Beaches.

Our gratitude to recreation officers Bob Frenes in Kernville and David Kotlarski at Big Bear Lake for taking time out of their busy schedules to meet with us. Ranger Jim in Santa Barbara helped us navigate the different land management arms for the Front Country hikes in the Los Padres National Forest. We are grateful to Ranger Ann Boggess at La Purisima Mission State Historic Park for her trail recommendations. Whether it was the Sierra Nevada's Mount Whitney Ranger Station and Visitor Center or the State Beach Parks Department, we found dog lovers eager to assist with *Best Dog Hikes Southern California*.

If a picture is worth a thousand words, we owe a special note of gratitude to the owners of all the photogenic pooches who wagged their way in front of the camera on so many of the trails.

Doodle does the desert on Homme-Adams Trail.

As dog owners and dog-loving hikers, the health and safety of four-legged furry family members and trail pals are of utmost importance. We feel privileged to have the continued generous cooperation of Dr. George Bishop, our family veterinarian of thirty years, as a resource for veterinary wisdom and first-aid on the trail.

Gem gives special thank-you wags to her friend and trainer, Andee Burleigh, CPDT-KA (Certified Professional Dog Trainer-Knowledge Assessed) for all the praises, not to mention tasty morsels, that helped her learn the good manners she practices on the trail as a role model for the fellow canine hikers she meets.

Last but not least, a heartfelt thank you to Sherri Del Pozo for bringing David, Gypsy, and me together with Gem, the eleven-month-old husky that joined our pack for the last twenty hikes of this book. We look forward to miles of trail and travel with her at our side. Gem was a born cover girl, who quickly became a jewel of a hiking companion.

In stride to Treasure Lakes

Introduction

The song "California Dreamin'," sang by the Beach Boys in 1989, never ceases to make people from all over the world sigh and long for a piece of the Golden State. From Fido's point of view, there's much to wag and bark about for dogs dreaming of California. There's a reason the third-largest state in the union is also the most populous. The diverse climate and geography, from beach and valleys to mountains and deserts, offers year-round hiking to suit every taste and caliber of hiker and their dog. The moisture-loving giant redwood and sequoia tree habitats at the northernmost boundary of the Southern California region covered in this book are a sharp contrast to the Mojave and Sonoran desert landscape of the southernmost region. At the heart of Southern California, you can travel between the highest point (Mount Whitney, 14,494 feet) and the lowest point (Death Valley, 282 feet below sea level) in the contiguous states in one day.

Although the Gold Rush of the mid 1800s may be the root of California's nickname, brilliant gold poppy as the state flower, the wild and rare golden trout, and an abundance of sunshine are reasons enough to know it as the Golden State.

The grizzly bear on the state flag, alas, is just a memory. Once considered a threat, grizzlies, like wolves, were hunted to extinction. Coincidentally, the last grizzly in Southern California was killed in 1908 near the Holy Jim Trail described in this book. Different habitat needs and their ability to coexist with humans saved the acorn- and berry-eating black bears.

The Native American, Mexican, and Spanish legacies—with even a trace of Russian heritage from the colonization of 1812 to 1842 on the North Coast—give California its unique flavor.

California was under Spanish rule from 1769 to 1821, when it became the property of Mexico. Monterey was actually the first capital of what was then Alta California from 1777 to 1846 under both Spanish and Mexican rule. Sacramento, the oldest incorporated city in California, did not become the official and permanent capital until 1879.

In 1846, settlers who had long been disenchanted with the Mexican government rebelled and formed the Republic of California. In the meantime the United States was at war with Mexico, and Californians supported their American neighbors. The armed combat lasted two years, and in 1848, when the US military stood at the gates of Mexico City, negotiations resulted in the Treaty of Guadalupe Hidalgo, which gave the United States much of the southwestern and western territories, including what is now California. Nine days after the signing of the 1848 treaty, gold was discovered in Sutter Mill, Coloma, in the foothills of the Sierra Nevada.

Back then, territories needed to have at least 60,000 habitants before they could have statehood status. California's population was sparse, but the news of gold in the area sparked a feverish emigration of 60,000 from around the world just in a few months. There was heated debate between the advocates for California as a slave state and those in support of a "free-soil" state. In 1850, California, rich in natural beauty and resources, became the thirty-first state and free of slavery.

It is a land whose rugged and poetic beauty is born of tumultuous geological events. It sits on the ring of fire where continental-plate grinding, volcanoes, and glaciers have sculpted a supernatural landscape between the Pacific Ocean and the Mojave Desert with a centerpiece of mountain ranges. The climate varies from Mediterranean to subarctic, which makes for diversity in vegetation and hiking ecosystems. Living on the Monterey Peninsula for the last thirty-three years, our pack, including my husband David, two spirited coyote/husky hybrids, a senior Queensland terrier rescue, and several furry trail pals borrowed from friends, spent most of our time exploring Central and Northern California trails with occasional forays into Southern California.

Best Dog Hikes Southern California was a welcome opportunity to better acquaint ourselves with the southern half's best dog-friendly jaunts and haunts. Some people need the ebb and flow of the ocean tides to feel alive, while others only breathe when cradled by the majesty of the mountains or warmth of the desert sun. Southern California serves an expansive eco menu for all tastes.

Although Southern California is much more arid than its northern sister and primarily a combination biome of low and high deserts with chaparral vegetation, it has several mountain ranges with distinct characteristics within the elevation range from 500 feet to 11,503 feet (Mount Gorgonio). This book defines Southern California's boundaries from the southern end of Big Sur on the coast, south to San Diego across the Central Valley, with Bishop at the northern end of the eastern boundary, then southward along the Southern Sierra to the Coachella Valley in the Mojave/Sonoran Desert. This landscape is gifted with high country meadows and glacial lakes, wetlands to forested peaks, wild rivers and wilderness areas, a surprising number of canyon waterfalls, and microclimates reaching from its legendary sun-drenched, surf-lapped beaches to the majestic California fan palm–studded desert oases.

Southern California's glorious national parks mostly restrict dogs to the parking lots and campgrounds, but dogs continue to be welcome in national forests adjacent to national parks boasting beauty worthy of park status. National recreation areas, some state parks, and national monuments offer limited but precious opportunities for exploring trails with your dog. Southern California also has its fair share of Bureau of Land Management open space designated as multiuse, including dog-compatible hiking trails.

It is only fair to say that Southern California's desirable climate for those craving winter warmth is greatly responsible for its heavily populated coastal communities, and there is no denying that it suffers from chronic urban sprawl for several miles inland. On the upside, residents with furry family members have helped create dog-friendly communities with a demand and supply of regional, city, and county parks with miles of trails to assuage the symptoms of nature deficit disorder. These

KNOW YOUR PUBLIC LANDS AND THEIR "USE" POLICIES

National forests and Bureau of Land Management land (the most rugged of landscapes, found mostly in the western United States) are designated "multiple use," which may include lumber, livestock grazing, mining, and recreation with and without vehicles. Pets are allowed on trails under "voice control," but can be required to be on a 6-foot leash in the developed areas of national forests.

National monuments can be managed by any of three different agencies: the US Forest Service, the National Park Service, or the Bureau of Land Management. They are created by presidential proclamation to protect specific natural or cultural features. The rules about dogs on the trails vary depending on the monument.

National parks strive to preserve the integrity of the landscape and its historical and natural features for future generations, while offering some limited recreational activities. Except for service dogs that meet the ADA criteria, dogs are not allowed on trails. They are permitted in developed areas (campgrounds, picnic areas, and paved roads) but must be on a leash less than 6 feet long.

Feeding Wildlife Is Prohibited in Any Area! Animals can become unnaturally dependent on handouts. Some may become brazen and develop habits that make them dangerous to hikers and campers. Some wildlife can carry disease. Problem wildlife, whether it's a bear, a coyote, deer, or squirrel, don't get rehabilitated or relocated. They get destroyed. Roadside beggars eventually become roadkill.

communities have creature comforts of restaurants, hotels and motels, cabins, or campgrounds to which you and your four-legged companion can retreat at the end of a satisfying day on the trail.

If you are not already fascinated by the cultural and natural history of the land under your hiking boots, traveling and hiking around Southern California is sure to be an adventure of discovery for you and your canine companion. On many trails, you will walk in the footsteps of the original inhabitants, subsequent Spanish explorers, and early settlers seeking a better life through farming, cattle ranching, logging, and mining precious metals, including gold. The stunning scenery and soul-stirring subtleties will inspire you in much the same way they did those who first witnessed them and those who continue to fight to preserve them.

This book will introduce you to some of Southern California's best dog hikes in every season. Be a good guest and dog-owner ambassador and let your boots and paws touch the land with a gentle caress as you pass through plants' and animals' homes. The landscape and its wildlife will work their slow seduction on you and your pooch, sometimes with bold beauty and other times revealing subtle splendor.

Don't Leave Home Without Him

There is no better pal for the trail than a canine companion. When it comes to hiking, you and your dog share some benefits, but your differences are what enhance and complement your nature experience.

Hiking is an inexpensive opportunity for you and pooch to stay physically active and trim while sharing quality time in the absence of everyday distractions and demands. The natural stimulation of sights, sounds, and smells is a great way for both of you to decompress from the daily urban sensory irritation. You both will be calmer and more relaxed at the end of a day on the trail. Hiking makes for a happy dog. The sensory experiences in addition to the physical exertion burn that excess anxiety and energy that builds up in some dogs. The result is a furry family member that focuses more easily and is more responsive to cues for the skills he has or is developing through training or obedience classes.

You may be more enthralled than your dog by panoramic vistas, soothed by the gurgling of brooks, excited about the significance of the historical landmarks on the trail, or intrigued by the sight of an unusual bird or blooming flower. But the highlight of any dog lover's hike is witnessing the simple unbridled joy of his or her dog wagging, sniffing, sauntering up a stream, or splashing into a lake. No trail companion is as enthusiastic about snack breaks as your dog. No trail companion will follow you as faithfully and eagerly or demonstrate as much gratitude as your dog for taking him on an outdoor adventure.

Why You Have to Step Up Before Your Dog Steps Out

In a perfect world, off-leash dogs would never chase wildlife and cattle or stamp strangers' shirts with muddy paws. In this imaginary world, all dogs would be best friends without ever the hint of an impatient growl or an angry snarl, and all humans would be dog lovers. It would be a Nirvana where all dog owners would be fastidious about picking up and appropriately disposing of their dogs' waste and there would be poop fairies standing by to distribute doggie waste bags or do the job themselves in an emergency potty pick-up situation. Dog owners would never leave their adored pal alone in a strange hotel room or tied up unattended at their campsite. Beloved bow-wows would never be subjected to barking, whining, and howling in fear and loneliness, risking sending Fido into an uncharacteristic frenzy of destructive antics.

Alas, the real world is a different place. Consequently, when good dogs exhibit bad behavior caused by ignorant, inconsiderate, or neglectful dog owners, signs that read "No Dogs" begin to appear at trailheads, beaches, city parks, campgrounds, hotels, restaurants, shopping malls, and in places that you remember being "dog friendly." The message is invariably, "We used to welcome well-behaved dogs with responsible owners, but our patience and tolerance were tested one too many times. Sorry, dogs are no longer welcome." A few bad apples so spoil the barrel.

The ASPCA (American Society for the Prevention of Cruelty to Animals) reports that there are about 70-80 million dogs in the United States. In response to the increase in furry family members in American households over the last twenty years, there has been a trend toward more "dog-friendly" attitudes in businesses. But more dogs at home also means more dogs on trails. Public lands (state and federal), even those open for recreation, must protect wildlife habitat. Rangers will tell you that off-leash dogs that chase and harass wildlife are a problem. Even the scent of leashed dogs can change wildlife behavior and cause unwanted stress to the animals that must conserve energy for survival. Dog waste also contributes to spreading disease and making your dog more vulnerable to picking up parasites and other health hazards.

Dogs off leash also face other hazards in certain regions. It is not unusual for livestock to graze on public lands in the west, and a dog harassing cattle can be injured by kicking hooves or, worse yet, get shot by a rancher. In the Sierra, closer to pack stations that sometimes use poison to manage rodent infestation, a dog can get seriously ill or die from snacking on a dead mouse. Back in the late 1990s, after years of hiking

Obedience classes help practice good trail manners.

on voice control without issues in the Eastern Sierra, I learned the hard way when Shiloh, our female husky/coyote hybrid, fell for the irresistible bonanza of sniffing out something tasty off-trail. She survived excruciating pain and damage to her organs, after weeks of treatment including blood transfusions and subcutaneous saline hydration. We suffered the agony of fear of losing our beloved furry family member as Aunt Visa pumped out the cash to the tune of $7,000. The veterinarian determined her illness was most likely caused by eating a poisoned rodent. Daily medication, her will to live, and lots of TLC gave us two more precious years together.

More dogs on trails also means more risk of conflicts between dogs and between hikers with dogs and other hikers.

Having said that, all the above potential problems can be mitigated if dog owners step up to the plate with three tools when they leave the house with their dog:

1. A leash to use whenever in doubt for the safety of your dog.
2. Dog-waste bags to model consideration for other trail users and respect for the wildlife's home you are in.
3. Any class that stresses good manners with positive reinforcement drills to create a solid foundation for Rover's training as a good trail companion.

Consider yourself and your dog ambassadors for the dog owner/hiker population at large so the privilege of having your four-legged pal at your side spreads to more rather than fewer trails and public as well as private venues. Respect posted signs on dog policy.

Meeting the World Out of the Whelping Box

Pups initially receive immunity from their mother's milk, but after they stop nursing they need protection through inoculation. Pups less than four months old must be protected from infectious disease until they receive all the immunizations recommended by their veterinarian. This is a good time to take your dog outdoors for play and exploring near your home.

By twelve weeks, with a minimum of two of the three DHLP-P shots (rabies vaccination at four months of age), it should be safe to begin socializing with romps with other pups that have been immunized and are current on rabies boosters. This is the ideal time to sign up for a group puppy class that is as much about practicing good manners and redirecting bad habits as it is about social skills. The sooner you can get started practicing the desired behaviors, the more easily your dog will absorb the conditioned behavior. A good trainer focused on positive reinforcement methods will help train you to train your dog.

It's now time to start building stamina and confidence in the outside world with daily short (twenty to thirty minutes) but frequent leash walks in a variety of settings. Begin introducing the pup to sights from the trail like backpacks, hiking sticks, tents. Begin by placing these items around the house, where the setting is familiar and non-threatening. If there is an opportunity to be around horses or cattle, take your dog on

Respecting other trail users

leash walks where he can see and smell these animals so they become part of your pal's repertoire of mundane sights and smells.

I was training a friend's super sweet husky for the trail for *Best Dog Hikes Northern California* when I discovered he had extreme anxiety about horses for lack of exposure. Chance was cool with everything and everybody and loved feeling like he had an important job carrying gear in his packs. But a narrow trail in the backcountry on the side of the mountain is not the ideal place to realize your docile happy-go-lucky dog has got it into his head that a pack train of horses and mules slowly clopping uphill is nothing short of a herd of wild savage beasts he's convinced are out to murder him. All the reassurances and distractions in my arsenal of training tips did not convince him to sit calmly and watch them walk past us. He totally lost his composure. I had to wrestle him to the ground inches above the trail and clench his harness with both hands to restrain his anxiety-wiggling body, with the added drama of his vocal protests. The hoofed beasts never missed a beat as they threw him a sideways glance filled with disgust at this pathetic display of unwarranted neurosis.

To Chance, this new element in his world had represented clear and present danger. He could only wonder at what was wrong with this human that she didn't react to it. The following pack train encounters were much less eventful now that he realized his worst fears had not come true, admitting to himself that maybe he had overreacted a tad.

In retrospect, I should have acquainted Chance with the horses and mules down at the pack station, with fencing between him and the enormous beasts to bolster his sense of safety. Had he been off leash and reacted aggressively toward the pack animals, he would have been at risk of being shot by the pack train wrangler.

It's never too soon to start getting used to car travel, since you will be driving to trailheads and campgrounds. Using a crate will make pup feel more secure and minimize the risk of sensory overload. Drive the car to nearby parks to build on the positive association of the crate and the car. Crate training, if done sensibly and sensitively, will produce long-term benefits for both you and your dog at home and on the road.

Four months (with rabies vaccination) to six months is the ideal time to venture farther afield to meadows or local trails on leash, but practice recalls at the end of a long rope with treats. Recalls off leash should be done in the house or in a fenced yard, and only when you are certain you have your dog's undivided attention. Beginner group obedience classes with a supportive trainer who practices positive reinforcement is the best investment you can make in your relationship with your hiking pal.

The number one rule, no matter how frustrated you may feel at times, is *never* to call your dog to you for a reprimand. Why would you run up to someone who calls you over to berate you and make you feel bad about yourself? You want your dog to associate his name being called with fun, pleasant, or tasty experiences.

Your one-on-one training sessions shouldn't last more than thirty minutes, and two fifteen-minute sessions with a play break in between might get better results if your dog is hyper and has a short attention span.

Getting in Hiking Form

Do not stress the healthy development of your dog's bones and muscles with overexertion during the first six months, or twelve to eighteen months for large dogs. Stick to a flat terrain and take frequent rest and water stops.

Adult dogs also need to condition their muscles and cardiovascular systems if they are new to the sport of hiking. Consult your veterinarian regarding the health and age of your dog. Overweight dogs work harder and overheat faster. Couch potatoes don't start with marathons, so why should house dogs be expected to leave the yard for a 5-mile hike the first time? In addition to cardio and muscular preparedness, your dog's paws must also gradually build up a rougher protective layer on his pads to prevent tenderness and abrasion.

Depending on how sedentary or active your dog has been, getting in shape for the trail can take from a couple of weeks to about a month of consistent twice-daily walking. Sprinting to retrieve a ball in the backyard or on the beach is not the same as a sustained walking pace on a trail for an hour or more, especially if you hike uphill.

Sample Fitness Regimen for Your Adult Pooch

Remember that different breeds have their particular physical limitations. Short-muzzled dogs with sinus issues like boxers and pugs can overheat more easily with sustained activity, especially in hot weather. Short-legged dogs work harder to keep pace. Dark-coated dogs can overheat more easily. These characteristics must be taken into consideration when thinking about hiking with your dog. The following is only a framework for you to design a training regimen based on your dog's health, age, and lifestyle with the input from your veterinarian.

Walk twice daily for 30 to 45 minutes per outing. Pick up the pace to brisk for 10-minute intervals, with time between to sniff and stroll. Carry water and offer your dog water after the brisk sprints. Increase your walk to one hour in the morning or evening at the end of the first week and continue with the more brisk intervals. Incorporate some uphill segments after the first week.

After two to three weeks, a healthy dog should be ready for a mostly level 3-mile hike. It's about the distance, not the speed. By the end of a month, it's not unreasonable to hike 5 miles once a week. As your dog becomes more fit and has the stamina based on his age, health, and breed, and if hiking becomes part of your regular lifestyle, he will enjoy the occasional longer, more-challenging hikes (up to 10 miles) with a rest day and easier hikes in between. Avoid injuries by not treating your dog like a weekend warrior.

Ideally, a dog in his prime (2 to 7 years old) should be going outdoors to exercise, socialize, and get mental stimulation two times a day and get at least two hours of physical activity each day. On hot days it is best to exercise early in the morning and after sundown. Make sure pooch has cool, fresh water regularly and has access to shade to cool down on hot days.

A Word of Caution About Food and Exercise

It is best to feed your dog at least a couple of hours before rigorous exercise, and perhaps divide his portion into two smaller portions (half two hours prior, the other half thirty minutes after). No one feels good jumping around on a full stomach. Puppies need frequent small feedings throughout the day, and adult dogs should be fed at least two times a day.

Gastric dilatation-volvulus complex (GDV) is commonly known as "bloat," because it causes the stomach to bloat and contort. There are different theories on the cause of bloat, but running and jumping after a large meal can compound the risks of the stomach twisting in the abdomen (especially in large breeds with deep chests), blocking the flow or absorption of gastric material. GDV can be fatal. Dividing daily portions into smaller, more frequent meals during rest periods on the trail or in camp can help prevent GDV and is a healthier way to fuel your dog's energy during physical activity.

Pacing and Body Language

Hiking with your dog should not be about forced marches. The whole idea is to get exercise and interact with your dog while your eyes and ears take in your surroundings. This is your best quality bonding time. Savor it. Three miles per hour is a good, steady pace on level terrain at sea level. If you can, time yourself on a local high-school track with your dog on leash to get an accurate idea of your pace in ideal conditions. Just remember that on a trail the terrain, weather, and elevation will slow that pace, not to mention your dog's sniff and spray stops, photo ops, and water and snack stops. Smelling the roses and all other scents only discernable to your dog's super snout is one of the highlights of hiking for your dog. Don't rush him out of his pleasure.

Also keep in mind the altitude factor. A 2-mile-an-hour pace at altitude and/or uphill would be a strong stride for a fit hiker. In the mountains, for every 1,000 feet of elevation gain, you can add an extra mile of walking time to your planned total. Walking downhill is about three quarters of the time, not the optimistic half of the time most people hope for.

Even on a "voice control" trail, keep your dog on leash for the first thirty minutes if you are planning to hike more than a couple of miles. Dogs out of the starting gate in a new, natural, stimulating setting can tucker themselves out running in circles. Most dogs' concept of pace is "run till you drop."

Watch your dog's body language for tail up and fluid movement to confirm he is feeling strong and happy. Tail down, stiff gait, and lethargy indicates fatigue or injury. When you see this, examine the dog's paws and between the toes for foreign bodies that may be causing discomfort. Stop and rest and offer your dog water and a snack. That might do the trick.

When you head out on the trail, don't forget that you have the distance back to the trailhead to cover, so don't go too far and get stuck having to carry your dog out. If your dog looks drained or demoralized, or stops, lies down, or behaves oddly, trust that something is wrong.

Dogs have an innate desire to please, and they will go till they blow. There have been instances of dogs dropping dead from exhaustion on a run with their trusted person. Some dogs just don't have body awareness. Some Labs will drown before they stop swimming out for that ball on the 150th throw. Be sensitive and conservative. Shorten the excursion or abort if necessary. Dogs are not machines or yardsticks for male machismo. Treat your dog as if he were a child dependent on his parent's loving better judgment.

If your dog is on hyper alert, with ears forward, tail up, or raised hackles (hair standing up on the back or neck), his tension and attention might have been triggered by a sound, smell, or sight that you have yet to notice. Put his leash on, look around, and wait a couple of minutes. Proceed cautiously.

Hiking is for dogs of all breeds, sizes, and ages.

If your dog appears jittery, barks, whines, or howls, he may be sensing a potential threat. Pat him and speak to him reassuringly, but respect his concern. Leash him until you identify the source of his concern, which could be as simple as the odd shape of a boulder ahead, another hiker with a dog around the bend, or a small critter darting in the bushes.

You want to share safe, positive experiences that will nurture a mutual enthusiasm for hiking. Once you have shared the trail with your dog, any other trail companion will seem uninspiring and a dogless hike will seem humdrum. Hiker dog lovers know that the "hi" in "hiking" begins with having a dog at your side, so prepare wisely— train him well so you never have to leave home without him!

Gearing Up for Safe Happy Trails

You are solely responsible for your dog's safety and well-being on the trail, as well as his behavior.

There's a hike for every dog (toy, giant, short legged, or fat), but you have to determine the length and pace of your outings based on the age, health, physical condition, and breed anatomic characteristics of your dog. While dogs with flatter faces and shorter sinuses—like pugs, for example—are more susceptible to breathing problems exasperated by heat and excessive physical activity, giant breeds like the great Dane have bones that grow more slowly, so exercise should be moderate until they reach skeletal maturity around 2 years old. Some giant breeds like St. Bernards and New-foundlands are strong but not excessively energetic. Chihuahuas and terriers, along with the spectrum of those breed mixes, are typically hardy types that motor along into their senior years. Annual checkups by your veterinarian help establish the status of your dog's health and what exercise regimen is appropriate.

Five Building Blocks for Good Trail Dogs

Behind every dog labeled "bad" is usually a naïve, oblivious, or irresponsible person with a dazed, glazed, or insouciant look on his or her face.

Good trail etiquette starts with good manners at home. Here are five tips for building the kind of human/dog partnership on the trail that will make hiking with your dog safe and fun, while promoting good stewardship of the land so our public lands can continue to be enjoyed by all:

1. Choose a dog that is compatible with your lifestyle and level of outdoor activity. Some things you need to consider are whether you want a puppy or adult dog and the breed health history, physical characteristics, tempera-ment, and grooming requirements that you want in a dog. Dogs are social pack animals and are not meant to be isolated at home alone for days on end while you work or play without them. They are not meant to sit in a yard by themselves, even if yours is the garden of Versailles. Isolation makes dogs bored, depressed, and sometimes destructive. It is nothing short of cruel. Dogs require time and attention for play, exercise, affection, training, and social interaction. Tasks associated with having a dog (and there are many) should be a labor of love rather than laborious obligations.

2. Spaying and neutering your canine companion won't make her fat or make him lazy. It reduces risks of mammary gland and prostate cancers. It saves dogs from being slaves to the hormonal drive to reproduce. He won't be obsessed with roaming, and she won't be scratching her address on fire hydrants. It will make them focus on you and their obedience training homework and make them more congenial with other dogs on the trail. Check with your veterinarian on the current recommended age range for spaying and neutering, as well as the health-related pluses and minuses of each school of thought on the matter.

3. Good manners matter. The only answer to your doubts about your dog's good behavior and responsiveness to your voice commands is a leash. No wildlife should be stressed by a run-amok dog, and no one likes to be rushed by an overexuberant dog. Some people fear dogs, and others dislike them—to put it mildly. Some dogs are social butterflies, while other less-gregarious canines despise the intrusion on their personal space by strange dogs in the running for Ms. Congeniality. Don't be surprised if uninvited greetings are

PERSONAL SPACE AND POLITE GREETINGS

According to Andee Burleigh, CPDT-KA (Certified Professional Dog Trainer-Knowledge Assessed), who has been using positive reward-based methods for twenty years, the biggest myth about dogs is that most dogs enjoy or need to meet other dogs on leash to be social. Most dogs actually would prefer *not* to have strange dogs rush into their personal space when they are trapped on a leash. A considerate dog owner advocates for their dog's sense of safety on leash by calmly avoiding dog encounters and teaching their dog to be polite and under control around other dogs and people.

met with surly snarls and snaps by the dog whose space was invaded. If your dog is the reserved kind on leash, it's your job to protect your dog from unwanted socializing by letting the owner of the other dog know it's not okay with your dog, and ask them to please reel Mr. or Ms. Perky Paws back into his or her own space.

In the case of dog issues, the easiest solution for park authorities and business owners who receive complaints is to ban dogs from trails, restaurants, hotels, and establishments. Being off leash is fun, and teaching your dog basic commands like sit, stay/wait, and come is his ticket to the mother of all privileges: off-leash playtime. Hikers and others with whom you share the trail appreciate a well-trained dog. Responsiveness to voice commands could someday save your dog's life. Signing up for positive-training obedience classes early on is an investment in your and your dog's relationship that you will never regret. If the only skill your dog learns is to walk at the end of a leash without strangling himself and pulling you off your feet, it will make strolling the neighborhood and the trail a joyful thrill rather than a dreaded exercise in frustration.

4. Socialize your dog around strangers and strange things to prevent overreaction when he first encounters them past the imprint stage in the tenth to twelfth week of life. Trashcans on the street corner should not be a threat, and neither should boulders on the side of the trail. Pack animals coming up the trail should not unglue your dog. Expose your dog to trail sights as early as possible. Pups should have had their series of vaccinations before venturing out, but who says you can't walk around the yard with a backpack and hiking sticks? Get your dog used to objects that move, like bicycles and cars, so he doesn't develop phobias that can trigger neurotic episodes that can endanger him, you, and others on the trail. Introduce your dog to water. Dogs don't have to like dipping in streams and swimming in lakes, but they should learn to walk near and across water without panicking. It requires time and sensitivity on your part.

5. Before hitting the trail, consult your veterinarian about required vaccinations, booster shots (rabies), and the most current preventives for ticks and Lyme disease, mosquitoes, and heartworm. Ask your veterinarian about the latest and safest flea and tick products for your dog's particular needs.

Pooch Essentials and Trail Readiness

The following will get your dog started on a safe paw.

The Essentials

1. Choose a harness. Hands down, harnesses are safer than collars. Dogs don't accidentally choke on harnesses. Harnesses make crossing streams and negotiating passages along precarious stretches of trail much safer. Harnesses allow for a quicker, safer, and more solid grab of your dog if necessary. If you don't use a harness, never let your dog run around off leash with a choke chain or martingale-type collar.

2. Lead your dog with a 6-foot leather or nylon leash. Retractable leashes are an invitation to chaos when passing people with dogs that like to do the "ring-around-the-rosy sniff-and-greet dance" on the trail. Leather leashes

Booties protect dogs' paws on rough trails.

last forever, but colorful nylon leashes can be easily located and dry quickly when wet.

3. Have your dog wear an identification tag. Tattooing and microchipping your dog is a great idea, but works better in urban areas. On the trail, an old-fashioned tag with your dog's name and your cell phone number is much more likely to reunite you with wayward Fido. Always attach a temporary tag with the name of your campground, cabin resort, or whatever lodging you are using as a base camp on your adventure. Some dog-friendly accommodations offer a temporary tag with the business's name and phone number and your room or cabin number.

4. Bring biodegradable dog-waste bags for pack-it-in, pack-it-out trails and campground areas.

5. Get your dog used to any gear or accessory he may eventually wear on a hiking or backpacking trip. That includes booties, raincoat, and life vests. Fit your dog with booties and let him get used to them in the house and on your neighborhood walks. Always have a set of booties in your or his pack for the unexpected tender tootsies on paw-bruising trails. It's one thing to have to carry a Chihuahua with raw paws out of the backcountry, but another to drape a German shepherd on your shoulders. Raincoats and life vests come in different sizes. Shop with your dog for a good fit. Life vests are an especially good idea for hiking the beaches with dogs that have more daredevil attitude than swimming skills, or if your outdoor adventures will include water sports.

6. Pack water and energy-boosting snacks. Never count on finding water on the trail. Instead, carry 8 ounces of water for every 1 hour or 2.0 miles of trail. Heat + Altitude + Exertion = Dehydration, which is the most common and preventable hiking hazard for both you and your dog.

Getting used to the wardrobe before a rainy-day hike

Properly trimmed nails make for happy paws on the trail.

Life vests come in many sizes.

7. Trim your dog's nails and cut dewclaws short to prevent snags that can tear the tissue.

8. Groom your long- or curly-coated dog for summer hiking for his comfort and your sanity. Choose function over fashion so his coat doesn't sweep up and trap burrs, foxtails, and dirt debris and turn your hike into a grooming nightmare.

9. Keep your dog's vaccinations current and carry proof of rabies vaccine in his pack, as you may be asked for this documentation at some park entrances.

10. Carry a basic first-aid kit (see Appendix B).

Dog Packs

There are several benefits to proper pack training. Some dogs are serious workaholics, and walking along the stream just to smell the wild roses just doesn't cut it. A sense of mission and purpose brings out the best in some of the more hyperactive dogs, while channeling the energies and focus of the smart and free-spirited ones. Carrying some of the load makes the cut-loose romping breaks that much more meaningful and ecstatic. A pack should be in proportion to your dog's build and height. It should fit his chest and shoulder contours comfortably without chafing and should be balanced. Dogs should never carry more than one fourth of their own weight.

To get your dog ready to carry a pack, let him get used to the weight of an empty pack. Use treats to reinforce the association of the pack with something pleasant.

Let your dog wear the pack on his daily walks. Gradually stuff the pack with paper, face cloths, treats, kibble, and dog-waste bags. Increase the balanced load over a couple of weeks in preparation for trail day. Take frequent snack breaks on the trail and remove the pack. Once your dog is comfortable with the pack and his muscles are toned to the appropriate weight, a frozen water bottle (of appropriate weight and balance) in his packs can help keep him cool on hotter days while providing cold water as the ice melts.

A well-fitting pack conforms to your dog's body type.

What to Expect on the Trail

Knowledge and information can make your excursions more positive and fun experiences for you and your dog, as they help prepare you for wildlife encounters, seasonal nuisances, other trail users, and Mother Nature's changing moods.

Plan Ahead

Always confirm ahead of time that dogs are welcome on the trail you plan to hike. Policies change, so call the managing agency about any restrictions and abide by the rules.

The managing agency or ranger district office can answer questions about permits, weather (critical information for the high country, where changes can be sudden and extreme even in the summer), road closures, trail damage and changes, campground availability, closures, and special advisories. Fire and flood are parts of life in Southern California's swings between drought and rains. Budget cuts reduce resources and manpower, which impact trail maintenance and campground operation. Visitor centers often depend on volunteers. National forest headquarters have recreation managers and some national forests have "district" recreation managers, who are typically the most informed. To get the most up-to-date information—especially early in the season—it is important to speak to someone who has recently hiked the trail and traveled the roads to the trailhead.

Know Where You Are

Carry relevant maps and know how to read a topographic map so you can study the terrain in the area of your hike and anticipate elevation changes, difficulty, shady spots, water sources, and suitability for your dog. It will help you pack and pace yourself. For every 1,000 feet of elevation, add about an extra mile of expected travel time.

USGS quad map(s) with a scale of 1:24,000 and a compass are the traditional means of navigation. USGS maps do not show road or trail changes that have occurred since their publication, but the USGS is in the process of updating and digitizing the "legacy" maps (USGS.gov/3DEP). Using a compass with a map requires some study and practice. Consider signing up for a navigation workshop at a local outdoor recreation store like REI or a local community college.

A good GPS (global positioning system) and maybe even a smartphone with a good map app should enable you to determine your approximate location along the trail. Usually, a GPS more accurately shows latitude and longitude, but is less accurate at showing elevation. Electronic devices have their limits. Reception of any electronic device depends on receiving correct signals from satellites or cell towers. Remember to fully charge your devices and carry spare batteries. However, even if you are a techno-savvy hiker, it is wise to also carry a map and compass.

Other Trail Users and Etiquette

On some hikes you will share the trail with people on horseback going out for a trail ride or on a backcountry trek with pack animals in tow. Mountain bikers may also be on some trails. And you will most definitely meet other hikers with or without dogs on and off leash.

Good trail etiquette breeds goodwill and positive relations with other trail users, especially those who may not be fans of dogs on the trail. Here are some general tips:

1. On or off leash, on the trail or in the campground, your dog must be under control.

2. Friendly exuberance or not, never let your dog charge or bark at other dogs, hikers, or horses. Some people are afraid of dogs. Dogs can also spook horses and jeopardize the safety of the rider. Always step off the trail to the upper side so the horse(s) can see you, keep a tight leash on your dog, and command him to sit until the riders have gone by. Use treats to encourage the sit and keep your dog's focus on your hand rather than the trail traffic if your dog is new at this.

3. Hike only where dogs are permitted, and abide by the posted regulations.

4. Stay on the trail, step lightly in pristine wilderness areas, and don't let your dog chase wildlife.

5. Pack out everything you pack in. At the very least, bury your dog's scat away from the trail and surface water. Better yet: Carry it out in

YOUR DOG MAY BE ON THE NO-ADMIT LIST

Some Southern California campgrounds, public lands, and private businesses post signs restricting certain breeds considered more prone to aggression. The signs always seem to include pit bulls, among other breeds. Dogs are not to blame, but the reality is that if you plan on getting a dog and having your four-legged pal share the trail and your everyday activities, consider making your life easier by choosing a non-controversial breed.

On the other hand, if you already own or love one of these stigmatized breeds, consider working to change public perceptions and policies through outreach, education, and, as with any dog, making sure your own dog is a good citizen and representative of his breed through training and socialization.

If you adopt from a shelter, pick a dog with some known history. Avoid supporting puppy mills by staying away from puppies advertised for sale. Locate a reputable breeder through word of mouth if you have your heart set on a purebred, and be aware of breed character traits and instinctive drives.

biodegradable poop-scoop bags. Dog doo on trails is the number one complaint by responsible dog owners as well as non–dog owners. Dog waste can transmit disease and it's a territory marker/intruder alert that can stress resident wildlife.

6. Camp in designated campsites in heavily used or developed areas. Never leave your dog unattended in the campground.

Leaving no trace means picking up after your dog.

Dogs That Want to Rumble

At one time or another, your dog may be a partner in a dominance dance with another dog. This occurs more frequently between males, especially intact males that reek of testosterone. Dogs well versed in pack hierarchy know to stay out of an alpha dog's face, or to assume the subordinate body language that stops the music.

To help avoid problems, neuter your male dog before 1 year of age or as soon as both testicles drop. Overt dominance may not appear until he is 2 years old. Neutering reduces macho and roaming instincts. Be aware that testosterone levels take several months to decrease after neutering. Spay your female. Breeding females can be instinctively more competitive around other females. A female in season should never be on the trail. She will create havoc, and her mating instincts will override her flawless obedience record every time.

A leashed dog can be overly protective. Avoid stress by taking a detour around other hikers with dogs or stepping off the trail with your dog at a sit while the other hiker and dog walk by. Do not panic at the hint of raised hackles and loud talk. Most of it is just posturing. If your dog is off leash, stay calm and keep walking away from the other dog while encouraging your dog to come in your most enthusiastic voice and with the promise of a biscuit. If she complies, reward her with a "good dog" and the promised biscuit for positive reinforcement.

Walking back toward the dogs, screaming, and interfering before they resolve their conflict can stoke the fires of a more serious brawl. If the squabble escalates into a dogfight, make sure you cover your arms and hands before trying to break it up. Pull the dogs by the tails, lift their hind legs off the ground, or throw water on them to distract them. As a last resort you may have to throw sand or dirt in the eyes of the one with the grip. One hiker, who uses a cane as a hiking stick, reports having broken up a dogfight or two by slipping the crook of his cane under the dog collar or harness to drag the thug away.

To help avoid dogfights, do not give treats to other hikers' dogs. Competition for food and protection of territory are the root of most dogfights.

Seasonal Nuisances

Foxtails

These arrowlike grasses are at their worst in late summer and early fall, when they are dry, sharp, and just waiting to burrow in some dog's fuzzy coat. A dry foxtail can be inhaled by a dog, lodge itself in the ear canal or between the toes, or camouflage itself in the dog's undercoat, puncturing the skin and causing infection. Foxtails have the potential to cause damage to vital organs.

Inspect your dog's ears and toes and run your hands through his coat, inspecting under the belly, legs, and tail. Brush out his coat out after excursions in areas where there were even hints of foxtails. Violent sneezing and snorting is an indication that the dog may have inhaled a foxtail. Even if the sneezing or shaking decreases in intensity or frequency, the foxtail can still be tucked where it irritates only occasionally while it travels deeper, causing more serious damage. If this happens, take your dog to a vet as soon as possible. He may have to be anesthetized to remove the foxtail.

Poison Oak

Poison oak is a three-leaved, low-growing vine or bush that ranges in color from green to red depending on the season. The plant can cause topical irritations on hairless areas of your dog's body. (You can apply cortisone cream to the affected area.)

Find out if there is poison oak where you plan to hike, and make sure to wash your hands with soap after handling your dog. The resin can rub off your dog onto you, your sleeping bag, your car seat, and your furniture at home. If you are very sensitive to these rashes, bathe your dog after the hike and sponge your arms and legs with diluted chlorine bleach, Tecnu soap, or anti-itch spray. Tecnu soap is an outdoor cleanser that removes plant oil from your skin and also can be used on your laundry.

Other Poisonous Plants

Unfortunately, your dog may be tempted to taste and chew hazardous plants. This includes plants found in your backyard, like rhubarb. In the wilderness, however, there are similar dangers—plants such as rhododendrons may cause considerable sickness and discomfort for your pet.

If you suspect poisoning, take note of what your dog ate and head back to the car. Once out of the woods, call your vet or an animal poison control center (see Appendix B for phone number).

Fleas and Ticks

Fleas are uncomfortable for your dog and carry tapeworm eggs, and ticks are one of nature's most painfully potent and tenacious creatures for their size. Some tick bites cause uncomfortable red, swollen irritation to the area of the skin where they attach and can make the area feel like it was pounded by a two-by-four. In some cases, tick bites can inflict temporary paralysis. Other types of ticks found in California can carry Lyme disease, which is reported to be the most common tick-carried disease in the United States.

Ticks thrive on wild hosts (deer are the most common) around lakes, streams, meadows, and some wooded areas. They cling to unsuspecting hikers and dogs. On dogs, they crawl under the fur and attach to the skin around the neck, face, ears, stomach, or any soft, fleshy cavity. They attach to their hosts by sticking their mouthparts into the skin and then feed on the host's blood and swell up until they dangle from the skin like an ornament.

Removing a Tick:

1. Try not to break off any mouthparts (remaining parts can cause infection), and avoid getting tick fluids on yourself by crushing or puncturing the tick.
2. Grasp the tick as close to the skin as possible with blunt forceps or tweezers, or with your fingers in rubber gloves, tissue, or any barrier to shield your skin from possible tick fluids.

3. Remove the tick with a steady pull.

4. After removing the tick, disinfect the skin with alcohol and wash your hands with soap and water.

There is an abundance of chemical and natural flea and tick products on the market, including collars, dips, sprays, powders, pills, and oils. Some products have the advantage of being effective on both fleas and ticks, remain effective on wet dogs, and require an easy once-a-month topical application or oral ingestion delivered in the form of a treat. Consult your veterinarian about a safe and appropriate product.

Mosquitoes

Avon's Skin So Soft is a less toxic and more pleasant-smelling option, but is not as effective as mosquito repellents containing DEET. Mix one cap of the oil with one pint of water in a spray bottle. Spray your dog and run your hands through her coat from head to toe and tail to cover her with a light film of the mixture. Be careful to avoid her eyes and nostrils, but do not miss the outer ear areas. Organic solutions containing eucalyptus, lavender, and tea tree oil can also be used as a mosquito repellent. Besides being annoying, mosquitoes carry heartworm. Consult your veterinarian about preventive medication.

Bees, Wasps, Hornets, and Yellow Jackets

These insect nests can be in trees or on the ground.

Moody Mother Nature and Seasonal Hazards

Every season has climatic constants, but Mother Nature can be temperamental, bringing additional unexpected challenges that can affect your safety and the safety of your dog.

Summer

Heat, albeit generally "dry" in Southern California valleys and lower elevation foothill regions, can be in the triple digits, and taxing to fatal for your dog. These conditions increase the risks of dehydration and heatstroke. (See Appendix B for Trail Emergencies and First Aid.) Here are some tips to help avoid heat-related trouble:

- Hike in the early morning or late afternoon and keep hikes under 5 miles.
- Don't burden your dog with a pack in hot weather.
- Carry at least 8 ounces of water per dog for each hour or 3.0 miles of trail.
- Rest in a shaded area during the intensity of the midday.
- Take frequent rest stops and offer your dog water.
- Let your dog take a plunge in a lake or lie belly-down in a stream or mud puddle to cool down.

Keep your dog hydrated on the trail.

Winter

Wintry conditions can affect your dog's feet, endurance, and body warmth. Crusty snow can chafe and cut your dog's pads, and walking in deep snow is exhausting and can put a short-haired dog at risk of hypothermia. Here are some ways to protect your dog from cold and extra exertion.

- Carry booties for icy conditions and use them on your dog if she is not accustomed to snow and ice. Even dogs accustomed to snow can get abraded paws. Check your pup's feet for chafing and carry a couple extras booties as replacements for any lost in the snow. Keeping your dog on leash while she is in booties makes it easier to know when to adjust them or to retrieve any that slip off.
- Clothing on dogs should be about function, not fashion. Consider a wool or polypropylene sweater for your short-haired dog, or down if your dog has no undercoat.
- Encourage your dog to walk behind you in your tracks. It is less strenuous.
- Carry a small sled or snow disk with an insulated foam pad so your dog can rest on the frozen ground.
- Unless your dog is a northern breed that thrives in cold, keep your outings shorter in transition seasons when there is some snow and ice to navigate. Carry your dog's favorite snacks and warm drinking water.

Winter in coastal Southern California, unlike in the mountains, is hike-friendly, but it can bring heavy rain. The desert temperatures are more comfortable, but Pacific storms sweeping down from the north or tropical moisture from the south can cause hazardous flash-flooding of the dry washes. Check the weather forecast and be prepared for potential threats to your dog's safety and comfort on the trail.

Spring

Following the cooler, wetter winter months, spring and sun in coastal Southern California bring fresh crops of wildflowers, but also offer ideal conditions for ticks, mosquitoes, poison oak, and foxtails to come to life and infest the summer months.

Fall

Fall brings shorter daylight hours. Adjust the length of your hikes accordingly. Hunting season in many parts of the backcountry requires extra caution. Check the hunting regulations and dates for the hiking area you have in mind. It is important that you and your dog wear bright colors when hiking anywhere in the fall. Orange hunting vests are available for dogs, and colorful harnesses and bandanas are also a good idea. When in doubt about hunting in forested areas, keep your dog on a leash.

The High Country

The high country is subject to variable and extreme weather year-round. Check for weather advisories at the ranger station, including thunderstorm warnings and fire danger. Afternoon thunderstorms are common in the afternoon. Rain can quickly turn to hail and snow. Stay below the timberline and off exposed ridges. In spring and fall, pay attention to sudden drops in temperature and shifts in wind with system clouds announcing snowfall. Wildfires are more common in the fall in Southern California during stretches of hot, dry, breezy days.

How to Use This Guide

The book divides Southern California into thirteen regions, taking geography and population centers into account. These regions include seven counties (San Luis Obispo, Santa Barbara, Ventura, Los Angeles, Orange, San Diego, and Riverside), four mountain ranges (Western Sierra, Eastern Sierra, White Mountains, and San Bernardino Mountains), and two distinct areas (Big Sur and Central Valley). The introduction at the beginning of each cluster of hikes describes the characteristics of the region.

Although Southern California conjures up images of Hollywood stars and palm-lined beaches, the reality is much more diverse. Sand, surf, rivers, desert, forests, and snow-capped peaks are all faces of Southern California.

This book could not possibly contain all the hikes in Southern California. But the hikes chosen are meant to introduce hikers and their dogs to Southern California's diversity while inspiring a desire of discovery. Some regions will speak more loudly than others to an individual hiker's soul and his or her furry pal's spirit.

Most of the hikes are moderate in distance, with shorter and more challenging trails sprinkled throughout the book. Since much of Southern California can be hot most of the year, your dog's comfort was a primary factor in choosing the hikes. Because the southernmost part of California is so heavily populated, many hikes are close to urban areas for welcome escape and quick jaunts when traffic cooperates. What some trails lack in solitude, they compensate with convenience of services for creature comforts.

We chose hikes of various distances and terrain to satisfy both the younger or more eager dog that already has some trail dust under his paws and the older, less-ambitious, or novice dog on his first foray out of the 'burbs. It is up to you to build up your dog's fitness with regular, consistent exercise and to monitor his body language for signs of discomfort, pain, or fatigue. Don't risk injuring your dog by making him a weekend warrior.

In choosing the fifty-one hikes, we gave preference to trails accessed from paved roads and those with historical highlights, water (lakes, streams, rivers, waterfalls), shade, and scenery. Unless there is specific reference to dirt or gravel roads, assume that the road access to the trail is paved.

Distances were calculated using USGS, forest, wilderness, and area-specific maps in tandem with a GPS unit for maximum accuracy. Be aware that it not uncommon for trails to be rerouted from their original USGS mapping as a result of floods, fires, and slides or changes in agency policy. At the time we hiked the trails for this book, California was in its fourth year of severe drought, which also contributed to more wildfires.

The Trail Finder section at the beginning of the book allows you to quickly sort hikes by distance, exertion level, leash policy, and suitable overnight trips. Hikes are divided into three categories: easy, moderate, and strenuous. A short hike may be more strenuous than a longer one because of elevation gain. Hikes under 5.0 miles will always mention if there are characteristics that would make the otherwise easy or moderate hike strenuous. The assumption in determining the degree of difficulty is that you and your dog have driven from sea level or low elevation to the trailhead, so hikes with elevations of 5,000 feet and above are labeled moderate, at best, or strenuous. You must exercise some personal judgment as to the suitability of a hike based on your and your dog's general fitness levels.

The Summary Block below the sketch overview of the hike is an outline to assist you in preparing for the hike. It includes the following features:

- **Distance** is the total round-trip distance of the hike, with a notation on whether the hike is an out and back, loop, or lollipop.

- **Hiking time** is based on a 2.0-mile-per-hour pace, taking into account water and snack breaks, pooch swim stops, and vista points. Hikers' pace will vary according to individual fitness levels, pack weight, terrain, and elevation range, especially if the hikes begin above 5,000 feet. When hiking uphill, add 1.0 mile or thirty minutes for every 1,000 feet gained in elevation. One way to estimate your average pace per mile on level ground for a baseline is to time yourself walking around a running track.

- **Difficulty** rates hikes as easy, moderate, or strenuous.

- **Trailhead elevation** and **Highest point** on the hike help you prepare for weather and exertion (pick hikes that are suitable to both yours and your dog's abilities and fitness levels). Whether you are an enthusiastic newcomer to hiking or introducing your dog to the joys of the trail, it's best to set the bar lower on a first outing and make it a positive, safe experience for both of you. This becomes particularly significant on the Sierra Nevada hikes, which are mostly above 6,000 feet.

- **Best season** to hike a trail is determined by the trail's accessibility during different times of the year, which depends on the regional weather. Too much snow or rain during certain months can make a trail hard to navigate. Spring can last anywhere from early March to late May or mid-June depending on whether you are on the coast, in the desert, or in the high country. Summer is typically late June through August. Fall can begin in early September with hot temperatures during the day and cooler nights. But in Southern California, daytime temperatures can run warm to hot into November. The desert doesn't cool off until December, and it is not uncommon to have a spike of temperatures even during the winter months. Rain, when it comes, arrives in December through March, with snow at higher elevations. The summer monsoons bring thundershowers in the mountains, and the warm, dry winds known as Santa Anas kick up in the fall, making Southern California more vulnerable to wildfires.

The opening of trails and campgrounds, especially in the Sierra, is subject to the length and intensity of the winter season, and that can vary by several weeks from year to year. Optimally the Sierra season runs from Memorial Day weekend to mid-October, but don't count on it. Trails above 7,000 feet frequently still have snow after Independence Day. Although the trail may be accessible year-round, "Best season" will list the preferable months or seasons for optimal enjoyment and comfort, influenced by temperature, trail traffic, water sources, seasonal highlights like wildflowers and fall foliage, as well as nuisances like excessive mosquitoes and poison oak. Always call the ranger station for trail status.

California has microclimates as well as seasons, which can make some hikes even within just a 20-mile radius in the same geographic region more desirable than others. On an August afternoon, for example, a hike along the coast may be breezy while the inland valleys are in triple-digit sweat. There can be significant temperature differentials between the northernmost boundary of Southern California in Big Sur, for example, and the beaches of San Diego.

- **Trail surface** indicates what you'll be walking on, which is especially important for dogs' paws. If a trail has a lot of rock or an especially abrasive surface, dogs' pads can become worn down to tender or raw in worst cases. Paw Alert! 🐾 lets you know when to use booties.

- **Other trail users** lets you know if you and pooch will be sharing the trail with horses, which include pack animals, and/or bikes. In Southern California, paved multi-use trails may include rollerbladers and skateboarders. Horses and bicycles are the two most common trail users and require dogs to be on exemplary behavior, especially if using voice control.

- **Canine compatibility** lets you know whether dogs must be on leash or under voice control.

- **Land status** clues you in on the maps you may need as well as the management agency. Different agencies have different policies regarding leashes versus voice control. In populated areas, even National Forest Service trails considered "developed" for recreation may require your dog be on leash.

- **Fees and permits** applies to parking, day hiking, or overnight camping fees. Many trailheads in Southern California with developed amenities for recreation (picnic tables, grills, water, toilets) on public land require an Adventure Pass be displayed on the windshield. These passes are sold at ranger stations and often at businesses close to the trailhead. There is no mention of "campfire" on this line, because it is assumed that campfire permits are required outside of developed campgrounds on all trails. In California, "campfire permits" are not restricted to just the building of a campfire. Permits also apply to cooking stoves and anything with a flame. Campfire permits are obtained from ranger stations, and it is essential to check with the managing ranger district as to what the campfire policy is along any given trail at any given time, since the policy changes throughout the season on different public lands based on the level of fire risk. Campfire and the use of anything with a flame are outright prohibited in some wilderness areas and above certain elevations.

- **Maps** refers you to the appropriate USGS topographical map and/or national forest, wilderness, or additional park or local maps. (Be sure to check the contour interval when using USGS maps. Although most are 40 feet, some are 20, 25, or 80 feet, and some are in meters.)

- **Trail contacts** leads you to the best source for information on permits, fees, dog policies, parking, and campgrounds, as well as current information on access to trails, restrictions, and closures. There is no such thing as asking too many questions when it involves your and your dog's safety. Never drive past a ranger station and the opportunity to verify your information.

- **Nearest town** lists the largest population center closest to the trail for services such as food and lodging. It is also often the town used as the anchor for Finding the trailhead. Other smaller but more convenient communities may be listed for access to basic supplies and campgrounds or other types of lodging.

- **Trail tips** includes what amenities may be found at the trailhead (toilet, picnic tables, and so on) and other useful information.

- **Finding the trailhead** gives you driving directions to the trailhead from a significant population base or community located along the principal highway route.

- **The Hike** describes the history and other interesting factoids related to the area of the trail, as well as a description of some of the natural or cultural highlights along the trail.

- **Miles and Directions** gets you from the trailhead to the turnaround point with concise directions between waypoints at trail junctions and significant points of interest.

- **Creature Comforts** lists noteworthy or convenient "Fueling up" stops for food (store, takeout, or eat in). It will specify if an establishment has a dog-friendly outdoor dining area. "Resting up" offers information about nearby campgrounds or other dog-friendly lodging, including cabins, inns, motels, or resorts, some with historic significance or "après hike" pampering amenities.

- The **Puppy Paws and Golden Years** section is not exclusively for puppies and very senior dogs, but the options focus on providing dogs with added opportunities for physical and mental stimulation that are definitely suitable for those groups.

Trail Finder

Easy Hikes

1. Pfeiffer Beach
2. Sand Dollar Beach
5. Salinas Riverwalk
7. Bob Jones City to Sea Trail
9. Jalama Beach
11. Sweetwater Trail
12. Arroyo Burro Beach
13. Santa Barbara Beach Way
17. San Buenaventura State Beach Park to Ventura River Estuary
18. Paradise Falls
20. Cold Creek Valley Preserve
22. Mount Hollywood
23. Horseshoe Loop
24. Holy Jim Falls
25. San Juan Loop
27. The Beach Trail
31. Cabrillo National Monument
34. Indian Pools
35. Hume Lake Loop
36. Trail of 100 Giants
37. Whiskey Flat Trail
47. Alpine Pedal Path
49. Canyon View Loop

Moderate Hikes

3. Salmon Creek Trail to Salmon Creek Falls and Spruce Camp
4. Fiscalini Ranch Preserve
8. La Purisima Mission Loop
14. Inspiration Point
15. San Ysidro Falls
16. Piedra Blanca Trail to Twin Forks Camp
19. Solstice Canyon
21. Trail Canyon Falls
26. Rancho San Clemente Ridgeline Trail
28. Bernardo Mountain
29. Blue Sky Ecological Reserve
30. Cowles Mountain

32. Lewis S. Eaton Trail
39. Long Lake
45. North Shore National Recreation Trail to PCT Bridge
48. Devil's Slide Trail
50. Araby Trail
51. Homme-Adams Park to Cahuilla Hills Park

Strenuous Hikes

6. Bishop Peak
10. Davy Brown Trail
33. Lewis Creek National Scenic Trail
38. Treasure Lakes
40. First and Second Lakes
41. Gilbert Lake
42. Lone Pine Lake
43. Cottonwood Lakes
44. Methuselah Walk
46. Children's Forest Exploration Trail

Less than 5 Miles

1. Pfeiffer Beach
2. Sand Dollar Beach
3. Salmon Creek Trail to Salmon Creek Falls and Spruce Camp
4. Fiscalini Ranch Preserve
5. Salinas Riverwalk
6. Bishop Peak
9. Jalama Beach
12. Arroyo Burro Beach
13. Santa Barbara Beach Way
14. Inspiration Point
15. San Ysidro Falls
17. San Buenaventura State Beach Park to Ventura River Estuary
18. Paradise Falls
19. Solstice Canyon
20. Cold Creek Valley Preserve
21. Trail Canyon Falls
22. Mount Hollywood
23. Horseshoe Loop
24. Holy Jim Falls
25. San Juan Loop
27. The Beach Trail

Voice Control

Part On-Leash/Part Voice Control

Big Sur Coast

S trict boundaries do not apply to Big Sur ("Big South"), or "El Sur Grande," as the Spanish explorers first described this ruggedly dramatic stretch of coastline between Carmel, California, at its northern border and Cambria at its southern end.

Native Americans had long called this coast home before the Spaniard mariners and explorers thought they "discovered" it. Mexico's independence from Spain created land grants in Big Sur, as it did in the rest of Mexico-owned California. The Homestead Act of 1862 lured a few hardy pioneer families to the remote, surf-sculpted coast following the victory of the United States in the Mexican-American War. Redwoods, tanoaks, and the Gold Rush brought jobs and boosted the local economy. The boom didn't last, and the remote and legendary wildlands, where the Santa Lucia Mountains meet the Pacific, remained barely accessible until the construction of the paved two-lane road known as the Roosevelt Highway, later incorporated into the state highway network and redesignated as Highway 1 (CA 1). In 1965 the road became California's first Scenic Highway. Multiple bridges requiring engineering feats along with the miles of guardrails still provide safe passage for the millions of tourists a year that come to be awed by CA 1 and the natural and cultural landmarks that make it unique.

Hidden Pfeiffer Beach, named after one of the original pioneer families, is one of Big Sur's many memorable highlights.

1 Pfeiffer Beach

This is an idyllic hike on dog-compatible national forest sand in the heart of an otherwise not-so-dog-friendly stretch of mostly state park land. You can snap a photo of your furry pal enjoying one of the most pristine coastal settings in the country, if not the world.

Start: From the trailhead at the west end of the Pfeiffer Beach parking lot
Distance: 1.2 miles
Hiking time: About 1 hour
Difficulty: Easy
Trailhead elevation: 23 feet
Highest point: 23 feet
Best season: Year round; summers are very busy and the parking lot is full by midday. No parking allowed on the road.
Trail surface: Sand
Other trail users: Horses
Canine compatibility: On leash
Land status: National forest
Fees and permits: Parking fee

Maps: USGS Pfeiffer Point; Los Padres National Forest
Trail contacts: Los Padres National Forest Monterey District, 406 Mildred Ave., King City 93930; (831) 385-5434; fs.usda.gov/lpnf; Big Sur Station (831) 667-2315
Nearest town: Carmel and Big Sur Community
Trail tips: There are 4 vault toilets at the trailhead, trashcans, and recycling. There is no drinking water at the trailhead. Bring water for pooch. The length of the hike depends on the tide. The hike described here is as far as you can go at a low tide and would be shorter at high tide. Be tide aware for a safe excursion.

Finding the trailhead: From Carmel at the intersection of CA 1 and Rio Road, drive 26 miles south to the unmarked Sycamore Canyon Road on the west side (right) of CA 1 just past the Big Sur Station on the east side of CA 1 (left). Turn right on the one-lane paved Sycamore Canyon Road and drive 2 miles to the Pfeiffer Beach entrance and day-use pay station, which usually has an attendant. The trailhead is at the west end of the last parking lot next to the interpretive panel and bench. **GPS:** N36 14.29' / W121 48.83'

The Hike

The irony of this hike is the fact that it's down an unmarked road with no public land signs on CA 1 to draw attention to it, which suggests a primitive access at best. But Pfeiffer Beach awaits just 2 miles down a narrow, paved easement across private property. The road ends in a fairly well-developed day-use area with a 500-foot-long sandy path gateway to the temperamental Pacific's edge. The photogenic arches sculpted by the crashing surf off shore have long seduced amateur and professional photographers who seek to capture the untamed beauty.

You set out from the trailhead under the cypress canopy through the riparian habitat created by the creek and walk to the beach. Turn left (south) at the beach and walk 0.1 mile (or as the tide allows) to the natural end at the southern-point cliff.

National forest beaches are generally dog friendly.

Turn around and walk north. Note that the creek coming out of Sycamore Canyon flows out to the ocean seasonally with good winter rains and may be a natural barrier preventing access to the south end of the beach at certain times of year.

At 0.4 mile you come to a cluster of rock at the foot of the cliffs. At certain high tides, this is as far as you can walk. If the tide is in your favor, continue walking another 0.3 mile to the rock shelf and turn around. The beach ends and the coastline is impassable beyond this point at any time. Pick a spot to hang out, indulge your inner Ansel Adams, and picnic with your dog before going back to the trailhead the way you came.

Miles and Directions

0.0 Start at the interpretive panel at the west end of the Pfeiffer Beach parking lot.

0.1 Arrive at the beach and turn left to walk south.

0.2 Arrive at the south end of the beach and turn around and walk north on the beach.

0.7 Arrive at the rocky shelf and your turnaround point. Go back to the trailhead the way you came after taking time to savor the stunning setting. Elevation: 5 feet. **GPS:** N36 14.50' / W121 49.29'

1.2 Arrive back at the trailhead.

Pfeiffer Beach

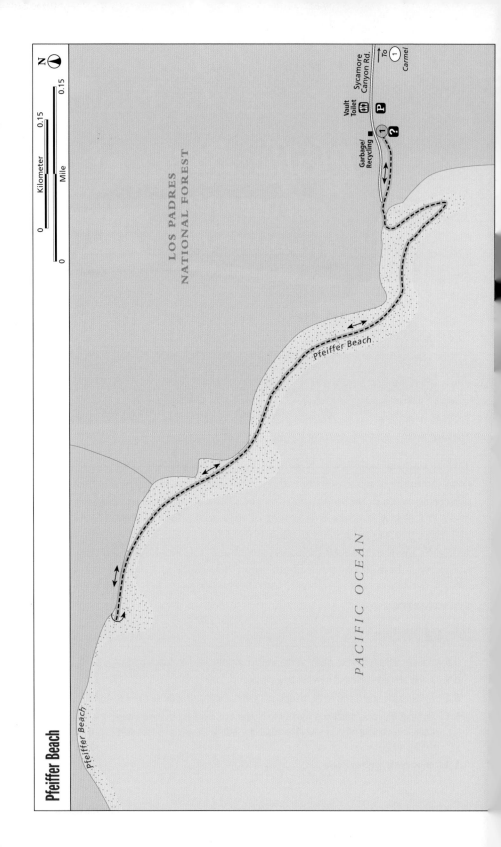

N

Kilometer
0   0.15

Mile
0   0.15

LOS PADRES
NATIONAL FOREST

Pfeiffer Beach

Pfeiffer Beach

PACIFIC OCEAN

Garbage/
Recycling

Vault
Toilet

P

1

Sycamore
Canyon Rd.

To
1
Carmel

Enjoying nature's sculpture

Creature Comforts

Fueling Up

Big Sur Bakery, 47540 CA 1, Big Sur 93920; (831) 667-0520; bigsurbakery.com. This is a must stop for fresh-baked goodies about 0.25 mile south of Sycamore Canyon Road on the west side of CA 1. The muffins are as divine as they are expensive.

Resting Up

Campgrounds

There are several large private campgrounds off CA 1 with cabins (no dogs in the cabins) and sites that accommodate tents and RVs.

Ventana Campground, 48123 on the east side of CA 1, Big Sur 93920; (831) 667-2712; ventanacamping.com. Tent camping only, or van camping site, in the 78 sites in the redwoods with creek setting. Sites have picnic tables and fire rings. The campground has showers and flush toilets as well as water faucets.

Pfeiffer Big Sur State Park, on the Big Sur River 26 miles south of Carmel on CA 1; parks.ca.gov; reserveamerica.com; (800) 444-7275. There are tent and RV sites (no hookups but dump station), flush toilets, showers, drinking water, picnic tables and grills, and a convenience store.

2 Sand Dollar Beach

This hike on national forest land is as superb as it is short. It is conveniently accessed from a day-use area off CA 1. The trail threads a scenic bluff with the bonus of a 0.25-mile-long sandy beach.

Start: From the northwest corner of the Sand Dollar Beach day-use parking lot off CA 1
Distance: 1.4-mile semi-loop
Hiking time: About 1 hour
Difficulty: Easy
Trailhead elevation: 138 feet
Highest point: 163 feet
Best season: Year-round
Trail surface: Dirt and sandy beach
Other trail users: Horses
Canine compatibility: On leash
Land status: National forest
Fees and permits: There is a parking pay station in the day-use area.
Maps: USGS Cape San Martin, Los Padres National Forest
Trail contacts: Los Padres National Forest Monterey District, 406 Mildred Ave., King City

93930; (831) 385-5434; lospadresnational forest.fs.usda.gov; Big Sur Station, (831) 667-2315
Nearest town: Cambria to the south and Carmel to the north
Trail tips: There are 2 vault toilets, picnic tables with grills, garbage and recycling cans. No water. The beauty of this hike is that it is on an isolated stretch of gorgeous coastline, but services are few and far between in this area. If you are driving south on CA 1, your last best bet for snacks and supplies is in Big Sur about 40 miles north of Sand Dollar Beach. If you are driving north on CA 1, there are limited services in Gorda about 4 miles south of Sand Dollar Beach.

Finding the trailhead: From Carmel at Rio Road and CA 1, drive 60 miles south on CA 1 and turn right at Sand Dollar Beach. The trailhead is at the northwest corner of the day-use parking lot. **GPS:** N35 55.32' / W121 28.02'
From Cambria on CA 1, drive 39 miles north on CA 1 and turn left at Sand Dollar Beach. The trailhead is at the northwest corner of the day-use parking lot. **GPS:** N35 55.32' / W121 28.02'

The Hike

This hike is on a sublime stretch off CA 1 south of Big Sur. Most of the beaches on the coast are in state parks that seldom welcome dogs. Luckily, Sand Dollar Beach is on dog-friendly national forest land. As a bonus, Plaskett Creek campground is just steps away on the southeast side of CA 1.

CA 1 is a world-famous scenic route, and the views from this hike's trailhead are astonishing. You begin the hike at the parking lot's northwest corner and walk north along the trail. The trail is narrow with low, green coyote brush, California blackberry vines, and sneaky three-leaf poison oak often camouflaged in the vines.

Looking north up the Big Sur Coast from the Sand Dollar Beach trail

You will come to a fork on the trail almost immediately. This left path with stairs heads down to the beach. This is where you will come up from the beach on the way back.

Just a few feet ahead is another short spur on the left leading to a viewpoint for photos. Bear right and continue walking north along the bluff trail. At 0.1 mile notice the spur trail on the left heading down to the beach. This is the spur trail where you will turn right to go down to the beach on the way back.

The last 0.3 mile of trail includes two steep but very short down-and-up dips across gullies on the way to the locked cattle gate.

Turn around at the gate and walk 0.3 mile back to the spur on your right. Walk down the path 0.2 mile to the beach.

At 0.9 mile you arrive on the 0.5-mile-long cove beach. Sand Dollar Beach stretches about 0.25 mile in each direction (north and south) from where you are standing. Turn left (south) to continue the hike to the stairs that will take you back up to the bluff. The white rock south of the stairs just off the coast is Plaskett Rock. Feel free to explore the beach and let pooch sniff to his nose's content before going back to the bluff up the 100 steps and short switchback path.

The left spur off the switchback between the steps and the bluff trail leads to a great viewpoint for photos and an interpretive panel about local bird life.

Strolling Sand Dollar Beach on a peaceful morning

You arrive back at the bluff trail and trailhead at 1.2 miles. Continue walking south past the trailhead a few steps. The day-use area fence is on your left with Monterey pines, Monterey cypress trees, and eucalyptus trees screening the headlands from CA 1. You will see a grassy path on the right heading toward Plaskett Rock. Turn right on the grassy path for about 0.1 mile and arrive at a viewpoint with a bench carved out of a tree trunk. Enjoy this unique picnic spot before going back to the trailhead the way you came.

Miles and Directions

0.0 Start at the Beach Area sign at the northwest corner of Sand Dollar Beach day-use parking lot and turn right.

0.1 Come to a spur path down to the beach on your left. This is the spur you will take to the beach on your return walk. Bear right on the bluff trail.

0.4 Arrive at the end of the bluff trail at cattle gate. Elevation: 141 feet. **GPS:** N35 55.64' / W121 28.06'. Walk back the way you came 0.3 mile to the spur on your right.

0.7 Arrive at spur on your right and walk down to the beach.

0.9 Arrive on the beach and turn left to walk south.

1.1 Come to stairs up to the bluff on the left. Walk up 100 steps and up the switchback path.

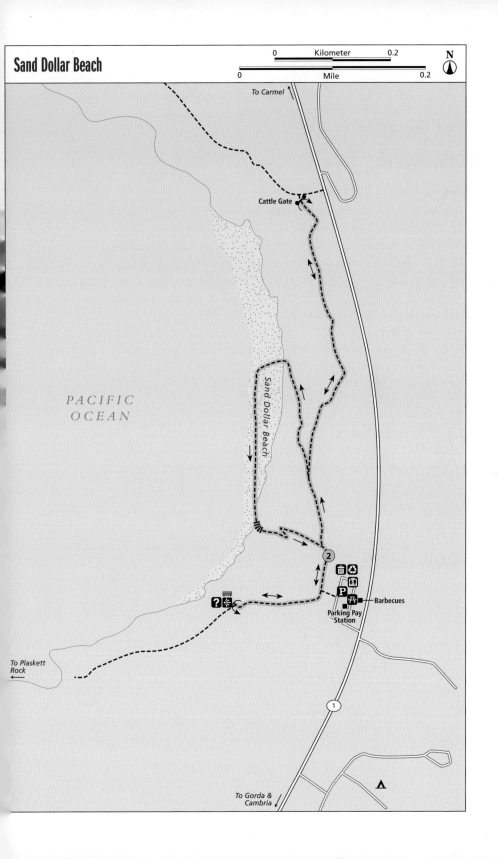

Sand Dollar Beach

To Carmel

0   Kilometer   0.2

0   Mile   0.2

N

Cattle Gate

PACIFIC
OCEAN

Sand Dollar Beach

2

Barbecues

P

Parking Pay
Station

To Plaskett
Rock

1

To Gorda &
Cambria

1.2 Arrive back at the trailhead and walk past the trailhead. Turn right on the grassy path.

1.3 Come to a viewpoint and a tree trunk bench on the right. Elevation: 114 feet. **GPS:** N35 55.28' / W121 28.14'. Soak up the stunning views while you and your dog enjoy a picnic. Go back to the trailhead the way you came.

1.4 Arrive back at the trailhead.

Creature Comforts

Fueling Up

Gorda General Store/Pacific Market and Gift Shop/Café, 3 miles south of Sand Dollar Beach on the east side of CA 1, 93920; (805)927-3918. This is the closest commercial business to Sand Dollar Beach. The outdoor patio is dog friendly.

Lucia Lodge Convenience Store, 62400 on the west side of CA 1, 10 miles north of Sand Dollar Beach, 93920; (831) 667-2391; lucialodge.com. This is a scenic spot for a deli snack at one of the three picnic tables down the hill. Janissa, the lodge's friendly staff member, claims the peanut butter cookies are "amazing!"

Big Sur Bakery, 47540 CA 1, Big Sur 93920; (831) 667-0520; bigsurbakery.com. If you are driving south to Sand Dollar Beach from Carmel, this is a must stop for fresh-baked goodies about 30 miles south of Carmel. The muffins are as divine as they are expensive.

Resting Up

Gorda Springs Resort on the east side of CA 1, about 3 miles south of Sand Dollar Beach, 93920; (805) 927-4600; gordaspringsresort.com. This small "oasis" has cottages and rooms that accommodate small dogs up to 15 pounds.

Campgrounds

Plaskett Creek Campground is a national forest campground with no hookups for RVs and trailers. Reservations can be made at reservation.gov; (877) 444-6777; campone.com. The campground is a few yards south and across the road from Sand Dollar Beach.

3 Salmon Creek Trail to Salmon Creek Falls and Spruce Creek

What could be more perfect than a hike that begins with a stunning waterfall, meandering through shady woodlands interrupted by open stretches for Pacific views before dropping you on the banks of a cool creek?

Start: From the Salmon Creek Trail sign on the east side of CA 1
Distance: 4.2 miles out and back
Hiking time: About 2.5 hours
Difficulty: Moderate
Trailhead elevation: 287 feet
Highest point: 1,123 feet
Best season: Year-round; winter and spring for most volume of water in waterfall and creeks
Trail surface: Dirt and rock
Other trail users: Horses
Canine compatibility: Voice control
Land status: National forest

Fees and permits: None
Maps: USGS Burro Mountain; Los Padres National Forest
Trail contacts: Los Padres National Forest Monterey District, 406 Mildred Ave., King City 93930; (831) 385-5434; fs.usda.gov/lpnf; Big Sur Station, (831) 667-2315
Nearest town: Cambria
Trail tips: There is a call box at the Los Padres National Forest Salmon Creek Station sign on CA 1 for emergencies. There are no amenities or water at the trailhead.

Finding the trailhead: From Cambria at the intersection of CA 1 and Windsor Avenue, drive 25 miles north on CA 1. The trailhead is tucked in the curve on the right (east side of the road) at the unmarked wide dirt shoulder parking area just before the Los Padres National Forest Salmon Creek Station, which will be on your right (east side of CA 1). Turn right onto the shoulder parking area and walk 100 feet south behind the metal guardrail to the trailhead. **GPS:** N35 48.93' / W121 21.51'

From Carmel at CA 1 and Rio Road, drive 70 miles south on CA 1 just past the Los Padres National Forest Salmon Creek Station, which will be on your left (east side). The trailhead is tucked in the curve just past the station. Turn left onto the wide dirt shoulder parking area and walk 100 feet south behind the guardrail to the trailhead. **GPS:** N35 48.93' / W121 21.51'

The Hike

Many of the hikes in the Los Padres National Forest on the east side of the Big Sur Coast require long, strenuous treks up canyons or steep, exposed slopes to reap the rewards of cool, shaded creeks or formidable views. Salmon Creek Trail is one of the few exceptions.

There's no fanfare to this trailhead, which is why the enchanting setting of the hidden waterfall, steps off the main trail before you barely get your steam up for the hike, is such an amazing sight. Even if that's as far as you and your dog have time or

Winter rains revive Salmon Creek Falls.

energy to go, it would be worth the drive. The sign at the junction at 0.1 mile points left for the falls and right to continue to S.C. Trail (Salmon Creek Trail). Almost immediately after turning left you enter a shady grove of tumbled boulders. Don't be perplexed by the faint spur trails that seem to fade at the foot of the maze of boulders. The path of least resistance to the base of the waterfall is to bear left and head down to the creek. Within 0.1 mile, depending on the season and the rainfall, you will hear and/or see the waterfall on your right up the creek bed at the head of the canyon. Your dog will probably be the first to spot the swimming holes along the creek.

If you don't get seduced into spending the afternoon at the waterfall, go back to the trail junction and continue uphill to Spruce Creek. This hike offers much shade from the bay, maple, and alder canopies with several seasonal creek crossings. The trail becomes more exposed with views toward the Pacific at about 0.4 mile and then again at 0.7 mile, where you come to a plateau with greenish rock and the evidence of jade mining in the Los Burros Mining District from earlier times. The trail winds up revealing grander vistas toward the Pacific and up the canyon. Chaparral yucca, spiny chaparral whitethorn, and sage dress the sun-blasted slopes. These viewpoints are perfect for water breaks.

You will reenter the shady woodland just ahead. At 1.4 miles the trail levels and you'll notice a sprinkling of Douglas fir trees. The trail begins a gentle descent over the next 0.5 mile with ferns mixed in with buckwheat, coffee berry, yellow sticky monkey, and wild California blackberry vines.

At 2.0 miles you come to a trail junction with two signs. The sign on the right is for Spruce Creek Trail. The sign on the left is for Salmon Creek Trail. Continue walking on Salmon Creek Trail to Spruce Creek, 0.25 mile. The trail steepens downhill to the creek bed. You arrive at Spruce Creek Camp at 2.2 miles. Spruce Creek and Salmon Creek converge just a few yards to the left downstream on Spruce Creek. This undeveloped shady campsite with swimming holes is your destination. Enjoy snacks with your four-legged companion before going back to the trailhead the way you came.

Miles and Directions

0.0 Start at the Salmon Creek Trail sign on the east side of CA 1.

0.1 Come to a trail junction with a small wooden sign for Falls with an arrow pointing left and SC to the right. Turn left toward the falls.

0.2 Arrive at the base of the falls. Elevation: 289 feet. **GPS:** N35 48.97' / W121 21.42'
Savor the magic of the boulder setting before walking 0.1 mile back to the trail junction to continue up Salmon Creek Trail (SC).

0.8 Come to an exposed rocky finger above the old jade mine at a viewpoint.

2.0 Come to a trail junction for the Spruce Creek Trail on the right. Bear left to continue walking on Salmon Creek Trail to Spruce Creek, 0.25 mile.

Salmon Creek Trail to Salmon Creek Falls and Spruce Creek

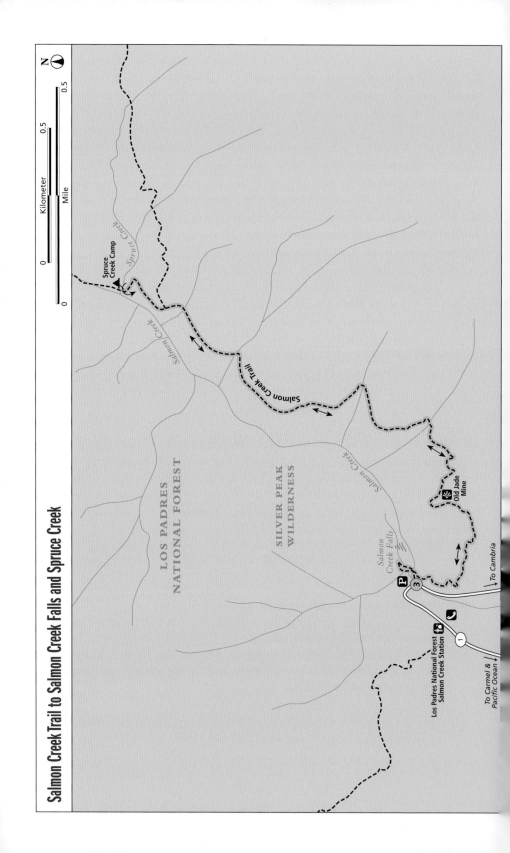

Arriving at Spruce Creek

2.2 Arrive at Spruce Creek Camp on Spruce Creek. Elevation: 904 feet. **GPS:** N35 49.58' / W121 20.70' Go back to the trailhead the way you came after enjoying the creekside solitude and snacks with pooch.

4.2 Arrive back at the trailhead.

Creature Comforts

Cambria Chamber of Commerce, 767 Main St., Cambria 93428; (805) 927-3624; cambriachamber.org. The chamber prints a "Yes, Dogs Allowed" list of restaurants, lodging, and some useful pooch services in the area.

Fueling Up

Sandy's Deli and Bakery, 604 Main St., Cambria's West Village 93428; (805) 927-3000; sandysdelicambria.com. The water bowl on the patio is a welcoming touch for pooches while you order one of their healthy sandwiches to share.

Robin's Restaurant, 4095 Burton Dr., Cambria's East Village 93428; (805) 927-5255; robinsrestaurant.com. Dogs are welcome in the garden seating area.

Centrally Grown Restaurant and Market, 7432 Exotic Gardens Dr., Cambria 93428; (805) 717-4379; centrallygrown.com. This 2015 commercial venture continues to evolve with relaxed rustic Big Sur flair. It's a stunning ocean-view setting with dog-friendly patio and grounds.

Resting Up

Cambria Shores Inn, 6276 Moonstone Beach Dr., Cambria 93428; (805) 927-8644; cambriashores.com. This inn across from Moonstone Beach boardwalk (dogs on leash) makes no bones about being dog friendly. The inn has 23 dog-friendly rooms out of 25. Check-in comes with a VIP ("very important pooch") welcome basket (very important pooch). Among other goodies, the basket includes a towel, a sheet, a flashlight, biscuits, pooch rules, and a list of dog-friendly restaurants as well dog-sitters and kennels.

Campgrounds

South of Salmon Creek Trail:

Hearst San Simeon State Park campground in San Simeon is about 19 miles south of Salmon Creek Trail on the east side of CA 1; (800) 444-7275; parks.ca.gov; reserveamerica.com. There are no hookups for RVs and trailers, but there is a dump station. During the 2015 drought, restrooms and sinks were closed, but there was water available at the campground faucets. There were portable toilets in the campground. Some sites have ocean views. Dogs are allowed on the paved roads but not on the trails or the beach.

North of Salmon Creek Trail:

Plaskett Creek Campground is a national forest campground with no hookups for RVs and trailers. Reservations can be made at reservation.gov; (877) 444-6777; campone.com. The campground is a few yards south and across the road from Sand Dollar Beach.

Puppy Paws and Golden Years

Salmon Creek Falls

Start at the trailhead for the above hike and walk 0.1 mile to the trail junction. Turn left at the sign and walk down to the creek for another 0.1 mile. The falls are to the right at the head of the canyon. This is a "cool" adventure in all ways for young and old pooches.

San Luis Obispo County

This region, often referred to as the Central Coast, is considered the transition area between Northern and Southern California. The county retains a rural feel with agriculture and vineyards as centerpieces. Grapes are the most cultivated crop after strawberries, making San Luis Obispo California's third-largest producer of wine. California Polytechnic State University helps make downtown San Luis Obispo a vibrant, dog-friendly hub for locals and visitors. From beaches to morros, there's a hike for every boot and paw.

4 Fiscalini Ranch Preserve

The bad news is that dogs are no longer allowed off leash. The good news is that dogs on leash are still welcome on this "five paw" network of trails.

Most hikes with as grand a view as the vistas from the Fiscalini Ranch would require serious sustained uphill panting to earn the reward. But this hike treats hikers and their dogs to meadows, a Monterey Pine forest, bluffs, and phenomenal coastal views after just a couple hundred feet of moderate grade up to the ridge.

Start: From the trailhead for the Santa Rosa Creek Trail on Windsor Boulevard
Distance: 4.6-mile lollipop
Hiking time: About 2.5 hours
Difficulty: Moderate
Trailhead elevation: 13 feet
Highest point: 240 feet
Best season: Year-round
Trail surface: Dirt, gravel, boardwalk
Other trail users: Bikes on some trails
Canine compatibility: On leash
Land status: Cambria Community Services District
Fees and permits: None
Maps: USGS Cambria
Trail contacts: Cambria Community Services District, 1316 Tamsen Dr., Suite 201, Cambria

92428; (805) 927-6220; ffrpcambria.org; cambriacsd.org
Nearest town: Cambria
Trail tips: There is a trashcan at the trailhead and a small map on the information board. Until spring 2015, dogs were permitted off leash under voice control on several of the trails in the Fiscalini Ranch. As a result of problem dogs (more accurately: problem dog owners), the rules have changed, requiring that dogs be on leash on all trails. As of fall 2015, the website cited the change but no signs had been posted at the trailheads. You may see dogs off leash with hikers who are not aware of the change in rules.

Finding the trailhead: From Cambria on CA 1 at Windsor Boulevard, turn west toward the coast and drive 0.1 mile before making an immediate left into a dirt parking area just past the bridge. There's a wastewater treatment plant on the south side of the parking area and the trailhead is at the southeast corner of the parking area. **GPS:** N35 34.07' / W121 06.23'

The Hike

The Fiscalini Ranch land was home to Chumash and Salinan tribes before the Fiscalini family grazed cattle on the land from the late 1800s until they sold it to a real estate developer in the 1980s. Plans for development stalled for thirteen years. In 1993 another real estate developer acquired the land at a bankruptcy auction. Thankfully, grassroots community efforts, with the help of land and coastal conservancies, raised $11.1 million and purchased the Fiscalini Ranch and adjacent parcels for preservation.

Of the ranch's 434 acres, 364 acres are located on the west side of CA 1. The Santa Rosa Creek West trailhead is the most convenient access from CA 1 with the best

Interpretive panels add interest along the trail.

parking. The trailhead has a small map board that you will see again at a couple of trail junctions. Although the trail and junctions are unmarked in the preserve, the area is easy to navigate since the ranch is braced by CA 1 on the east border and the ocean on the west side, and the residential neighborhoods at the north and south ends also serve as landmarks.

You begin the hike along a wide, shady stretch of dirt and gravel trail with Santa Rosa Creek on your left and the wastewater treatment plant on the right. The trail undulates with a couple of short but stiff up-and-downs over the first 0.5 mile. The creekside trail is lush with a carpet of ivy and some primeval-looking asparagus ferns at the foot of willows, eucalyptus, and oak trees.

At 0.7 mile, just past a bench and interpretive panel about steelhead trout and across from a sign about restricted fishing on the left, you turn right up a trail to the ridge. You leave CA 1 road noise behind as you climb. The view quickly opens up to the east toward the Santa Lucia Range. Turn left at the next unmarked trail junction and reach the ridge boasting expansive views of the Pacific. The wooden dolphin bench on the left marks the beginning of the loop for this lollipop hike. Turn right downhill toward the ocean. You will see a residential neighborhood on the right at the north end of the ranch.

Arriving back at the trailhead

At 1.5 miles you come to the fire lane and the gate with a couple of parking spaces reserved for the physically disabled. There is a dog-waste bag dispenser and some maps at the gate. The boardwalk is to your left about 10 yards ahead. Walk around the gate and continue on the boardwalk, which is an ADA-accessible trail and part of the Bluff Trail. This is a stunning stretch of trail with several unusual benches along the way perfect for scanning the surf for whale migration.

You leave the boardwalk just short of a mile ahead near the residential neighborhood at the south end of the preserve. Turn left on the dirt trail at 2.3 miles, walk through the opening in the fence about 50 yards up the trail, and continue uphill to the ridge and the fire lane, which is also the unmarked Marine Terrace Trail. Turn right at the bench and then left at the unmarked trail junction to continue uphill with the forest on your right.

At the ridge and bench, turn right until you reach a fork just ahead. Bear left at the fork and walk through the Monterey pine grove. Continue walking straight through the next unmarked trail junction to another fork. This is the farthest point south on this hike. Turn left to begin heading back toward the trailhead. At 3.1 miles, bear right downhill into the forest, bear right past a bench, and then bear left to merge into the unmarked Ridge Trail heading back to the wooden dolphin bench, where you will close the loop of your lollipop.

Enjoy the views from the dolphin bench and take time to offer your dog water and a snack before going back to the trailhead the way you came. Your trail down off the ridge is just 0.2 mile ahead on the right.

Miles and Directions

0.0 Start at the Fiscalini Ranch trails information board and trailhead for the Santa Rosa Creek Trail.

0.4 Come to an unmarked fork on the trail and bear right uphill past the bench.

0.7 Come to an unmarked trail junction with a Restricted Fishing sign on the left. Turn right and walk uphill to the ridge.

0.9 Arrive at the ridge and an unmarked trail junction. Turn left on the ridge trail.

1.1 Come to an unmarked trail junction on the right across from a wooden dolphin bench. Turn right and walk downhill on the trail. This junction at the bench is where you will return to close the loop of your lollipop.

1.3 Come to an unmarked trail junction with a trail crossing your path. Turn right and walk downhill toward the ocean.

1.5 Come to a trail junction at a fire lane, also the unmarked Marine Terrace Trail, and gate at a parking lot for the physically disabled. Walk around the gate and connect to the board-walk part of the unmarked Bluff Trail on the left about 10 yards ahead.

2.3 Leave the boardwalk and turn left on the dirt trail. Walk about 50 yards to reach the opening in the fence and continue walking uphill toward the ridge.

2.5 Come to the fire lane and unmarked Marine Terrace Trail and a bench. Turn right on the trail.

2.55 Come to an unmarked trail junction and turn left uphill on a narrow dirt trail. Trees will be on your right.

2.7 Arrive at a bench on the unmarked Ridge Trail. Turn right.

2.75 Come to a fork. Bear left through the Monterey pine grove.

2.8 Come to an unmarked trail junction. Continue walking straight.

2.9 Come to an unmarked trail junction. Make a sharp left on the trail.

3.1 Come to a fork. Bear right downhill on the forested trail and bear right past the bench.

3.3 Bear left and merge with the unmarked Ridge Trail.

3.5 Come to the wooden dolphin bench on the right. This is the close of your loop on the lollipop. The bench makes a perfect rest and snack stop for you and pooch while you savor the view before going back down to the trailhead the way you came.

4.6 Arrive back at the trailhead.

Creature Comforts

Cambria Chamber of Commerce, 767 Main St., Cambria 93428; (805) 927-3624; cambriachamber.org. The chamber prints a "Yes, Dogs Allowed" list of restaurants, lodging, and some useful pooch services in the area.

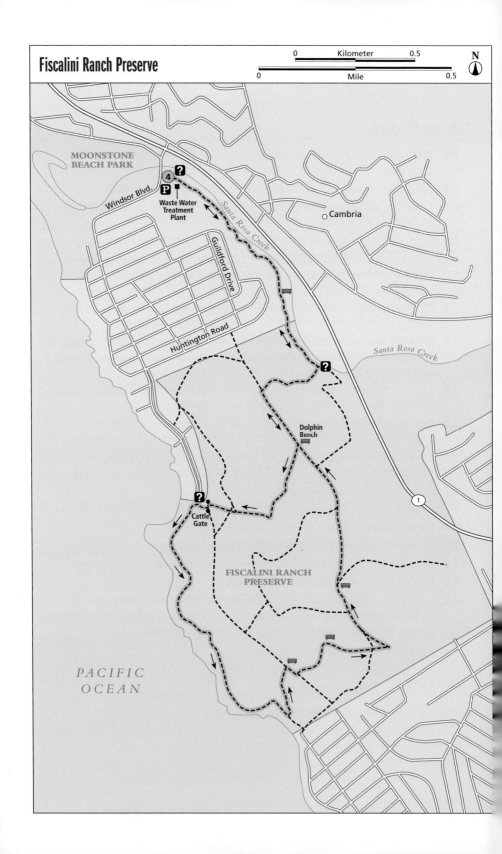

Fiscalini Ranch Preserve

0   Kilometer   0.5

0   Mile   0.5

N

MOONSTONE
BEACH PARK

Windsor Blvd.

Waste Water
Treatment
Plant

Santa Rosa Creek

Guildford Drive

Cambria

Huntington Road

Santa Rosa Creek

Dolphin
Bench

Cattle
Gate

FISCALINI RANCH
PRESERVE

1

PACIFIC
OCEAN

Fueling Up

Sandy's Deli and Bakery, 604 Main St., Cambria's West Village 93428; (805) 927-3000; sandysdelicambria.com. The water bowl on the patio is a welcoming touch for pooches while you order one of their healthy sandwiches to share.

Robin's Restaurant, 4095 Burton Dr., Cambria's East Village 93428; (805) 927-5255; robinsrestaurant.com. Dogs are welcome in the garden seating area.

Centrally Grown Restaurant and Market, 7432 Exotic Gardens Dr., Cambria 93428; (805) 717-4379; centrallygrown.com. This 2015 commercial venture continues to evolve with relaxed rustic Big Sur flair. It's a stunning ocean-view setting with dog-friendly patio and grounds.

Resting Up

Cambria Shores Inn, 6276 Moonstone Beach Dr., Cambria 93428; (805) 927-8644; cambriashores.com. This inn across from Moonstone Beach boardwalk (dogs on leash) makes no bones about being dog friendly. The inn has 23 dog-friendly rooms out of 25. Check-in comes with a VIP ("very important pooch") welcome basket (very important pooch). Among other goodies, the basket includes a towel, a sheet, a flashlight, biscuits, pooch rules, and a list of dog-friendly restaurants as well dog-sitters and kennels.

Campgrounds

Hearst San Simeon State Park campground is the closest campground to Cambria, about 2 miles north on the east side of CA 1; (800) 444-7275; parks.ca.gov; reserveamerica.com. There are no hookups for RVs and trailers but there is a dump station. During the 2015 drought, restrooms and sinks were closed, but there was water available at the campground faucets. There were portable toilets in the campground. Some sites have ocean views. Dogs are allowed on the paved roads but not on the trails or the beach.

Puppy Paws and Golden Years

Moonstone Beach Boardwalk, part of the California Coastal Trail, begins at Leffingwell Landing Park at the north end of Cambria on Moonstone Beach Drive off CA 1. Enjoy interpretive panels, benches, and migrating whale sightings from above Moonstone Beach with your leashed pal. The path is about 1.5 miles long, and you can extend your stroll north on the dirt path accessible from Leffingwell Landing parking lot. Vault toilet and picnic tables are in the parking lot.

5 Salinas Riverwalk

This urban hike alternates between dirt and pavement as it traces the banks of the Salinas River. Tucked above the river's floodplain, it meanders discreetly through Lawrence "Larry" Moore Neighborhood Park past newer home developments and a commercial center as it weaves through a chaparral landscape interrupted by cottonwood trees and willows.

Start: From the Salinas Riverwalk Trailhead at the Riverbank Lane cul-de-sac
Distance: 4.2 miles out and back
Hiking time: About 2 hours
Difficulty: Easy
Trailhead elevation: 709 feet
Highest point: 724 feet
Best season: Year-round, but can be very hot in the summer
Trail surface: Dirt and pavement
Other trail users: Bicycles
Canine compatibility: On leash

Land status: City
Fees and permits: None
Maps: USGS Paso Robles, Templeton
Trail contacts: City of Paso Robles, 1000 Spring St., Paso Robles 93446; (805) 237-2388; prcity.com
Nearest town: Paso Robles
Trail tips: There is no water at the trailhead, but there is a bench, trashcan, and recycling. Locals often let their dogs romp off leash in the dry floodplain.

Finding the trailhead: From US 101 in Paso Robles south of CA 46, take Pine Street exit 230 and drive under the railroad overpass. Drive 0.1 mile and turn left on 4th Street. Drive 0.1 mile on 4th Street and turn left on Spring Street. Drive 0.1 mile to Niblick Road and turn left at the traffic signal. Drive 0.5 mile on Niblick Road over US 101 to South River Road. Turn right on South River Road and drive 0.3 mile to Riverbank Lane. Turn right on Riverbank Lane and drive 0.5 mile to the end of the cul-de-sac at the south end of Lawrence "Larry" Moore Neighborhood Park. Park on the street in the cul-de-sac. The Salinas Riverwalk Trailhead is on the river side (west side) of the cul-de-sac across from the houses. **GPS:** N35 36.41' / W120 41.31'

The Hike

The hike begins in a residential neighborhood on a multi-use trail that alternates between dirt and pavement. This urban hike is an example of the trend for communities to integrate nature and restore habitat alongside residential and commercial development. There are plans to extend the trail system to 40 miles, connecting communities along the way. The Salinas River is unique in that it is one of the few rivers in the western United States that flows north and flows entirely underground in several places on its 170-mile journey through the Salinas Valley's agricultural lands before flowing into the Pacific at the Monterey Bay.

Accounts by the Juan Bautista de Anza expedition from Mexico through California in 1776 confirm that steelhead salmon thrived in the Salinas River. Now only a

Setting out at the trailhead

few tributaries in the upper Salinas River support steelhead populations that migrate between their spawning grounds and an area west of the Aleutian Islands.

The trail begins on dirt, and the dry riverbed is on your left the entire way, passing several interpretive panels explaining the importance of the Salinas River's ecology as well as the geology of the watershed. There are benches along the way and a few foot-bridges over seasonal streams in riparian zones. There is a water fountain and flush toilets in the Lawrence "Larry" Moore Park, but California was in its fourth year of severe drought at the time of this hike, so restrooms were locked and the drinking fountain was turned off. The picnic tables in this park make a pleasant stop for a snack on the return.

The trail is fairly exposed for the first 0.75 mile and transitions from dirt to pavement at 0.5 mile. The hum from US 101 to the west can seem intrusive at times, and the stretch of trail that passes under Niblick Road with a mall to the right is noisy but short. At Niblick Road bear left along the fence where the trail drops down before rising up and across a bridge over a pipe system for seasonal drainage. The shade of cottonwood trees welcomes you and pooch under its cooler canopy at 0.8 mile on the other side of Niblick Road.

At 1.1 miles the trail comes to a street of newer homes. Surprisingly, this more recent paved extension with a dirt shoulder is the start of the quietest stretch until the trail ends at Union Street 1 mile farther north. This mile-long section is primarily

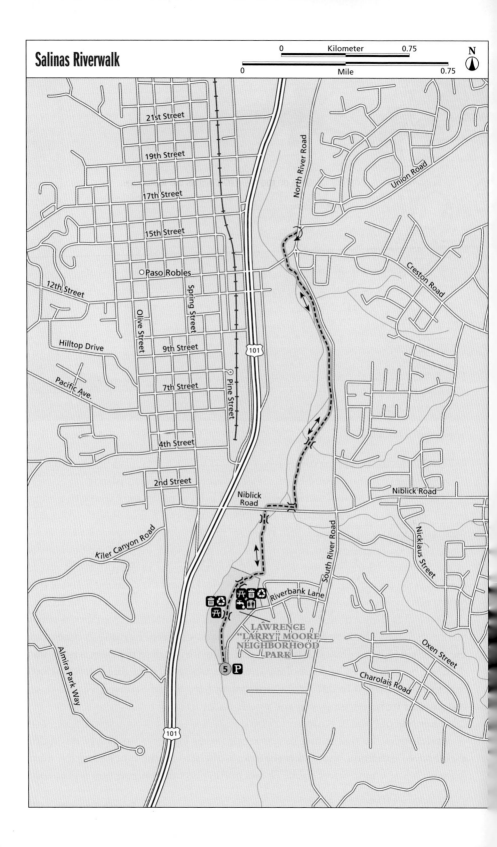

0   Kilometer   0.75

0   Mile   0.75

N

21st Street

19th Street

17th Street

15th Street

North River Road

Union Road

Creston Road

Paso Robles

12th Street

Spring Street

Olive Street

Hilltop Drive

9th Street

Pacific Ave.

7th Street

Pine Street

101

4th Street

2nd Street

Niblick Road

Niblick Road

Kiler Canyon Road

South River Road

Nicklaus Street

Riverbank Lane

LAWRENCE
"LARRY" MOORE
NEIGHBORHOOD
PARK

Almira Park Way

101

5 P

Oxen Street

Charolais Road

low chaparral brush bordered by North River Road on the right and the expansive dry floodplain on the left.

Miles and Directions

0.0 Start at the Riverbank Lane Cul-de-sac and Salinas River Walk Trailhead sign.

0.2 Walk across footbridge.

0.3 Come to an unmarked trail junction on the right going into Lawrence "Larry" Moore Neighborhood Park. Continue walking on the main trail across the footbridge.

0.7 Walk across the footbridge and under Niblick Road. Bear left along the fence.

0.8 Walk across footbridge over seasonal drainage and enter the cottonwood woodland.

1.1 Come to a street. Follow the trail north.

1.5 Come to Creston Road. Continue on the trail under the road.

2.1 Come to intersection of Union Road and North River Road. Trail ends. Go back to the trailhead the way you came. Elevation: 703 feet. **GPS:** N35 37.83' / W120 40.95'

4.2 Arrive back at the trailhead.

Creature Comforts

Fueling Up

Artisan Restaurant, 843 12th St., Paso Robles 93446; (805) 237-8638; artisanpaso robles.com. Dog-friendly patio.

Resting Up

Dunning Ranch Guest Suites, 1945 Niderer Rd., Paso Robles 93446; (800) 893-1847. Canine guests with sensible owners are welcome in this intimate bed and breakfast buffered by 40 acres overlooking a vineyard.

Oaks Hotel, 3000 Riverside Ave., Paso Robles 93446; (805) 237-8084; pasooaks .com. A hotel that welcomes dogs in the bar area and restaurant patio. Pet fee.

Hotel Cheval, 1021 Pine St., Paso Robles 93446; (805) 226-9995; hotelcheval.com. A luxurious boutique hotel in downtown Paso Robles that calls itself "dog loving." Dogs are welcome to join their owners for a bite and a drink on the bar patio. Pet fee.

Paso Robles Inn, 1103 Spring St., Paso Robles 93446; (805) 238-2660; paso roblesinn.com. Historic hotel with dog-friendly bar and restaurant patio. Pet fee.

Puppy Paws and Golden Years

Wine lovers will love **Paso Robles,** in the heart of vineyard country where furry visitors enjoy strolling the charming downtown area and park between wine-tasting rooms. Try Anglim Winery, anglimwinery.com, and Arroyo Robles, arroyorobles.com. **Travelpaso.com** has an extensive list of pooch-friendly wineries, businesses, and activities.

Doggie Splash Days (parks4pups.org) in September is a unique event for water-loving bow-wows.

Learning about the local habitat

6 Bishop Peak

This is a rare opportunity to hike up the slope of a more than 20-million-year-old volcanic plug. Your dog will be all wags from the smells in the lower oak woodland, while you'll be thrilled with the panoramic views on the exposed slope.

Start: From the City of San Luis Obispo Ferrini Ranch Open Space sign at the top of Highland Drive

Distance: 3.4 miles out and back

Hiking time: About 2 hours

Difficulty: Strenuous

Trailhead elevation: 600 feet

Highest point: 1,462 feet

Best season: Year-round

Trail surface: Dirt and rock

Other trail users: Hikers only

Canine compatibility: On leash

Land status: City

Fees and permits: None

Maps: USGS San Luis Obispo

Trail contacts: City of San Luis Obispo Parks and Recreation, 1341 Nipoma St., San Luis Obispo 93408; (805) 781-7300; slocity.org

Nearest town: San Luis Obispo

Trail tips: There are no toilets or water on this trail. In the summer, this hike is best enjoyed early in the morning when the sun is not so brutally hot on the exposed slope.

Finding the trailhead: From San Luis Obispo at the intersection of US 101 and CA 1, drive north on CA 1/Santa Rosa Street for 1 mile and turn left (west) at Highland Drive. Drive 1 mile to the top of Highland Drive. The road ends in a cul-de-sac. The Ferrini Ranch Open Space memorial plaque and City of San Luis Obispo Ferrini Ranch Open Space rules information board on the left side of the street mark the trailhead. Park on the street and walk to the trailhead. **GPS:** N35 18.07' / W120 41.35'

The Hike

Bishop Peak is the highest of nine morros (volcanic plugs) in this pocket of Southern California. The Bishop Peak land was donated by the Ferrini family in 1995 and became one more gem in the city of San Luis Obispo's crown of open-space parklands.

The Bishop Peak trail begins in a residential neighborhood at the top of Highland Drive. Fence lines define the corridor off the street for about 100 yards before entering the oak woodland. At 0.1 mile you come to a fork on the right. Follow this trail between large boulders to the clearing. You will see a wooden post and trail sign just beyond the boulders. Bear left at the trail sign. The morro with rocky Bishop Peak is up ahead on the left. The grade is moderate as you walk up to the trail junction for Felsman Loop Trail and Bishop Peak.

Continue walking uphill and bear left, walking past a bench and the Open Space map. Come to another trail sign with a faded arrow pointing left. Follow the trail left toward the water tank. The trail gets steeper as you approach the water tank on the

Studying the map with Bishop Peak in the background

left and a fence on your right up to a cattle gate. Turn left at the cattle gate and the sign for Bishop Peak. Enter the shade of the oak woodland just ahead and the morro is now on your right as the trail traces the base of Bishop Peak.

At 0.6 mile you come to a plaque for the Bishop Peak Natural Reserve. This is a good spot to offer your dog water before leaving the shade of the woodland. The last mile of the hike is totally exposed on a narrow dirt and rock trail with some steeper stretches as the trail spirals upward from the east side to the west before reaching a saddle and a bench marked End of Trail.

Although it may be tempting to scramble the boulders to the highest point, the saddle is a safer perch to enjoy the unique perspective of San Luis Obispo tucked between the surrounding volcanic morros, the Santa Lucia Range, and the Pacific Ocean. Share some snacks and water with your dog before going back to the trailhead the way you came.

Miles and Directions

0.0 Start at the wooden sign for the City of San Luis Obispo Ferrini Ranch Open Space at the top of Highland Drive.

0.1 Come to a fork. Turn right on the trail between large boulders. The trail leads out of the woodland into the open to a wooden trail sign. Bear left at the wooden trail sign.

Enjoying a moment at the top of Bishop Peak

0.2   Come to a trail junction for Felsman Loop Trail and Bishop Peak. Bear left past the bench and Open Space map to a trail sign with a faded arrow pointing left. Continue walking left toward the water tank.

0.3   Come to a water tank on your left. Continue walking past the water tank.

0.4   Come to a cattle gate and a sign for Bishop Peak. Turn left at the cattle gate.

0.6   Come to a plaque for the Bishop Peak Natural Reserve.

1.7   Arrive at a bench on the saddle with an End of Trail sign. Breathe in the views on either side of the saddle and reward yourself and your dog with some snacks and water before going back to the trailhead the way you came. Elevation: 1,462 feet. **GPS:** N35 18.12' / W120 41.81'

Creature Comforts

Fueling Up

Novo, 726 Higuera St., San Luis Obispo 93401; (805) 543-3986; novorestaurant .com. Enjoy fresh, local ingredients on the dog-friendly creekside patio.

Luna Red, 1023 Chorro St., San Luis Obispo 93401; (805) 540-5243; lunaredslo .com. The restaurant patio treats customers to Latin flavors and a view of the historic mission.

Bishop Peak

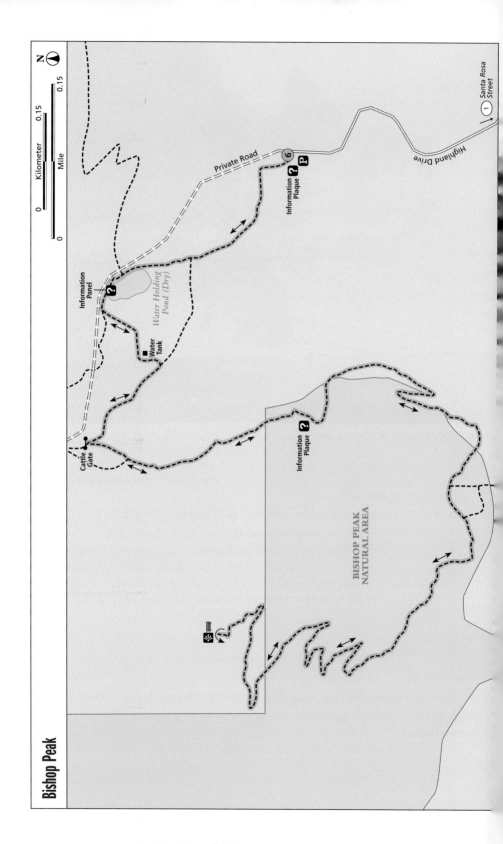

Big Sky Café, 1121 Broad St., San Luis Obispo 93401; (805) 545-5401: bigskycafe .com. If you are up for a blend of modern international cuisine and comfort food, there are two outdoor tables for canine guests at this popular cafe open for breakfast, lunch, and dinner.

Resting Up

San Luis Obispo has several chain motels that are pet friendly, but if your pal is in the mood for a more intimate tail-wagging experience, there are a couple of dog-loving bed-and-breakfast inns downtown.

Garden Street Inn, 1212 Garden St., San Luis Obispo 93401; (805) 545-9802; garden streetinn.com. This historic Victorian inn built in 1887 on land that was once part of the mission vineyard has two rooms reserved for well-behaved canines.

Petit Soleil B&B, 1473 Monterey St., San Luis Obispo 93401; (805)544-0321; petitsoleilslo.com. Dogs don't have to bark in French to ask for one of the fresh-baked "petits bone appetits" dog treats.

Campgrounds

El Chorro Regional Park, 4.5 miles north of San Luis Obispo off CA 1 on the east side; (805) 781-5930; slocountyparks.org. There are tent, trailer, and RV sites with partial and full hookups.

Puppy Paws and Golden Years

El Chorro Regional Park, 4.5 miles north of San Luis Obispo off CA 1 on the east side; (805) 781-5930; slocountyparks.org. There is an off-leash dog park.

Take your dog on stroll back in time around the **Mission Plaza** in downtown San Luis Obispo between Chorro and Broad Streets. Mission San Luis Obispo, the fifth of the twenty-one California missions, was founded in 1772. There's rich history and charming Spanish colonial architecture for you and lots of smells and sights for your pal in the park and by the nearby creek.

7 Bob Jones City to Sea Trail

This easy, level hike begins in a convenient Park and Ride lot just off CA 1 and ends at charming Avila Beach Community Park. Most of the trail in the Avila Valley traces the San Luis Obispo Creek, lined with eucalyptus trees, oaks, and willows. This is a paved multi-use path along an old Pacific Coast Railroad right-of-way with a dirt shoulder that treats dogs to a banquet of natural smells.

Start: From the Bob Jones City to Sea trail sign at the entrance to the Park and Ride lot
Distance: 5.6 miles out and back
Hiking time: About 3 hours
Difficulty: Easy
Trailhead elevation: 35 feet
Highest point: 35 feet
Best season: Year-round
Trail surface: Pavement
Other trail users: Bicycles
Canine compatibility: On leash
Land status: County

Fees and permits: None
Maps: USGS Pismo Beach
Trail contacts: San Luis Obispo County Parks, 1087 Santa Rosa St., San Luis Obispo 93408; (805) 781-5930; slocountyparks.org
Nearest town: Pismo Beach and Avila Beach
Trail tips: There is a vault toilet and trashcan in the parking lot for the trailhead. There are dog-waste bag dispensers and trashcans along the trail. Avila Beach Community Park at the end of the hike has flush toilets, sinks, picnic tables, grills, and cold-drink vending machines.

Finding the trailhead: From Pismo Beach on CA 1, drive 4 miles north and turn off at exit 195. Drive 0.4 mile west on Avila Beach Drive. Turn right on Ontario Road and drive 0.3 mile to the Park and Ride lot and Bob Jones City to Sea Trail sign on the right. The Park and Ride driveway is just past the bridge over San Luis Obispo Creek. **GPS:** N35 11.13' / W120 42.18'

The Hike

This trail is named in honor of Bob Jones, considered an environmental pioneer who was committed to protecting natural habitats. Bob Jones was president of the Land Conservancy of San Luis Obispo County from 1987 to 1989. The trail is a result of his vision and dedication to restoring and protecting the San Luis Obispo Creek. Bob Jones died in 1994 and the trail opened in 1998. Plans are to eventually extend the trail by an additional 4.4 miles to San Luis Obispo.

From the Park and Ride lot at the large Bob Jones City to Sea Trail sign, you begin the excursion by crossing Ontario Road in the crosswalk to the start of the paved path. The moment you step on the tree-lined path, it's as if a curtain drops and you leave the nondescript world of urbanization behind. Twenty TIPs (Trail Information Project) markers along the path describe the cultural and natural history (sibme .org/TrailMarkers.aspx).

The first mile of trails wanders between San Luis Obispo Creek on the left and large residential parcels with orchards against a backdrop of rolling hills on the right.

Making friends along the trail

There are a few benches shaded by leafy canopies for rest stops along the way. You cross a bridge over See Canyon Creek around 0.8 mile and walk under the San Luis Bay Drive overpass at 1 mile. The trail passes Avila Village's small commercial development, complete with a dog-friendly market/wine bar patio and inn, on the right just before the Avila Bay Athletic Club gated residential community.

At 1.5 miles, the recreational trail merges into Blue Heron Drive where hikers and cyclists share the lightly traveled road that ends at the gated community. San Luis Obispo Creek is still on your left. Notice the fish ladder in the creek and the interpretive panel describing the life cycle of the steelhead, an oceangoing trout listed under the 1997 Endangered Species Act. Steelhead trout migrate up to their native freshwater creek in the winter to spawn.

At 1.9 miles you come to the Avila Beach Golf Resort as you continue along Blue Heron Drive tucked between the golf course on the left and valley hills on the right.

At 2.3 miles you come to a junction on Blue Heron Drive and turn left off the road downhill where the Bob Jones path crosses the golf course and over the bridge. San Luis Obispo Creek becomes Avila Beach Estuary. Golf carts may also use the bridge. The water is now on your right as you continue along the path for about 0.2 mile to the traffic light at Avila Beach Drive and the end of the Bob Jones City to Sea Trail. You have arrived at the town of Avila Beach. Walk across Avila Beach Drive

Crossing over the Avila Beach Estuary

and follow the sidewalk into Avila Beach Community Park on your left and the sandy beach ahead. You'll find the park is a perfect terminus for a picnic with a view in a small green space appointed with picnic tables, grills, restrooms, drinking water, and cold beverage vending machines. Note that the beach is only dog friendly before 10 a.m. and after 5 p.m.

If this little beach community appears to exude a fresher quaintness than its neighbors, it's because much of it was rebuilt after an ecological disaster less than twenty years ago. A decades-old oil leak in a rusted pipeline running under the town resulted in litigation and a multimillion-dollar settlement with the oil company. It took a quarter-mile-wide swath of excavation to remove contaminated soil before rebuilding much of the town. Take time to explore the charming promenade beachfront downtown stretching south of the park and appreciate the commercial and ecological restoration.

If you and pooch have extra energy and time, walk 1 mile north over the bridge across the estuary to the Olde Porte Beach, which is an off-leash gift of a small beach for well-behaved canines and their responsible owners. This will add 2 miles to the hike before heading back to the trailhead the way you came.

Miles and Directions

0.0 Start at the Bob Jones City to Sea Trail sign at the entrance to the Park and Ride lot and walk to the crosswalk along the gravel path toward the bridge on Ontario Road. Walk across Ontario Road to the trail sign on the right of the bridge.

0.8 Walk across the bridge over See Canyon Creek.

1.0 Walk under the San Luis Bay Drive overpass.

1.5 Come to Blue Heron Drive and turn left on Blue Heron Drive with San Luis Obispo Creek on your left.

1.9 Come to Avila Beach Golf Resort on your left.

2.3 Come to a junction and turn downhill, left off of Blue Heron Drive toward the path crossing the bridge.

2.4 Walk across the Avila Beach Estuary on the bridge.

2.6 Come to Avila Beach Drive traffic light. Walk across the road and follow the sidewalk into Avila Beach Community Park.

2.8 Arrive at Avila Beach Community Park picnic area. Enjoy this idyllic dog-friendly patch with a snack and a stroll before going back to the trailhead the way you came. Elevation: 10 feet. **GPS:** N35 10.78' / W120 44.18'

5.6 Arrive back at the trailhead.

Creature Comforts

Fueling Up

Avila Grocery and Deli, 354 Front St., Avila Beach 93424; (805) 595-2500; avila grocery.com. It's a convenient stop for snacks.

Woodstone Marketplace in Avila Village, 6675 Bay Laurel Place, Avila Beach 93424; (805) 595-1018; woodstoneavila.com. Imagine a market/deli/cafe with dog-friendly patio for breakfast, lunch, and dinner just off the Bob Jones Trail about half-way between the trailhead and Avila Beach.

Avila Valley Barn, 560 Avila Beach Dr., San Luis Obispo 93405; (805) 595-2816; avilavalleybarn.com. This country farmstand/deli/bakery off Avila Beach Drive minutes from the trailhead has been delighting locals since 1985. Leashed pooches are welcome at the picnic tables and around the petting farm. The pies are expensive but a special treat worth taking back to the campground.

Olde Port Fisheries, 3 Avila Beach Pier, Avila Beach 93424; (805) 541-3474; old eportfish.com. A great spot to buy fresh seafood for a campground feast.

Custom House Restaurant, 404 Front St., Avila Beach 93424; (805) 595-7555; oldcustomhouse.com. Enjoy breakfast, lunch, or dinner on the patio with pooch.

Avila Beach's promenade has several food venues with outdoor seating areas where you and pooch can enjoy light bites with a view.

Bob Jones City to Sea Trail

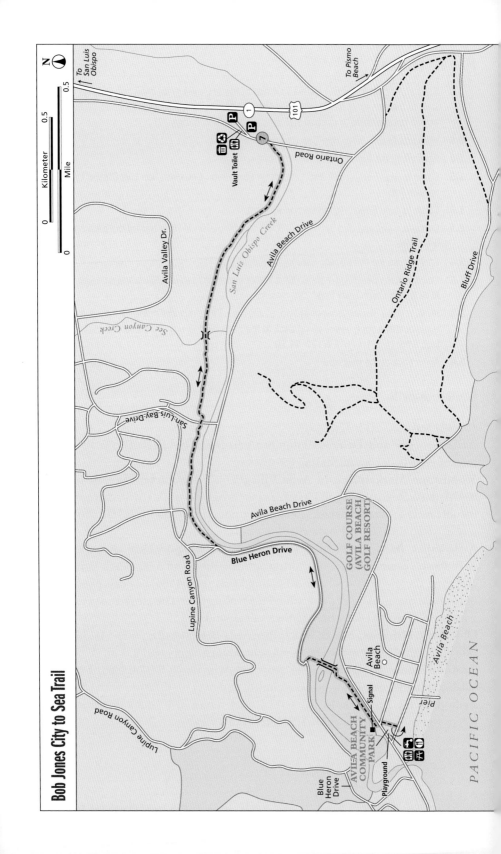

Resting Up

Avila La Fonda Hotel, 101 San Miguel St., Avila Beach 93424; (800) 595-1700. Both you and pooch will feel pampered at this quiet boutique hotel with kitchen conveniences in the guestrooms.

Campgrounds

Port San Luis RV Camping, Port San Luis Harbor District, 3950 Avila Beach Dr., Avila Beach 93424; Camp Host (805) 903-3395; camphost@portsanluis.com. The downside is that it's RV parking lot–style camping (dry and some hookups) but the upside is the cul-de-sac waterfront location almost across from an off-leash dog beach.

Pismo Coast Village RV Resort, 165 S. Dolliver St., Pismo Beach 93449; (888) 782-3224; pismocoastvillage.com. About 5 miles south of the trailhead off CA 1, it's luxury at the dog-friendly Pismo Beach with hookups and Wi-Fi.

North Beach Campground, 399 S. Dolliver St., Pismo State Beach 93449; (805) 473-7220; parks.ca.gov; reservations: (800) 444-PARK; reserveamerica.com. No hookups. Reservations accepted May 15 through Nov 30. First-come, first-served basis the rest of the year. This state park campground behind the dog-friendly beach dunes is about 5 miles south of the trailhead off CA 1. This is a great place to see wintering colonies of monarch butterflies.

Puppy Paws and Golden Years

Pismo State Beach's dunes and flat, firm sand stretches over three communities off CA 1 and can be accessed from the pier area in Pismo Beach and south from the bottom of Grand Avenue in Grover Beach for day use. Pismo Beach Conference and Visitors Bureau, 760 Mattie Rd., Pismo Beach 93449; pismobeach.org or classic california.com. Pismo Beach Chamber of Commerce, (800) 443-7778. Grover Beach, grover.org. Oceano Dunes Park District, (805) 773-7170.

Santa Barbara County

Santa Barbara County was one of the original twenty-six counties that divided up California's territory when it was admitted as a state in the union in 1850. The geography of this county offers hikers an abundance of options, from the Los Padres National Forest's mountains in the interior to the coastal plains and its beaches. The romantic Spanish architecture of the city of Santa Barbara and its scenic setting, on the south-facing coastline with the steep Santa Ynez mountains as a backdrop, have earned it the nickname "American Riviera." The area is a popular tourist destination and dog-friendly portal to the surrounding hikes.

8 La Purisima Mission Loop

Pooches can't miss out on hiking in a state park that actually allows them off the blacktop and on the trails. Walk in the footsteps of the Chumash, this land's first inhabitants, and the Spanish conquerors who Christianized them. The hike takes you along the southern tip of the Pismo sand dunes covered in mixed chaparral, weaving along the Burton Mesa with views of the surrounding hills, before dropping into an oak woodland and then looping past the mission's historic compound.

Start: At the north end of the Mission La Purisima parking lot and interpretive panel
Distance: 5.5-mile loop
Hiking time: About 3 hours
Difficulty: Moderate
Trailhead elevation: 130 feet
Highest point: 418 feet
Best season: Year-round; summers are hot; spring for wildflowers, winter and spring for water in creeks
Trail surface: Soft sand, loose dirt, and old pavement

Other trail users: Horses and mountain bikes on some sections
Canine compatibility: On leash
Land status: State park
Fees and permits: Day-use parking fee
Maps: USGS Lompoc; State Park map
Trail contacts: California Department of Parks and Recreation, parks.ca.gov; (805) 733-3713
Nearest town: Lompoc
Trail tips: There is a visitor center, flush toilets, drinking fountain, and picnic tables.

Finding the trailhead: From Lompoc on CA 1 and CA 246, drive north 1.7 miles to Mission Gate Road and bear left onto Mission Gate Road. Drive 0.3 mile on Mission Gate Road to the entrance to La Purisima Mission State Historic Park. **GPS:** N34 40.22' / W120 25.25'

The Hike

Mission Purisima State Historic Park sits on almost 2,000 acres of mixed chaparral-covered sand dunes with mesas (plateaus) surrounding oak woodlands and riparian canyons. You cannot talk about California's rich history without thinking about the thousands of indigenous people, which included Southern California's Chumash tribe, and Spanish conquerors' mission settlements. The original mission (Mission Vieja) was established in Lompoc in 1787 by Father Lasuen, but was destroyed by an earthquake in 1812. The compound was moved to its present location, and construction of the new adobe buildings took seven years to complete. La Purisima was the eleventh of twenty-one missions built in California during the height of Spanish colonization. The Mexican Revolution and subsequent loss of California to the Americans in 1846 left many of the missions neglected and in ruins. In 1934 the land and what was left of the La Purisima compound was donated to the State of California. A joint effort between the state, Santa Barbara County, and the Civilian Conservation Corps under national park management eventually accomplished the most complete restoration project of the California missions. It's a remarkable gem architecturally and culturally. But the 25 miles of backcountry hiking, biking, and equestrian trails are a unique boon for dogs and their human companions.

The new visitor center, opened to the public in 2009, is a great place to get an overview of earlier times at the mission. Pooch will have to wait for you outside while you peruse the indoor exhibits.

The hike begins at the north end of the parking lot across from the visitor center at the interpretive panel next to the water fountain. From there, as you face the visitor center you will spot the trailhead for Vista de la Cruz Trail just to the left of the building. Since much of the land here sits on sand dunes covered by chaparral vegetation, many of the trails are on soft sand surface like this 0.3-mile stretch of trail to the top of the mesa viewpoint marked by a cross. Be prepared for a slower pace on the soft sand trails. The main trails and dirt roads are fairly well marked, but there are several spur trails and forks that are labeled on the park map but not necessarily at the junctions once on the trail.

The unmarked Rita Mesa Trail is mostly level along the mesa as it parallels a fence line on your right for about another mile. The trail is lined with chamise, manzanita, scrub oak, and some coast live oaks. The views reach across canyons to the hills and a ridge scorched by the July 2015 fire. Some of the trails in the park are closed to minimize the risk of introducing invasive species while the vulnerable landscape recovers from the fire with native vegetation.

At 1.7 miles the trail makes a gentle descent into a swale before emerging back up an exposed hillside. At 2.2 miles you continue straight downhill into a shady oak canyon with ferns and reeds at the edge of the mission pond and original aqueduct. There's a bench here inviting you to contemplate the setting and take a water break with your dog before crossing the narrow aqueduct and coming to a dirt road. You turn right on the dirt road paralleling an open field. At the fork bear left to another open field.

At 2.9 miles you come to a trail junction with a wooden gate and sign for the State Historic Park on the right. The unmarked old paved road at the junction is the historic El Camino Real (Royal Highway) the Spanish traveled between the California missions. Turn left on the Camino Real. It traces a large field on your left.

At 3.2 miles, about two-thirds of the way down to the end of the field, turn right on the narrow, sandy El Chaparral Trail as it curves uphill. Come to the next trail junction and turn right on Cuclillo de Terre Trail, which is a dirt road. The trail sign is actually on your left on the road and you turn right. At about 3.8 miles you will see a stand of Torrey Pines towering above the oak woodland. Continue walking on Cuclillo de Terre Trail until you come to a paved road at 5.0 miles. Walk across the paved road and continue on a narrow, soft-sand trail to a T intersection. Turn left at the T. The historic mission buildings will be on your left and the creek on your right. Walk across the aqueduct and continue on the trail toward the corral.

Historic mission buildings across Los Burros Creek bridge

At 5.5 miles you come to a wooden footbridge. Walk across Los Burros Creek on the footbridge and arrive back at the trailhead.

Although four-legged visitors are not allowed inside the historic buildings, it is worthwhile to walk around the compound and courtyards and take a peek at the impressive craftsmanship and interior restoration that replicates a significant era in California history.

Miles and Directions

0.0 Start at the interpretive panel next to the water fountain at the north end of the parking lot. Walk toward the visitor center and up the narrow Vista de la Cruz Trail on the left heading to the cross on the mesa.

0.3 Come to a cross on the mesa and viewpoint with a picnic table on the left. Walk 60 feet to a trail junction. Turn left at the unmarked trail junction and bear left on the trail.

0.4 Come to an unmarked trail junction and bear left. Fence will be on your right.

0.9 Come to a trail junction for La Artemisia Trail. Continue straight on Santa Rita Mesa Trail.

1.7 Come to an unmarked trail junction. Continue walking straight and uphill.

2.2 Come to a fork on the left. Continue walking straight and downhill.

2.5 Come to a marsh and pond with a bench on the left at the aqueduct. Walk across the aqueduct and come to a dirt road. Turn right on the dirt road.

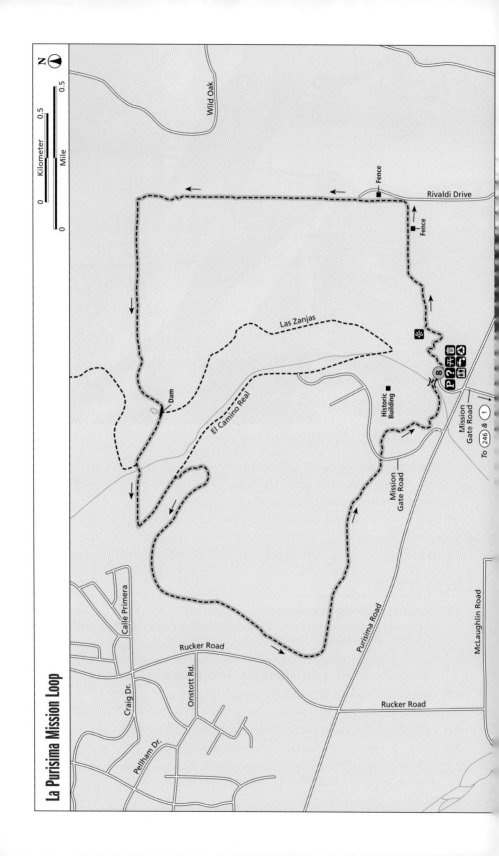

La Purísima Mission Loop

2.6 Come to a fork at the edge of a field. Bear left on dirt trail and come to another field.

2.9 Come to an unmarked trail junction at an old paved road. This is the El Camino Real. Turn left on the El Camino Real.

3.2 Come to the El Chaparral Trail sign on the right. Turn right and walk up the sandy trail.

3.3 Come to a trail junction at a dirt road. The Cuclillo de Terre Trail sign is on your left. Turn right on the Cuclillo de Terre Trail.

3.9 Come to a trail junction for the Huerta Mateos Trail on the left. Continue straight on the Cuclillo de Terre Trail.

5.0 Come to a paved road. Cross the paved road to the narrow, soft-sand trail.

5.3 Come to a T intersection. Turn left at the T. Historic buildings are on your left. Walk across the aqueduct. The creek is on your right. Corrals are straight ahead.

5.5 Come to a wooden footbridge on the right over Los Burros Creek. Walk across the footbridge and arrive back at the trailhead.

Creature Comforts

Fueling Up

South Side Coffee Company, 105 S. H St., Lompoc 93436; (805) 737-3730. Dog-friendly patio for cafe menu, 5:30 a.m. to 9 p.m.

Resting Up

Motel 6, 1521 N. H St., Lompoc 93436; (855) 265-2185. No pet fee.
Embassy Suites Hotel, 1117 N. H St., Lompoc 93436; (805) 735-8311.

Puppy Paws and Golden Years

Walk around the **La Purisima Mission**'s historic compound and courtyards for a taste of early California life.

9 Jalama Beach

How often does a paved road take you off the beaten path to hike an isolated scenic stretch of wild Pacific coastline? Did I mention that the road ends at a dog-friendly county park beach, where you and pooch can share quality time exploring several miles of surf and sand if you get the tide chart right?

Start: From the north end of Jalama Beach County Park parking lot
Distance: 3.3 miles
Hiking time: About 2 hours
Difficulty: Easy
Trailhead elevation: 15 feet
Highest point: 15 feet
Best season: Year-round; fall and winter weekdays for maximum solitude; spring for wildflowers on the drive to the Jalama Beach County Park
Trail surface: Sand
Other trail users: None
Canine compatibility: On leash
Land status: County

Fees and permits: Day-use fee
Maps: USGS Tranquillo Mtn., Lompoc Hills, and Point Conception
Trail contacts: Santa Barbara County Parks Department, 610 Mission Canyon Rd., Santa Barbara 93105; (805) 568-2461; sbparks .org; Jalama Beach Park office, (805) 736-3504
Nearest town: Lompoc
Trail tips: There are flush toilets, drinking fountains, showers (open until sunset; coin operated), picnic tables, grills, store and grill. It is essential to check the tides for your safety. There is a tide chart posted outside at the Jalama Beach Grill.

Finding the trailhead: From Lompoc at CA 1 and CA 246, drive 4.2 miles south on CA 1 to Jalama Road. Turn right on Jalama Road and drive 14 miles to the end of the road and entrance to Jalama Beach County Park. **GPS:** N34 30.70' / W120 30.12'

The Hike

The sense of remoteness from the undeveloped, rolling, oak–studded open space on the drive to Jalama Beach from Lompoc is just a prelude to Jalama Beach's stunning solitary setting. There's only one road in and out of here, and a railway that skirts the coast with no rail stops between Lompoc and Santa Barbara. The county park and beach are braced by secluded Vandenberg Air Force Base's 98,000 acres, including 35 miles of coastline to the north and sprawling cattle ranch land to the south. Vandenberg Air Force Base is headquarters for the 30th Space Wing and 14th Air Force. It is Air Force Space Command's premier missile base for missile testing and launching of satellites into polar orbit. This wild coast is out of sight in every way possible.

The trick is to check your tide chart to maximize your adventure time. This hike describes the optimal excursion at an average tide, allowing you to sample a stretch of beach north and south from Jalama Beach County Park and Campground.

Enjoying the solitude of a sunrise hike

The hike begins at the north end of Jalama Beach County Park between the store and the estuary at the dog-waste bag dispenser. Walk down the short dune path to the beach and turn right, heading north for 0.5 mile with the eroded cliffs on your right (you can walk farther if tides permit). Turn around and walk south past the county park to the eroded cliffs on your left toward the exposed rock shelf jutting out to sea. Watch your step as you leave the sand and step up on these slices of rock slabs. The kelp and wet surface can be very slippery. Notice the patches of hardened tar. Contrary to what you might think, this is not evidence of an oil spill. Explorers in the Juan Bautista de Anza party of 1776 reported seeing tar on rocks and beaches "thrown up by the sea."

At 2.1 miles, look down the coast and see if you can spot a faint white speck on a ledge. That's Point Conception Lighthouse.

If the tides are with you, you can continue walking farther south before going back to the trailhead the way you came. Pick a protected spot from the wind and enjoy a snack in solitude with your furry pal. It's important to be aware of the tide chart to ensure a safe and dry return. Your four-legged pal depends on you.

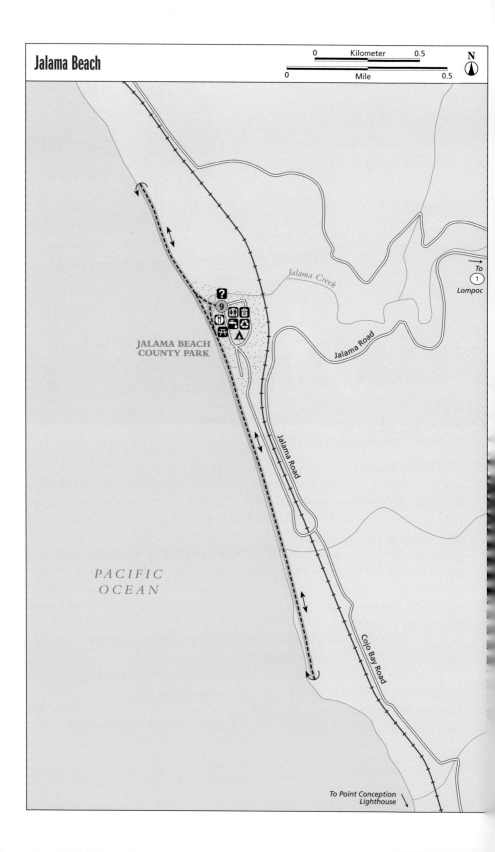

Jalama Beach

Miles and Directions

0.0 Start from the trailhead at the dog-waste bag dispenser just past the Jalama Beach store and before the estuary. Walk to the beach and turn right.

0.5 Come to a location where the eroded cliff comes to a point and turn around. Walk south and continue walking on the beach past Jalama Beach County Park. Elevation: 3 feet. **GPS:** N34 31.01' / W120 30.40'

2.1 Come to the rocky shelf with Point Conception Lighthouse within sight south in the distance. Turn around and go back to the trailhead the way you came. Elevation: 4 feet. **GPS:** N34 29.73' / W120 29.78'

3.3 Arrive back at the trailhead.

Creature Comforts

Fueling Up

Jalama Beach Store and Grill, Jalama Beach County Park, 9999 Jalama Rd., Lompoc 93436. They pride themselves on making a "famous" burger. Order to take out and dine with pooch in the day-use area or have yourself a beach picnic. **South Side Coffee Company,** 105 S. H St., Lompoc 93436; (805) 737-3730. Dog-friendly patio for cafe menu, 5:30 a.m. to 9 p.m.

Resting Up

Motel 6, 1521 N. H St., Lompoc 93436; (855) 265-2185. No pet fee. **Embassy Suites Hotel,** 1117 N. H St., Lompoc 93436; (805) 735-8311.

Campgrounds

Jalama Beach County Park, 9999 Jalama Rd., Lompoc 93436; (805) 736-3504; (805) 736-6316; reservations at (805) 568-2460; sbparks.org/reservations. Tent, trailer, and RV sites. Some electrical hookups. The cabins are dog friendly for an extra fee. Limit two dogs per cabin.

Puppy Paws and Golden Years

Jalama Beach County Park's beach and day-use area.

10 Davy Brown Trail

This uphill canyon hike rewards pooches and their companions with a year-round creek, swimming holes, and a good dose of shade under sycamore canopies. The views of the San Rafael Mountains are just an added bonus.

Start: From Davy Brown Creek Campground
Distance: 5.4-mile lollipop
Hiking time: About 3 hours
Difficulty: Strenuous
Trailhead elevation: 2,064 feet
Highest point: 3,501 feet
Best season: Year-round; summers can be hot; fall colors are stunning
Trail surface: Dirt and rock
Other trail users: Horses and mountain bikes
Canine compatibility: Off leash
Land status: National forest
Fees and permits: Adventure Pass fee

Maps: USGS Bald Mountain, Figueroa Mountain
Trail contacts: Los Padres National Forest, Santa Lucia Ranger District, 1616 N. Carlotti Dr., Santa Maria 93454; (805) 925-9538; fs.usda.gov/lpnf
Nearest town: Los Olivos
Trail tips: There are 2 vault toilets, trash container, and an information panel at the entrance to the campground. There is no drinking water. The gnats can be annoying in the summer and early fall, so bring insect repellent.

Finding the trailhead: From Buelton on US 101, take the CA 246 exit and drive 8.5 miles east on CA 246 to the junction for CA 154. Continue straight across CA 154 onto Armour Ranch Road, drive 1.5 miles to Happy Canyon Road, and turn left on Happy Canyon Road. Drive 13.5 miles on Happy Canyon Road (the road is paved except for a 1-mile stretch of well-graded dirt road at approximately 9 miles) to the road junction at the Cachuma Saddle information board. You enter the Figueroa Mountain Los Padres National Forest Recreation Area at this junction. Continue straight on the paved, unmarked Sunset Valley Road/FS8N09. Drive 3.6 miles down to the unsigned Davy Brown campground on the left. Enter the campground and park on the left side just beyond the vault toilets. Walk 0.1 mile down the paved road on the right past 3 campsites. The trailhead is at the end of the pavement just past the last campsite on the right. **GPS:** N34 45.50' / W119 57.29'

From Santa Barbara on US 101, take exit CA 154 and drive 22 miles northwest on CA 154 to Armour Ranch Road. Turn right on Armour Ranch Road, drive 1.3 miles to Happy Canyon Road, and turn right. Drive 13.5 miles on Happy Canyon Road (the road is paved except for a 1-mile stretch of well-graded dirt road at approximately 9 miles) to the road junction at the Cachuma Saddle information board. You enter the Figueroa Mountain Los Padres National Forest Recreation Area at this junction. Continue straight on the paved unmarked Sunset Valley Road/FS8N09. Drive 3.6 miles down to the unsigned Davy Brown campground on the left. Enter the campground and park on the left side just beyond the vault toilets. Walk 0.1 mile down the paved road on the right past 3 campsites. The trailhead is at the end of the pavement just past the last campsite on the right. **GPS:** N34 45.50' / W119 57.29'

The Hike

The drive to the trailhead from CA 154 is a picturesque treat of horse ranches and meadows against the backdrop of Santa Ynez and San Rafael stadium of mountain ridges. The Davy Brown Trail, named after Davy William Brown, a pioneer who lived in a cabin here from 1879 to 1895, is a perfect introduction to Santa Barbara County's backcountry and the Los Padres National Forest Recreation Area. The creek runs year-round, and even after four years of drought, this creek had a healthy gurgle and several inviting swimming holes. This hike is especially picturesque in the fall, when sycamore trees are dressed in gold.

The trail starts off level just after crossing Munch Creek and walking through the cattle gate at a meadow. At 0.4 mile you come to Davy Brown Creek and your first of three crossings of this creek and several seasonal stream crossings as you begin to climb up the canyon on the narrow trail. You cross Davy Brown Creek again at 0.5 and 0.7 mile.

Fall colors light up the trail.

Catching a view toward the San Rafael Mountains

At 1.0 mile you come to an unmarked trail junction. The trail on the left is where you will close the loop part of your lollipop on the return. The Forest Service trail sign is often lying on the ground, and therefore not always visible. Bear right on the trail and continue walking uphill past the Forest Service trail sign. Davy Brown Creek is on your left. Follow the well-worn trail as it laces uphill with several seasonal stream crossings.

At 1.9 miles, the trail becomes more exposed, revealing an expansive view toward the San Rafael Mountains and Wilderness. You leave the cooler sycamore and oak woodlands behind with more manzanita and chaparral vegetation flanking the slopes.

At 2.1 miles you come to a trail junction and a Forest Service trail sign. Bear left on the trail to continue the loop of your lollipop. Just 1 mile ahead you come to another trail junction at Davy Brown Creek, where you cross the creek and bear left downhill with Davy Brown Creek on your left. The descent is steep in some stretches and you will have to negotiate some rocky sections. At 4.4 miles you cross Davy Brown Creek and rejoin the main trail to close the loop of your lollipop. Turn right on the main trail and continue walking down, back to the trailhead the way you came.

Davy Brown Trail

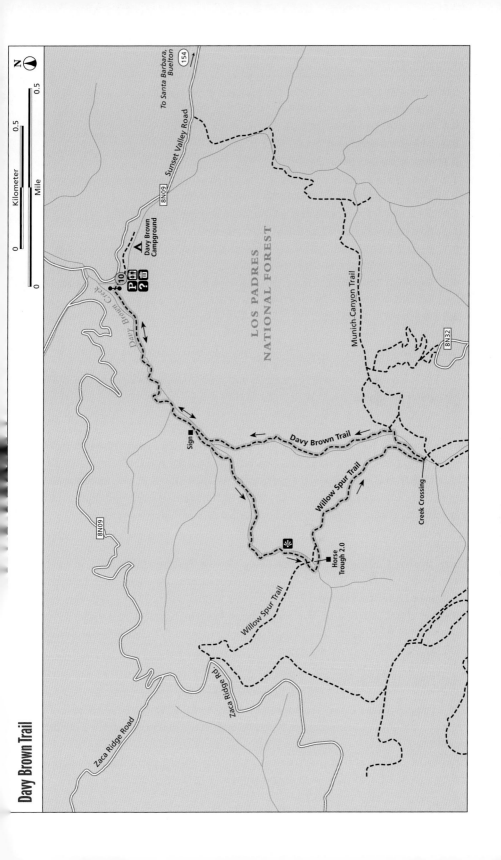

Miles and Directions

0.0 Start at the cattle gate just past the last campsite at the west end of the campground down the paved road on the right.

0.4 Walk across Davy Brown Creek.

0.5 Walk across Davy Brown Creek.

0.7 Walk across Davy Brown Creek.

1.0 Come to a trail junction with a trail sign. The trail on the left is the close of your lollipop loop on the return. Bear right and continue walking up the trail.

1.9 Come to a viewpoint overlooking the San Rafael Mountains and Wilderness.

2.1 Come to a trail junction. Bear left to continue the loop of your lollipop.

3.1 Come to a trail junction at Davy Brown Creek. Bear left, walk across the creek, and walk downhill with Davy Brown Creek now on your left.

4.4 Cross Davy Brown Creek and turn right to join main trail and close the loop of your lollipop. Continue walking down the trail the way you came to the trailhead.

5.4 Arrive back at the trailhead.

Creature Comforts

The closest largest urban areas for services and more lodging and dining are in Santa Barbara and Solvang.

Fueling Up

Cachuma Lake Recreation Area General Store, 2225 Hwy. 154, Santa Barbara 93105; (805) 686-5055; sbparks.org. Groceries and snacks available.

Sides Hardware and Shoes, 2375 Pintado Ave., Los Olivos 93441; (805)688-4820; mobiledudamobile.com. Pooches can join their humans for lunch and dinner on the patio of this historic building in the heart of Santa Ynez Valley's wine country.

Resting Up

Davy Brown Campground at the Davy Brown Trailhead; RV and tent sites; no water, no hookups; vault toilets; picnic tables; no reservations, only first-come, first-served.

Cachuma Lake Recreation, 2225 Hwy. 154, Santa Barbara 93105; (805) 686-5055, (805) 568-2460; sbparks.org. The campground has tent as well as trailer and RV sites with hookups. The cabins ($20 nightly pet fee) and yurts ($3 nightly pet fee) are dog friendly.

Puppy Paws and Golden Years

The **Mohawk Mesa Loop Trail** at the Mohawk Fishing Pier at the south end of the campground in the Cachuma Lake Recreation Area is a short trail tracing a peninsula in the lake.

Cachuma Lake Recreation Area has a large fenced dog park in the campground for dogs to enjoy a safe area to sniff and saunter.

11 Sweetwater Trail

This is a delightful, undulating trail to a vista point overlooking the Bradbury Dam on scenic, albeit man-made, Cachuma Lake. The mostly chaparral-covered landscape is set against the picturesque backdrop of the Santa Ynez and San Rafael Mountains in the Los Padres National Forest.

Start: From the Sweetwater Trailhead in the Harvey's Cove picnic area parking lot
Distance: 5.2 miles out and back
Hiking time: About 2.5 hours
Difficulty: Easy
Trailhead elevation: 768 feet
Highest point: 899 feet
Best season: Year-round; summers are hot
Trail surface: Dirt and short stretch of concrete
Other trail users: Mountain bikes
Canine compatibility: On leash
Land status: County

Fees and permits: Day-use fee
Maps: USGS Lake Cachuma; Cachuma Lake Recreation Area
Trail contacts: Santa Barbara County Park, 2225 CA 154, Santa Barbara 93105; (805) 686-5054 for recorded info; (805) 686-5055 (gate); (805) 568-2460 (reservations)
Nearest town: Los Olivos
Trail tips: There is no water at the trailhead or trail end. There is a portable toilet at the trailhead and vault toilet at the trail end.

Finding the trailhead: From US 101 at Santa Maria, drive 27 miles south on US 101 to the Cachuma Lake/CA 154 exit. Drive 15 miles east on CA 154 to the Cachuma Lake Recreation Area entrance on your left (2225 CA 154, Santa Barbara 93105); Turn left after you enter the park and follow the sign for Harvey's Cove. Drive 0.3 mile to the trailhead at the north end of the parking area. **GPS:** N34 34.40' / W119 57.70'
From US 101 at Santa Barbara, take the Cachuma Lake/CA 154 exit and follow the signs for the recreation area. Drive approximately 18 miles northwest on CA 154 to the Cachuma Lake Recreation Area entrance on your right. Turn left after you enter the park and follow the sign for Harvey's Cove. Drive 0.3 mile to the trailhead at the north end of the parking area. **GPS:** N34 34.40' / W119 57.70'

The Hike

Cachuma Lake is fed by the Santa Ynez River and is the result of the Bradbury Dam, built in 1953. Besides creating a reservoir for drinking water, Cachuma Lake was developed into a splendid 9,000-acre recreation area for hiking, camping, and boating, complete with a nature center and general store. The 1930s classic white ranch houses the Neal Taylor Nature Center and is named after the park's first naturalist and founder of the nature center. There are a couple of picnic tables on a brick patio behind the nature center for visitors to enjoy a picnic with their four-legged companions. Although your furry pal is not allowed inside the nature center, the mounted wildlife specimens and various exhibits are well worth at least a brief visit while a

Bridge across seasonal stream

leashed bowser sits outside patiently. There are naturalist-led lake cruises for wildlife and bald eagle watching, but unfortunately, four-legged companions are not welcome. The County of Santa Barbara administers the Cachuma Lake Recreation Area. Humans and dogs are prohibited from swimming or wading in the lake, but dogs are permitted on the rental watercraft (canoes, kayaks, and other boats).

Sweetwater Trail begins in the Harvey's Cove parking area just 0.25 mile from the entrance. Harvey's Cove has an ADA-accessible boat ramp when the reservoir levels allow. The reservoir was only at 16 percent capacity in the fall of 2015 after a fourth year of drought and the water was not accessible from this ramp at that time. In spite of the reservoir's lower water levels, Cachuma Lake Recreation Area offered a surprisingly scenic setting.

The first 0.1 mile of the Sweetwater Trail is ADA accessible on a concrete path to a shaded picnic area overlooking the water. This is a perfect spot to end the excursion with a picnic on the return. The trail heads left away from the picnic area on a single-track corridor of dirt and rock flanked by chaparral vegetation of chamise, rabbit bush, chaparral yucca, and manzanita. There are several seasonal streams feeding riparian woodlands along the way.

At 1.5 miles the landscape transitions to more oaks, providing welcome shade for pooch on a warm day, and you come to two signs: Sweetwater and Vista Point. The

View of Cachuma Lake from vista point

large Sweetwater sign would lead you to believe there is a developed site of some kind here, but there isn't. You can turn right and loop around the knob for more water views of Sweetwater Cove or veer left downhill at the junction toward the Vista Point, which is your destination.

You will cross a footbridge at 1.9 miles and the trail will rise on the left about 0.5 mile ahead. At 2.6 miles you arrive at the Vista Point parking area where there are two vault toilets on your right. The Vista Point overlooking the dam is at the far end by the Bradbury Dam information panel. There is a single picnic table under the oak trees to the right of the Vista Point.

Soak in the views of the San Rafael Mountains across the lake before going back to the trailhead the way you came.

Miles and Directions

0.0   Start at the Sweetwater Trailhead in the Harvey's Cove parking lot.

0.1   Come to the Harvey's Cove picnic area.

0.8   Come to a spur trail to the right and bear left walking uphill.

1.5   Come to the Sweetwater junction and Vista Point 1.5 sign. Bear left and walk downhill toward the Vista Point.

Sweetwater Trail

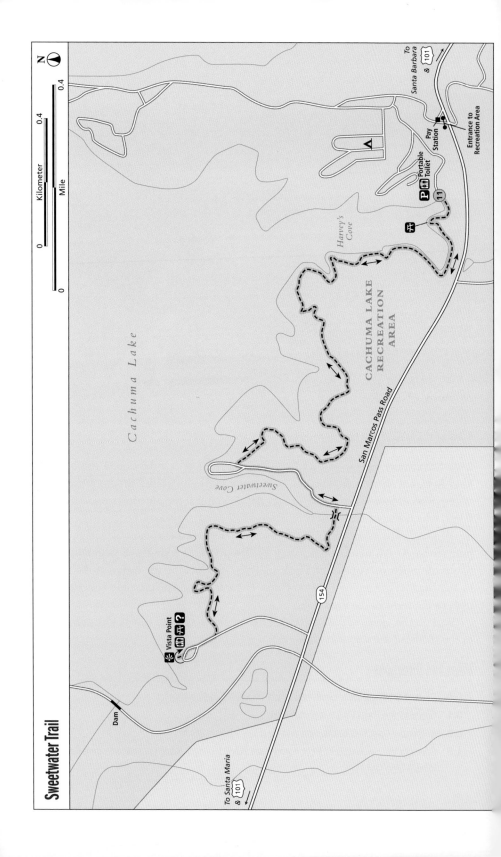

1.9 Walk across the footbridge.

2.4 Come to a spur trail on the right. Bear left and walk uphill.

2.6 Arrive at the Vista Point parking lot and the Bradbury Dam Vista Point. Go back to the trailhead the way you came.

5.2 Arrive back at the trailhead. Elevation: 840 feet. **GPS:** N34 34.85' / W119 58.73'

Creature Comforts

Cachuma Lake Recreation Area sits between Santa Barbara (18 miles to the south) and Solvang (9 miles to the north) for the closest additional lodging, dining, and provisions options.

Fueling Up

Cachuma Lake Recreation Area General Store, 2225 Hwy. 154, Santa Barbara 93105; (805) 686-5055; sbparks.org. Groceries and snacks available.

Sides Hardware and Shoes, 2375 Pintado Ave., Los Olivos 93441; (805) 688-4820; mobiledudamobile.com. Pooches can join their humans for lunch and dinner on the patio of this historic building in the heart of Santa Ynez Valley's wine country.

Resting Up

Cachuma Lake Recreation, 2225 Hwy. 154, Santa Barbara 93105; (805) 686-5055, (805) 568-2460; sbparks.org. The campground has tent as well as trailer and RV sites with hookups. The cabins ($20 nightly pet fee) and yurts ($3 nightly pet fee) are dog friendly.

Puppy Paws and Golden Years

The **Mohawk Mesa Loop Trail** at the Mohawk Fishing Pier at the south end of the campground in the Cachuma Lake Recreation Area is a short trail tracing a peninsula in the lake.

Cachuma Lake Recreation Area has a large, fenced dog park in the campground for dogs to enjoy a safe area to sniff and saunter.

12 Arroyo Burro Beach

This is an equal opportunity beach that screams love of four-legged locals and visitors without discriminating against the two-legged ones. The hard-packed sand beach at the mouth of Arroyo Burro Creek is divided into two stretches. East of the estuary, dogs can hike and gallivant off leash for several miles (tide-depending). West of the estuary, dogs can also hike for several miles (tide-depending), but on leash, so their frolicking doesn't intrude on the humans who love beach hikes but may be lacking in dog-loving genes.

Start: From the information panel at the south end of the parking lot
Distance: 1.6 miles out and back
Hiking time: About 1 hour
Difficulty: Easy
Trailhead elevation: 17 feet
Highest point: 17 feet
Best season: Year-round (spring, fall, and winter weekdays for most solitude)
Trail surface: Sand
Other trail users: None
Canine compatibility: Voice control and on leash
Land status: City and county

Fees and permits: None
Maps: USGS Santa Barbara
Trail contacts: City of Santa Barbara, (805) 564-5418; santabarbaraca.gov; County of Santa Barbara, (805) 568-2461
Nearest town: Santa Barbara
Trail tips: This is a full-service beach park with flush toilets, drinking fountains, showers, trash and recycling, two picnic areas, grills. The most unique amenity is a self-service dog-wash station at the entrance to the park, complete with shampoo, rinse, and blow dry for $10 (credit card payment).

Finding the trailhead: From Santa Barbara on US 101 take Los Positos Road/CA 225 exit. Drive 1.7 miles on Los Positos Road south toward the ocean (away from the mountains) to Cliff Drive. Turn right on Cliff Drive and drive 0.2 mile to the entrance of Arroyo Burro Beach on the left. The trailhead is at the south end of the parking lot. **GPS:** N34 24.18' / W119 44.61'

The Hike

The city and county of Santa Barbara have made Arroyo Burro Beach a win-win experience for dogs and people. The east end of the beach past the Arroyo Burro Creek estuary is city beach and dogs are welcome off leash. The beach on the west side of the creek's estuary is county beach and dogs are also welcome, but on leash.

The beauty of this special stretch of coastline is that once you leave the area, immediately at the foot of the parking lot near the estuary, and begin walking in either direction, there's a real sense of solitude and being in a natural world far from urban hustle and bustle. To make it even more unique, you and pooch get to claim that you hiked along the California Coastal Trail.

Strolling the beach at low tide

The hike described here is limited to an 0.8-mile stretch of beach, sampling a bit of both the off-leash and on-leash worlds. This stretch is the most likely to be accessible during average tides. Safe access to the other several miles of beach at your dog's paws, east to Shoreline Park and west to Goleta Beach County Park, are dependent on the tides.

Begin your jaunt at the information panel and dog-waste bag dispenser at the south end of the parking lot left of the restaurant and walk down the five wooden steps. Keep your dog on leash for about 100 yards to the left until you are past the estuary. Snap off the leash and free your dog's spirit as you both stride for 0.4 mile to the rocks past the huge eucalyptus tree at the base of the cliff, evidence of ongoing coastal erosion. Turn around and head back toward the estuary. By now your furry friend should have gotten his edge off and will be content to continue savoring the surf and sand on leash as you walk west to the turnaround point. Pick a spot for a picnic lunch while communing with nature at the edge of the Pacific's endless horizon.

Check the tides ahead of time if you decide to extend the adventure in either direction.

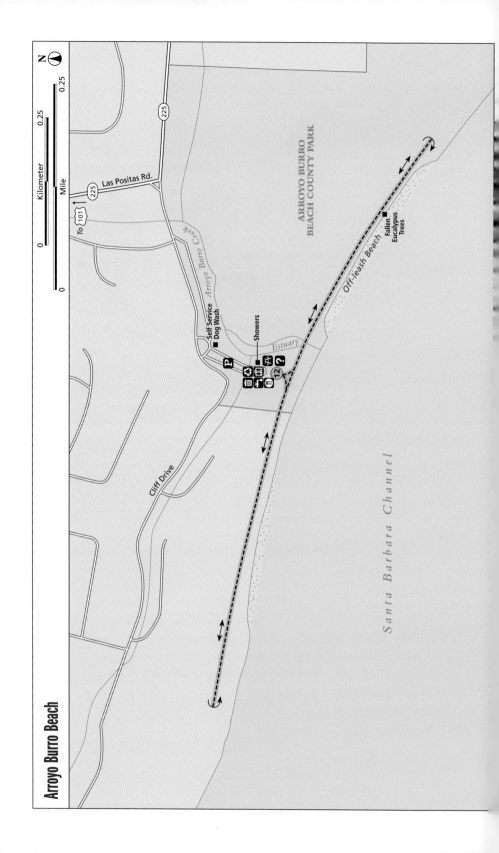

Arroyo Burro Beach

N

To 101

225

Las Positas Rd.

225

Kilometer
0   0.25

Mile
0   0.25

Cliff Drive

Arroyo Burro Creek

Self Service
Dog Wash

Showers

Estuary

P

12

ARROYO BURRO
BEACH COUNTY PARK

Off-leash Beach

Fallen
Eucalypus
Trees

Santa Barbara Channel

Miles and Directions

0.0 Start at the information panel and dog-waste bag dispenser by the steps at the south end of the parking lot. Walk 100 yards east just past the estuary before snapping off your dog's leash.

0.3 Come to the fallen eucalyptus trees at the foot of the bluff.

0.4 Come to some large rocks and your turnaround point at the east end. Walk back to the estuary and snap on the leash to continue walking west. Elevation: 4 feet. **GPS:** N34 24.02' / W119 44.29'

1.2 Come to a point of land where you turn around to go back to the trailhead at the parking lot. Elevation: 5 feet. **GPS:** N34 24.25' / W119 45.07'

1.6 Arrive back at the trailhead in parking lot.

Creature Comforts

Fueling Up

Whole Foods Market, 3761 State St., Santa Barbara 93105; (805) 837-6959. If your furry pal is hooked on organic, the chain food market has everything you'll need for snacks and picnics.

Boathouse, Hendry's Beach, 2981 Cliff Dr., Santa Barbara 93109; (805) 898-2628. The patio does not welcome the furry, wet four-legged beachcombers, but you and pooch can enjoy the bar menu to go and sit at one of the beach picnic tables.

The Brewhouse, 229 W. Montecito St., Santa Barbara 93101; (805) 884-4664. The staff wants you and your pooch to come and have a burger and cold brew on the patio.

Santa Barbara Shellfish Co., 230 Stearns Wharf, Santa Barbara 93101; (805) 966-6676; shellfishco.com. You can order your food to go and enjoy it at the picnic tables on the wharf.

Char West Fast Food Restaurant, 221 Stearns Wharf, Santa Barbara 93101; (805) 962-5631. It's a convenient place for fish and chips and enjoying the sea air with pooch at one of the wharf picnic tables.

Carlitos Café Y Cantina, 1324 State St., Santa Barbara 93101; (805) 962-7117; carlitos.com. End the hiking day with a margarita and fresh guacamole on the dog-friendly patio. You and pooch can window-shop if you decide to walk up State Street from the beach area.

Resting Up

Fess Parker Wine Country Inn and Spa, 633 E. Cabrillo Blvd., Santa Barbara 93103; (800) 879-2929; fessparkersantabarbarahotel.com. Pooch gets his own room-service menu here and is welcome everywhere on the property except in the interior food venues and the swimming-pool area.

The Old Yacht Club Inn, 431 Corona Del Mar, Santa Barbara 93103; (805) 962-1277; oldyachtclubinn.com. Well-mannered dogs are welcome in some of the rooms of this historic Craftsman house. Pet fee.

Santa Barbara Biltmore Four Seasons Resort, 1260 Channel Dr., Santa Barbara 93108; (805) 969-2261; fourseasons.com. This iconic Spanish-style property welcomes furry guests under 50 pounds in the garden cottage rooms. They are not permitted in any of the dining venues, but the menu is available at the lobby tables. They will even arrange for a sitter for your four-legged child if you want to dine *sans chien*. Doggie massage is also available, so don't worry about those post-hike sore muscles.

Campgrounds

Ocean Mesa RV and Campground, 100 El Capitan Terrace Ln., Santa Barbara 93117; (805) 879-5751; oceanmesa.com. This is a deluxe facility, between the views, heated pool, and spic and span restrooms and showers.

Romping in the winter surf

El Capitan State Beach Park, 10 Refugio Beach Rd., Goleta 93117; (805) 968-1033; parks.ca.gov; reserveamerica.com; (800) 444-7275. Fabulous setting on the bluff. The Aniso Trail that once connected El Capitan and Refugio State Parks between the railway and the beach is closed from the El Capitan side due to severe erosion along about a 0.5-mile section between the two state beach parks.

Refugio State Beach Park, 10 Refugio Beach Rd., Goleta 93117-9717; (805) 968-1033; (800) 444-7275; parks.ca.gov; reserveamerica.com. Beachfront campsites. The 2.5-mile paved hike/bike path running above the beach paralleling the railway that used to connect Refugio and El Capitan State Beach Parks is closed due to severe erosion damage and hazardous conditions. Nevertheless, it's a lovely, flat 1.5-mile-long hike or bike north from Refugio to the fence where the trail now ends.

Puppy Paws and Golden Years

Douglas Family Preserve is a 70-acre parcel acquired by the Trust of Public Lands and transferred to the City of Santa Barbara in 1997. Pooches enjoy off-leash romps in select areas on this blufftop property. The access is at the intersection of Medcliff and Selfrose Streets off Mesa Drive on the south side of Cliff Drive just east of the Arroyo Burro Beach.

Sam's Doggie Dude Ranch Boarding and Day Care, 12750 Calle Real, Goleta 93117; (805) 968-7337; samsdoggieduderanch.com. Susie Tautrim and her husband have gladly let the family's 300-acre working ranch go to the dogs. Dogs of all sizes are welcome to spend as little as a few hours at this canine-camp boarding kennel, while their owners go off on boring human-only activities around Santa Barbara. Sam's is about 30 miles north of Santa Barbara near the coastal campgrounds of Ocean Mesa RV and Campground, El Capitan State Beach Park, Refugio State Park, and Gaviota State Park.

13 Santa Barbara Beach Way

It's as far from the wilderness as you can get, but it's classic Southern California, and your dog won't want to miss a chance to experience the palm-lined beachfront scene along this 1.4-mile-long paved multi-use trail including a mile of paw-friendly turf.

Start: From the Santa Barbara Harbor parking lot
Distance: 2.8 miles out and back
Hiking time: About 1.5 hours
Difficulty: Easy
Trailhead elevation: 7 feet
Highest point: 11 feet
Best season: Year-round
Trail surface: Pavement and turf
Other trail users: Bicycles, rollerblades
Canine compatibility: On leash

Land status: City
Fees and permits: Parking fee
Maps: USGS Santa Barbara
Trail contacts: City of Santa Barbara Parks and Recreation Department, (805) 564-5418
Nearest town: Santa Barbara
Trail tips: There are restrooms in the parking lot and a small store for snacks. There is a drinking fountain and outdoor showers, as well as trash and recycling containers at the trailhead along with a dog-waste bag dispenser.

Finding the trailhead: From US 101 driving north in Santa Barbara, take exit 96B/Garden Street. Turn left on Garden Street and drive 2 blocks to East Cabrillo Boulevard. Turn right on East Cabrillo Boulevard, which becomes Shoreline Drive, and drive 0.8 mile to Santa Barbara Harbor on the left. Turn left into the Santa Barbara Harbor parking lot and turn left to park at the far end closest to the beach (northeast end of lot). The trailhead is at the northeast end of the parking lot at the beach. **GPS:** N34 24.52' / W119 41.51'

From US 101 driving south in Santa Barbara, take exit 97/Castillo Street. Turn right onto Castillo Street and drive 4 blocks to Shoreline Drive, turn right on Shoreline Drive, and drive 0.2 mile to the Santa Barbara Harbor on the left. Turn left into the Santa Barbara Harbor parking lot and turn left to park at the far end closest to the beach (northeast end of lot). The trailhead is at the northeast end of the parking lot at the beach. **GPS:** N34 24.52' / W119 41.51'

The Hike

The bad news is that dogs are not allowed on the beach. The good news is that the Beach Way path lets pooches, fit and fat, spry and slow, close enough to the beach to enjoy the smells of sand and surf. The wide strand of turf tracing most of the path on the left side is a cornucopia of natural scents, and is soft enough for the most delicate canine pads. The Santa Ynez Mountains' backdrop to the palm-lined path and south-facing sandy playground is not too shabby either.

From the harbor parking lot you begin on the Beach Way at the north (beach) end of the parking lot and follow the path left, tracing the beach toward Stearn's Wharf. The beach will be on your right all the way.

Starting the hike

Getting fit on the trail

You walk across the entrance to the wooden Stearn's Wharf at 0.3 mile. A stroll along Stearn's Wharf for a snack at one of the dog-friendly eateries is a perfect side excursion on the way back to the trailhead. Stearn's Wharf is 0.4 mile long to the end.

There are restrooms with flush toilets and sinks just across the entrance to Stearn's Wharf. You can refill your pooch's water bottle here before continuing on.

At 0.4 mile you cross a bridge over Mission Creek. The estuary on the right is always busy with egrets and other bird life. At 0.6 mile you come to the wide greenbelt sprinkled with palm trees that creates a buffer from Cabrillo Road. The turf area borders the path all the way to your turnaround point at the traffic light and crosswalk at Milpas Street and Cabrillo Boulevard.

If pooch is pawing for more, you can keep walking on the ocean side of Cabrillo Boulevard through the parking lot past East Beach Grill to East Beach Park about 0.3 mile farther. East Beach Park has a 0.2-mile dirt path with picnic tables.

You can also cross Cabrillo Boulevard at the Milpas Street traffic light and crosswalk to pick up the path on the other side of Cabrillo Boulevard to a lagoon. Unfortunately the traffic noise on the stretch of path on the other side of Cabrillo Boulevard is intrusive.

Santa Barbara Beach Way

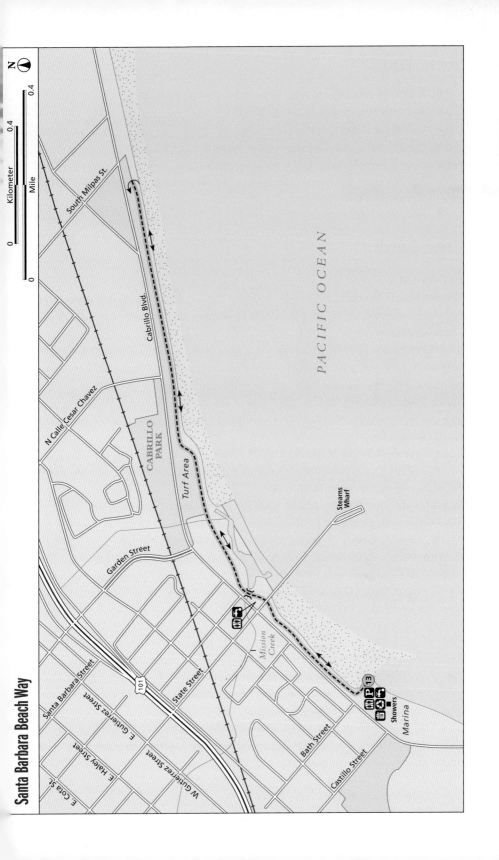

Kilometer
0   0.4   0.4

0   Mile

N

PACIFIC OCEAN

South Milpas St.

Cabrillo Blvd.

N Calle Cesar Chavez

CABRILLO PARK

Turf Area

Garden Street

Stearns Wharf

Mission Creek

Santa Barbara Street

Santa Barbara Street

E. Haley Street

E. Gutierrez Street

W Gutierrez Street

State Street

Bath Street

Castillo Street

Marina

Showers

E Cota St.

101

13

Miles and Directions

0.0 Start at the northeast end of the Santa Barbara Harbor parking lot.

0.3 Walk across the entrance to Stearn's Wharf.

0.4 Walk across Mission Creek on a footbridge.

0.6 Come to the beginning of the turf area on the left of Beach Way path.

1.4 Arrive at your turnaround point at the corner of Cabrillo Boulevard and Milpas Street traffic light and crosswalk. Go back to the trailhead the way you came. Elevation: 11 feet. **GPS:** N34 24.99' / W119 40.33'

2.8 Arrive back at the trailhead.

Creature Comforts

Fueling Up

Whole Foods Market, 3761 State St., Santa Barbara 93105; (805) 837-6959. If your furry pal is hooked on organic, the chain food market has everything you'll need for snacks and picnics.

The Brewhouse, 229 W. Montecito St., Santa Barbara 93101; (805) 884-4664. The staff wants you and your pooch to come and have a burger and cold brew on the patio.

Santa Barbara Shellfish Co., 230 Stearns Wharf, Santa Barbara 93101; (805) 966-6676; shellfishco.com. You can order your food to go and enjoy it at the picnic tables on the wharf.

Char West Fast Food Restaurant, 221 Stearns Wharf, Santa Barbara 93101; (805) 962-5631. It's a convenient place for fish and chips and enjoying the sea air with pooch at one of the wharf picnic tables.

Sambo's on the Beach, 216 W. Cabrillo Blvd., Santa Barbara 93101; (805) 965-3269; sambosrestaurant.com. Breakfast and lunch are served all day at this local institution (sidewalk tables).

Carlitos Café Y Cantina, 1324 State St., Santa Barbara 93101; (805) 962-7117; carlitos.com. End the hiking day with a margarita and fresh guacamole on the dog-friendly patio. You and pooch can window-shop if you decide to walk up State Street from the beach area.

Resting Up

Fess Parker Wine Country Inn and Spa, 633 East Cabrillo Blvd., Santa Barbara 93103; (800) 879-2929; fessparkersantabarbarahotel.com. Pooch gets his own room-service menu here and is welcome everywhere on the property except in the interior food venues and the swimming pool area.

The Old Yacht Club Inn, 431 Corona Del Mar, Santa Barbara 93103; (805) 962-1277; oldyachtclubinn.com. Well-mannered dogs are welcome in some of the rooms of this historic Craftsman house. Pet fee.

Santa Barbara Biltmore Four Seasons Resort, 1260 Channel Dr., Santa Barbara 93108; (805) 969-2261; fourseasons.com. This iconic Spanish-style property welcomes furry guests under 50 pounds in the garden cottage rooms. They are not permitted in any of the dining venues, but the menu is available at the lobby tables. They will even arrange for a sitter for your four-legged child if you want to dine *sans chien.* Doggie massage is also available, so don't worry about those post-hike sore muscles.

Campgrounds

Ocean Mesa RV and Campground, 100 El Capitan Terrace Ln., Santa Barbara 93117; (805) 879-5751; oceanmesa.com. This is a deluxe facility, between the views, heated pool, and spic and span restrooms and showers.

El Capitan State Beach Park, 10 Refugio Beach Rd., Goleta 93117; (805) 968-1033; (800) 444-7275; parks.ca.gov; reserveamerica.com. Fabulous setting on the bluff. The Aniso Trail that once connected El Capitan and Refugio State Beach Parks between the railway and the beach is closed from the El Capitan side due to severe erosion along about a 0.5-mile section between the two state beach parks.

Refugio State Beach Park, 10 Refugio Beach Rd., Goleta 93117-9717; (805) 968-1033; (800) 444-7275; parks.ca.gov; reserveamerica.com. Beachfront campsites. The 2.5-mile paved hike/bike path running above the beach paralleling the railway that used to connect Refugio and El Capitan State Beach Parks is closed due to severe erosion damage and hazardous conditions. Nevertheless, it's a lovely, flat 1.5-mile-long hike or bike north from Refugio to the fence where the trail now ends.

Puppy Paws and Golden Years

If your pooch is less adept as a landlubber, but has good sea legs, consider paddling him around in a kayak from **Sea Landing Rentals,** and don't leave home without his life vest. 301 W. Cabrillo Blvd., Santa Barbara 93101; (805) 963-3564; sealanding .net.

Sam's Doggie Dude Ranch Boarding and Day Care, 12750 Calle Real, Goleta 93117; (805) 968-7337; samsdoggieduderanch.com. Susie Tautrim and her husband have gladly let the family's 300-acre working ranch go to the dogs. Dogs of all sizes are welcome to spend as little as a few hours at this canine-camp boarding kennel, while their owners go off on boring human-only activities around Santa Barbara. Sam's is about 30 miles north of Santa Barbara near the coastal campgrounds of Ocean Mesa RV and Campground, El Capitan State Beach Park, Refugio State Beach Park, and Gaviota State Park.

14 Inspiration Point

This uphill trail is popular with well-behaved dogs that love the freedom of hiking off leash. The hike rewards their human companions with views at the start from the dramatic caramel sandstone bluffs and peaks to the sweeping vistas over Santa Barbara and across to the Channel Islands. As a bonus, during normal wet winters and springs, seasonal creeks flush through the chaparral landscape.

Start: From the top of Tunnel Road at the gate
Distance: 4.0 miles out and back
Hiking time: About 2 hours
Difficulty: Moderate
Trailhead elevation: 1,010 feet
Highest point: 1,852 feet
Best season: Year-round (summers are hot; winter and spring for water in the creeks)
Trail surface: Dirt and sandstone
Other trail users: Horses and mountain bikes
Canine compatibility: Voice control
Land status: National forest
Fees and permits: None

Maps: USGS Santa Barbara; Los Padres National Forest
Trail contacts: Los Padres National Forest Santa Barbara Ranger District, 3505 Paradise Rd., Santa Barbara 93105; (805) 967-3481; fs.usda.gov/lpnf. County of Santa Barbara, (805) 568-2461. City of Santa Barbara, (805) 564-5418
Nearest town: Santa Barbara
Trail tips: There is a dog-waste bag dispenser at the gate. There are no amenities at the trailhead. There is no water. Pack out all the trash you pack in.

Finding the trailhead: From Santa Barbara on US 101 take exit 99/Mission Street. Drive 0.7 mile on Mission Street to Santa Barbara Street toward the mountains and follow the signs for Mission Santa Barbara. Turn left on Santa Barbara Street, drive 0.1 mile to Los Olivos Street, and turn right on Los Olivos Street. Drive 0.4 mile on Los Olivos Street, where it becomes Mission Canyon Road. Bear left on Mission Canyon Road, drive 0.3 mile on Mission Canyon Road to Foothill Road, and turn right on Foothill Road. Drive 0.1 mile on Foothill Road and bear left to reconnect to Mission Canyon Road and drive 0.2 mile on Mission Canyon Road to Tunnel Road. Bear left on Tunnel Road. Drive 1.0 mile on Tunnel Road and park on the right side of the road just short of the end of Tunnel Road. Walk uphill approximately 100 feet to the trailhead. **GPS:** N34 27.90' / W119 42.76'

The Hike

This hike is a perfect example of how the south-facing front country slopes of the Santa Ynez Mountains offer hikers with dogs a quick escape with a backcountry feel.

The Los Padres National Forest and the Santa Barbara City and County Parks Departments work together to manage this formidable swath of open space. Like most of the hikes in the Santa Barbara area front country, this trailhead is located in a residential neighborhood at the edge of a rugged canyon.

Trail starts on the service road.

You begin the hike at a gate with hiker safety advisories about fire hazards, carrying water, packing in and packing out trash, and keeping boots and paws on the trail. The dog-waste bags dispenser emphasizes owners' responsibility to pick up after their dogs. Make sure to take plenty of water for pooch and offer him water at the trail junctions.

The trail starts on an old paved service road with some oak trees. The trail transitions to dirt at the trail junction for Jesusita Trail shortly after crossing Mission Creek on a wooden bridge at 0.7 mile. The trail becomes more exposed through the chaparral landscape highlighted by sandstone uplifts and faces. Continue walking straight on Jesusita Trail at the 0.9-mile junction.

At 0.95 mile the trail bears left and drops down into a gorge. Mission Creek is on your left and you cross the creek at 1.1 miles. Watch for an unmarked spur trail on your right at 1.15 miles as you begin climbing out of the creek bed. This spur follows an unnamed seasonal creek that leads to what locals call the "seven falls." Although it sounds idyllic, as of autumn 2015 even the first 0.25 mile to what would be the first cascade when there's water flowing was a very primitive, rocky, and somewhat overgrown path in the dry creek bed.

Walk past the spur trail and continue walking uphill to the unmarked trail junction at 1.8 miles. Cross the dirt service road and walk 100 feet straight ahead to the

Inspiration Point rewards hikers with a view of the Channel Islands.

viewpoint. This is not the official Inspiration Point, but the panoramic views of the coastline with Santa Barbara below and the Channel Islands looking mystical draped in fog on the Pacific horizon are breathtaking. This perch is cradled by the Santa Ynez's sandstone ridgeline behind you. Make this a water break for you and your dog before walking back to the dirt service road. Turn right at the service road. Walk about 180 feet and look to the right for the narrow primitive path. Turn right on the path and walk about 0.1 mile to a cluster of sandstone boulders and be inspired. Enjoy the sweeping views before going back down to the trailhead the way you came. If you have time for a mountaintop snack, the first viewpoint is a much better location to sit with pooch and refuel.

Miles and Directions

0.0 Start at the gate at the top of Tunnel Road. Walk around the gate onto the old paved road.

0.7 Walk across wooden bridge over Mission Creek.

0.8 Come to a trail junction and information panel about the multi-use trail. The trail transitions to dirt. Turn left on Jesusita Trail.

0.9 Come to a trail junction. Continue walking straight on Jesusita Trail.

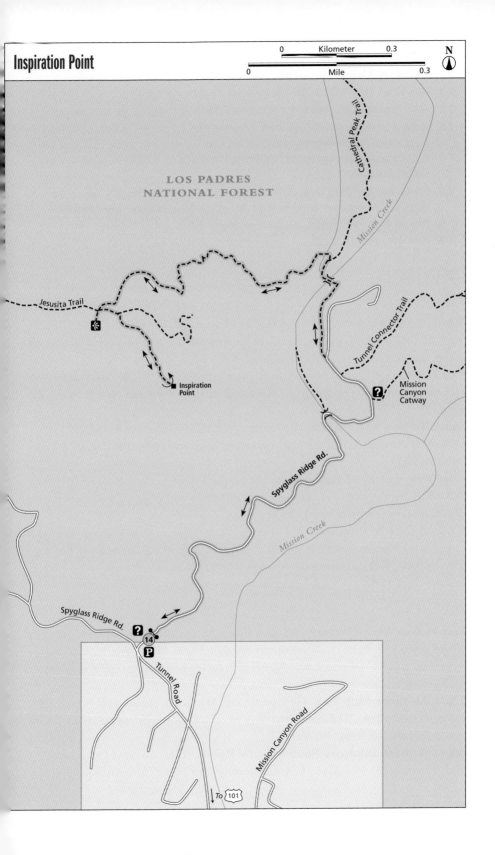

0   Kilometer   0.3

0   Mile   0.3

N

LOS PADRES
NATIONAL FOREST

Cathedral Peak Trail

Mission Creek

Jesusita Trail

Tunnel Connector Trail

Inspiration
Point

Mission
Canyon
Catway

Spyglass Ridge Rd.

Mission Creek

Spyglass Ridge Rd.

14

P

Tunnel Road

Mission Canyon Road

To 101

0.95 Come to an illegible trail junction. Bear left on a narrow trail descending into the gorge. Mission Creek is below on your left.

1.1 Walk across Mission Creek and bear left uphill out of the creek bed.

1.15 Come to primitive spur trail on the right. Continue walking straight up the main trail.

1.8 Come to a junction at a dirt road. Walk across the dirt road 100 feet to a viewpoint. Enjoy the coastal views before going back to the dirt road. Turn right onto the dirt road. Walk 180 feet to a faint, narrow trail on the right. Turn right and walk 0.1 mile on the faint trail to the cluster of boulders.

2.0 This is Inspiration Point, overlooking Santa Barbara and revealing sweeping views of the coastline. Go back down to the trailhead the way you came. Elevation: 1,852 feet. **GPS:** N34 28.23' / W119 42.72'

4.0 Arrive back at the trailhead.

Creature Comforts

Fueling Up

Whole Foods Market, 3761 State St., Santa Barbara 93105; (805) 837-6959. If your furry pal is hooked on organic, the chain food market has everything you'll need for snacks and picnics.

The Brewhouse, 229 W. Montecito St., Santa Barbara 93101; (805) 884-4664. The staff wants you and your pooch to come and have a burger and cold brew on the patio.

Santa Barbara Shellfish Co., 230 Stearns Wharf, Santa Barbara 93101; (805) 966-6676; shellfishco.com. You can order your food to go and enjoy it at the picnic tables on the wharf.

Char West Fast Food Restaurant, 221 Stearns Wharf, Santa Barbara 93101; (805) 962-5631. It's a convenient place for fish and chips and enjoying the sea air with pooch at one of the wharf picnic tables.

Carlitos Café Y Cantina, 1324 State St., Santa Barbara 93101; (805) 962-7117; carlitos.com. End the hiking day with a margarita and fresh guacamole on the dog-friendly patio. You and pooch can window-shop if you decide to walk up State Street from the beach area.

Resting Up

Fess Parker Wine Country Inn and Spa, 633 E. Cabrillo Blvd., Santa Barbara 93103; (800) 879-2929; fessparkersantabarbarahotel.com. Pooch gets his own room-service menu here and is welcome everywhere on the property except in the interior food venues and the swimming pool area.

The Old Yacht Club Inn, 431 Corona Del Mar, Santa Barbara; (805) 962-1277; oldyachtclubinn.com. Well-mannered dogs are welcome in some of the rooms of this historic Craftsman house. Pet fee.

Santa Barbara Biltmore Four Seasons Resort, 1260 Channel Dr., Santa Barbara 93108; (805) 969-2261; fourseasons.com. This iconic Spanish-style property welcomes furry guests under 50 pounds in the garden cottage rooms. They are not permitted in any of the dining venues, but the menu is available at the lobby tables. They will even arrange for a sitter for your four-legged child if you want to dine *sans chien*. Doggie massage is also available, so don't worry about those post-hike sore muscles.

Campgrounds

Ocean Mesa RV and Campground, 100 El Capitan Terrace Ln., Santa Barbara 93117; (805) 879-5751; oceanmesa.com. This is a deluxe facility, between the views, heated pool, and spic and span restrooms and showers.

El Capitan State Beach Park, 10 Refugio Beach Rd., Goleta 93117; (805) 968-1033; (800) 444-7275; parks.ca.gov; reserveamerica.com. Fabulous setting on the bluff. The Aniso Trail that once connected **El Capitan to Refugio State Parks** between the railway and the beach is closed from the El Capitan side due to severe erosion along about a 0.5-mile section between the two state beach parks.

Refugio State Beach Park, 10 Refugio Beach Rd., Goleta 93117-9717; (805) 968-1033; (800) 444-7275; parks.ca.gov; reserveamerica.com. Beachfront campsites. The 2.5-mile paved hike/bike path running above the beach paralleling the railway that used to connect Refugio and El Capitan State Parks is closed due to severe erosion damage and hazardous conditions. Nevertheless, it's a lovely, flat 1.5-mile-long hike or bike north from Refugio to the fence where the trail now ends.

Puppy Paws and Golden Years

Alice Keck Park and Memorial Gardens make a pleasant stroll on Arrellagra Street between Garden Street and Santa Barbara Street.

Sam's Doggie Dude Ranch Boarding and Day Care, 12750 Calle Real, Goleta 93117; (805) 968-7337; samsdoggieduderanch.com. Susie Tautrim and her husband have gladly let the family's 300-acre working ranch go to the dogs. Dogs of all sizes are welcome to spend as little as a few hours at this canine-camp boarding kennel, while their owners go off on boring human-only activities around Santa Barbara. Sam's is about 30 miles north of Santa Barbara near the coastal campgrounds of Ocean Mesa RV and Campground, El Capitan State Park, Refugio State Park, and Gaviota State Park.

15 San Ysidro Falls

This easily accessible multi-use trail on the south-facing slopes of the Santa Ynez Mountains near Santa Barbara, where hikes are often dry, uphill schleps, has the distinction of climbing alongside a creek to a seasonal waterfall. Even at the height of a four-year drought, this creek had a trickle and two small but limpid swimming holes inviting dogs for a splash. Responsive pooches can scamper off leash.

Start: From trailhead on right side of East Mountain Drive
Distance: 3.8 miles out and back
Hiking time: About 2 hours
Difficulty: Moderate
Trailhead elevation: 450 feet
Highest point: 1,520 feet
Best season: Year-round; winter and spring for best swimming holes and waterfall; summer can be hot; annoying face flies in early fall
Trail surface: Dirt and rock
Other trail users: Horses and mountain bikes
Canine compatibility: Voice control
Land status: City, county, and national forest

Fees and permits: None
Maps: USGS Carpinteria; Los Padres National Forest
Trail contacts: Los Padres National Forest Santa Barbara Ranger District, 3505 Paradise Rd., Santa Barbara 93105; (805) 967-3481; fs.usda.gov/lpnf. County of Santa Barbara, (805) 568-2461. City of Santa Barbara, (805) 564-5418
Nearest town: Montecito Village and Santa Barbara
Trail tips: There is a trashcan and dog-waste bag dispenser at the trailhead. No amenities and no water.

Finding the trailhead: From Santa Barbara heading south on US 101, take Exit 93/San Ysidro Road. Turn left at the stop sign on San Ysidro Road and head toward the mountains. Drive 1 mile on San Ysidro Road to East Valley Road/CA 192 and turn right onto East Valley Road/CA 192. Drive 0.9 mile on East Valley Road/CA 192 to Park Lane and turn left onto Park Lane. Drive 0.3 mile on Park Lane to where the road forks. Bear left at the fork onto East Mountain Drive and drive 0.1 mile to the trailhead on the right. Park on the right side of East Mountain Drive. **GPS:** N34 26.76' / W119 37.33'

The Hike

This hike is in an area known as the "front country" on the southern slopes of the Santa Ynez Mountains. The city and county of Santa Barbara in cooperation with the Los Padres National Forest manage the front country trails. Like many of the front country trails, this one begins in a residential neighborhood. Montecito is posh and lush and the trail is dotted with posted reminders to "stay on the trail" wherever you cross private roads until you leave civilization for the heart of the canyon.

The hike begins along a corridor between two fence lines under a leafy canopy. The well-marked trail crosses two private paved roads within the first 0.5 mile and weaves around two gates on the first mile of trail. Although San Ysidro Creek is on your left the entire length of the hike, the swimming holes are only accessible at a few locations along the way. Eucalyptus stands transition to oaks and sycamores as you continue upward.

The trail merges into a fire road from 0.5 mile to 1.0 mile. At 1.0 the trail veers right, away from the fire road, and resumes its narrower backcountry character. At 1.4 miles you come to a swimming hole on the left. Even after a string of four severely dry years, this was a small but limpid pool waiting to reward a hot doggie. Just past the swimming hole, the trail spurs to the right and begins to switchback above the creek. There is a short, ribbed-concrete pathway on this steeper stretch with some metal handrails on the left. This section of

Spring blossoms frame the trailhead.

the trail could be slippery and precarious in wet weather. The trail emerges higher above the creek and views open across the creek to stunning sandstone escarpments.

At 1.8 miles you cross a seasonal stream just before coming to an unmarked trail junction. Bear left at the junction and arrive at the base of the towering cliff at 1.9 miles. The sheer wall is impressive when it is dry, and a true spectacle draped in a waterfall. Take time to enjoy the setting before going back down to the trailhead the way you came.

Miles and Directions

0.0 Start at the trailhead on East Mountain Drive.

0.1 Come to private paved road and turn left uphill. Follow signs for dirt trail paralleling road. San Ysidro Creek is on your left.

0.4 Come to private paved road. Continue walking on dirt trail to gate and trail junction ahead. Walk left around the gate.

0.5 Trail merges into fire road and you come to a trail junction for McMenemy Lower Trail on the left. Continue walking straight.

0.6 Come to a gate. Walk around the gate.

0.9 Unmarked trail comes in from the right. Continue walking straight.

1.0 Leave the fire road and bear to the right up the narrow trail.

1.4 Bear right onto spur trail rising above creek and begin switchbacks.

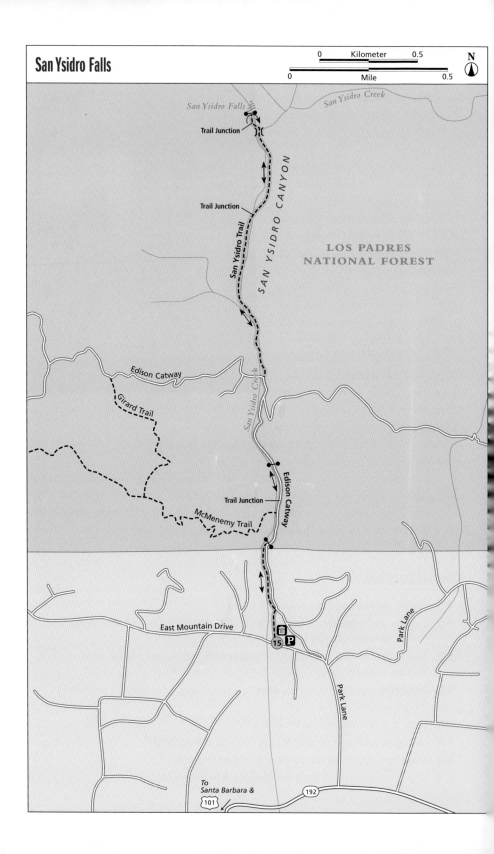

San Ysidro Falls

San Ysidro Creek

San Ysidro Falls

Trail Junction

SAN YSIDRO CANYON

Trail Junction

San Ysidro Trail

LOS PADRES
NATIONAL FOREST

Edison Catway

Girard Trail

San Ysidro Creek

Edison Catway

Trail Junction

McMenemy Trail

East Mountain Drive

Park Lane

15 P

Park Lane

To
Santa Barbara &
101

192

1.8 Cross a seasonal creek.

1.85 Come to an unmarked trail junction. Bear left toward seasonal waterfall.

1.9 Arrive at base of seasonal waterfall. Elevation: 1,520 feet. **GPS:** N34 28.15' / W119 37.40'. Turn around and return to the trailhead the way you came.

3.8 Arrive back at the trailhead.

Creature Comforts

Fueling Up

Montecito Village Grocery, in Montecito Village at the corner of San Ysidro Road and East Valley Road. 1482 E. Valley Rd., Santa Barbara 93108; (805) 969-7845; montecitogrocery.com. Organic products and novel items.

Montecito Coffee Shop, in Montecito Village on the corner of San Ysidro Road and East Valley Road. 1498 E. Valley Rd., Santa Barbara 93108; (805) 969-6250; montecitocoffeeshop.com. Breakfast and brunch. House-made muesli is a favorite.

Resting Up

San Ysidro Ranch, 900 San Ysidro Ln., Montecito 93108; (805) 969-5046; sanysidroranch .com. This historic property is rich-and-famous territory where dogs are valued family members under the Privileged Pet Program. Prepare for sticker shock.

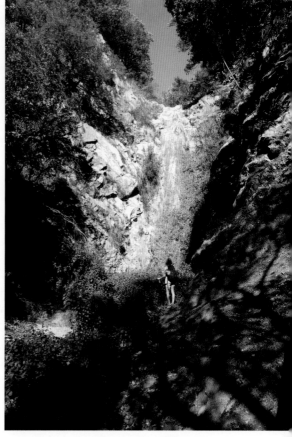

Waterfall runs dry during drought years.

Ventura County

Until 1873, Ventura County was part of Santa Barbara County. Although the split of the land's boundaries resulted in creating new communities, it is no big surprise that Ventura County shares similar geography to Santa Barbara with mountainous territory, coastal plains, and enviable beaches. Fifty-three percent of the county's area is Los Padres National Forest and contains some of the most pristine and remote wilderness in Southern California.

Ojai, from the Chumash language meaning "moon," is a gateway to rugged, mountainous hiking terrain. San Buenaventura, commonly known as Ventura or the "city of good fortune" and founded by Father Junípero Serra in 1782, benefits from a gentle beach-traced coastline and small-town atmosphere. Ventura was named "one of the 10 Best Places to Live Now" in a 2015 issue of *Men's Journal*. Based on how welcoming the town is to furry four-legged tourists, your dog would give it a five-paw rating as well.

16 Piedra Blanca Trail to Twin Forks Camp

This hike through mostly chaparral lets you and pooch sample a stretch of the Gene Marshall–Piedra Blanca National Recreation Trail into the Sespe Wilderness past the eye-catching Piedra Blanca (white rock) unique sandstone mounds. The hike concludes along the Piedra Blanca Creek to the undeveloped Twin Forks Camp.

Start: From the Sespe Trailhead between the two interpretive panels
Distance: 6.8 miles out and back
Hiking time: About 3.5 hours
Difficulty: Moderate
Trailhead elevation: 3,079 feet
Highest point: 3,633 feet
Best season: Year-round depending on the flow of the Sespe and Piedra Blanca Creeks. Early spring to avoid summer heat and late fall to avoid the face flies and enjoy the most comfortable temperatures.
Trail surface: Dirt, rock, and sand
Other trail users: Horses
Canine compatibility: Voice control
Land status: National forest; wilderness
Fees and permits: Adventure Pass fee for parking (passes available at ranger stations, visitor centers, and some local businesses or online at fs.usda.gov/adventurepass)

Maps: USGS Lion Canyon; Los Padres National Forest South; National Geographic Los Padres National Forest East; Tom Harrison Maps Sespe Wilderness
Trail contacts: Ojai Ranger Station, 1190 E. Ojai Ave., Ojai 93023; (805) 646-4348; fs .usda.gov/lpnf. Wheeler Gorge Visitor Center, 17017 Maricopa Hwy., Ojai 93023; (805) 640-9060; lpforest.org
Nearest town: Ojai
Trail tips: There are several interpretive panels at the trailhead about endangered species, local wildlife, and the history of the Sespe Creek watershed. There are 2 vault toilets, trash containers, and picnic tables. There is no water at the trailhead. Watch for poison oak on parts of the trail, and leash your dog to prevent a nosy pooch from surprising a rattlesnake.

Finding the trailhead: From Ventura at US 101 and CA 33, drive 13 miles north on CA 33 towards Ojai to the traffic signal and junction of CA 33 and CA 150. From the junction, continue driving north on CA 33 for 14.5 miles. CA 33 is part of the Jacinto Reyes National Forest Scenic Byway and passes through a couple of tunnels before climbing and twisting up the Sespe Gorge. Turn right onto paved Forest Service Road 6N31 at the sign for Rose Valley Recreation Area. Drive 4.6 miles to a junction and continue for 1 mile past the junction to the Sespe Trailhead parking lot. **GPS:** N34 33.61' / W119 09.90'

The Hike

The Gene Marshall–Piedra Blanca National Recreation Trail is an 18-mile-long trail in the Sespe Wilderness, the largest wilderness area in the Los Padres National Forest (219,000 acres). Chumash Indians had summer hunting camps along the Sespe Creek long before European settlers arrived in the late 1800s.

1947 was a significant milepost for natural habitats when the Sespe Condor Sanctuary was established as part of the ongoing efforts to preserve California condors. In 1992 the Los Padres Condor Range and River Protection Act designated 400,450 acres of the Los Padres National Forest as wilderness, including 31 miles of Sespe Creek as a Wild and Scenic River. The 53,000 acres protected as the Sespe Condor Sanctuary are closed to the public to minimize the negative impacts of human activity.

Condors are scavengers and their diet consists of dead animals. But human food and litter not only disrupt the raptors' natural foraging patterns, but also increase the risk of ingesting or feeding non-digestible particles of litter to their young.

This hike takes you along a 3.4-mile sample of the national recreation trail. Depending on the season and whether Southern California is in a wet or dry cycle, the landscape and the experience can be quite different.

The rounded white sandstone formations jut out above the dry chaparral landscape to the north immediately as you set off from the trailhead. Your excursion begins with three seasonal creek crossings in the first mile before entering the Sespe

Hiking across the white sandstone hills of Piedra Blanca

Wilderness. During drought years, these crossings will be dry. Conversely, during very wet years, flooding can make the crossings hazardous. Be sure to check with the ranger station on the current flow status of Sespe Creek.

You come face to face with the Piedra Blanca formations at 1.2 miles. These sandstone mounds and boulders of varying size and shapes invite you and pooch to scamper around. If you don't have time or gusto for the longer hike, Piedra Blanca is a very satisfying adventure for hikers and dogs looking for a picnic spot with a view.

To continue to Twin Forks Camp, follow the worn, sandy trail as it weaves around the boulders for about 0.2 mile before the trail begins to descend on the other side of the Piedra Blanca. On this side you will see a few more oaks, cottonwoods, and an occasional pine tree. You will cross two more seasonal creeks before the trail veers upward to the right. Even in drought there is evidence of robust riparian habitat, lush with willows and bunch grass along Piedra Blanca Creek below on your right. The view opens back toward the Piedra Blanca boulders at the bend in the trail.

You come to Piedra Blanca undeveloped campsite at 3.0 miles on the Piedra Blanca Creek, which runs year-round at this location. The trail becomes more primitive over the next 0.4 mile along the creek to Twin Forks camp with Pine Mountain Ridge as a backdrop.

You come to a trail junction at 3.35 miles and one last creek crossing before arriving at the undeveloped Twin Forks Campsite on the right. Fossil lovers will be delighted by what is encrusted in the large boulder at this camp.

Take the time to share a snack with your pal before going back to the trailhead the way you came.

Miles and Directions

0.0 Start at the trailhead between the two interpretive panels.

0.3 Walk across Lion Canyon Creek.

0.35 Walk across the wide Sespe Creek (seasonally dry or spread over two branches).

0.4 Come to a trail junction for the Middle Sespe and Gene Marshall-Piedra Blanca Trails to the left and Sespe River to the right. Turn left.

0.8 Walk across a seasonal creek.

0.9 Come to a trail junction with a wooden sign. Turn right on the Gene Marshall-Piedra Blanca NRT to the right.

0.95 Enter Sespe Wilderness.

1.2 Come to the Piedra Blanca sandstone formations.

1.4 Begin descent on trail.

1.5 Walk across seasonal creek.

2.8 Walk across seasonal creek.

3.0 Come to Piedra Blanca undeveloped campsite.

3.1 Walk across seasonal creek.

3.3 Walk across Piedra Blanca Creek.

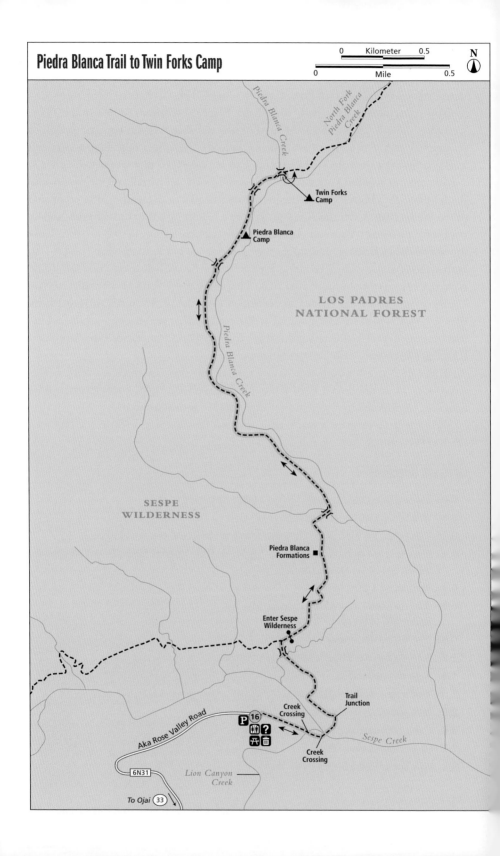

3.35 Come to trail junction. Turn right to Twin Forks and cross North Fork Piedra Blanca Creek.

3.4 Arrive at undeveloped Twin Forks Camp. Go back to the trailhead the way you came. Elevation: 3,633 feet. **GPS:** N34 35.27' / W119 09.77'

6.8 Arrive back at the trailhead.

Creature Comforts

Fueling Up

Ojai Beverage Company, 655 E. Ojai Ave., Ojai 93023; (805) 646-1700; ojaibevco .com. It's casual and hip with a dog-friendly patio. Pooch may want to try one of the signature burgers.

Knead Baking Company, 469 E. Ojai Ave., Ojai 93923; (310) 770-3282; knead bakingcompany.com. Pick up picnic goodies or take Fido out to breakfast or lunch on the patio.

The Oak Grill and Jimmy's Pub at the Ojai Valley Inn and Spa, 905 Country Club Rd., Ojai 93023; (855) 697-8780; ojairesort.com. Pooches are welcome on their patios.

Resting Up

Blue Iguana Inn and Suites, 11794 N. Ventura Ave., Ojai 93023; (805) 646-5277; blueiguanainn.com. The classic inn has charm and character. Some rooms welcome well-mannered canines. Nightly fee and refundable deposit.

Ojai Valley Inn and Spa, 905 Country Club Rd., Ojai 93023; (855) 697-8780; ojairesort.com. It's a perfect place to luxuriate after a hike if you are willing to splurge on the non-refundable $150 pet fee for a "pet-friendly room," or $200 if all the pet-friendly rooms are occupied.

Puppy Paws and Golden Years

The **Ojai Valley Trail,** a national recreation trail, is a 9.5-mile rails-to-trails multi-use paved path that runs along the Ventura River paralleling CA 33. There is a wood-chip shoulder. The easiest access in Ojai is from the town's green centerpiece, Libbey Park, on East Ojai Avenue.

17 San Buenaventura State Beach Park to Ventura River Estuary

There's nothing Southern California canine locals and visitors love more than a chance to sniff that rich Pacific air and sink their paws in the sand. This paved multi-use trail, suitable for dogs of all sizes, shapes, and stamina, offers both.

Start: From the trailhead on the left (west) side of the San Buenaventura State Beach Park entrance on Pierpont Boulevard at San Pedro Street
Distance: 4.0 miles out and back
Hiking time: About 2 hours
Difficulty: Easy
Trailhead elevation: 19 feet
Highest point: 27 feet
Best season: Year-round
Trail surface: Pavement and sand
Other trail users: Bicycles and rollerblades
Canine compatibility: On leash and voice control
Land status: State

Fees and permits: Parking fee at the state beach park
Maps: USGS Ventura
Trail contacts: California Department of Parks and Recreation, (805) 968-1033; parks.ca .gov. California State Parks Channel Coast District, (805) 585-1850. City of Ventura Parks Department, (805) 652-4550. County of Ventura Parks Department, (805) 654-3951.
Nearest town: Ventura
Trail tips: There are restrooms with flush toilets and sinks, picnic tables, and barbecue areas in the state beach park. There is a dog-waste bag dispenser at the trailhead.

Finding the trailhead: At Ventura on US 101 going south, take the Seaward Avenue exit 68 onto Monmouth Boulevard going west. Drive 0.1 mile to Pierpont Boulevard and turn right. Drive 0.1 mile on Pierpont Boulevard and cross San Pedro Street into the San Buenaventura State Beach Park. Turn left into Picnic Lot A after entering the park. The trailhead is at the southwest corner of Pierpont Boulevard and San Pedro Street west of the park entrance. **GPS:** N34 16.08' / W119 16.63'

At Ventura on US 101 going north, take Seaward exit 68 and drive 0.2 mile west on Seaward Avenue to Pierpont Boulevard. Turn right on Pierpont Boulevard; drive 0.5 mile on Pierpont Boulevard and cross San Pedro Street into the San Buenaventura State Beach Park. Turn left into Picnic Lot A after entering the park. The trailhead is at the southwest corner of Pierpont Boulevard and San Pedro Street west of the park entrance. **GPS:** N34 16.08' / W119 16.63'

The Hike

Dogs give Ventura and its beachfront multi-use trail five wags. The paved path has a dirt shoulder with natural vegetation, which sends Fido into scent heaven while you feast on Mother Nature's canvas of surf, sand, and palm trees.

There are civilized conveniences along the way, including benches and restrooms with flush toilets and sinks for water to serve hikers, walkers, cyclists, and rollerbladers.

The trail widens to a promenade midway.

There are several dog-waste bag dispensers along the path. As a matter of fact, Ventura is so determined to welcome canine visitors, while making it easy for you to be a responsible human companion, that the dispensers are sprinkled around town in all the public parks and are sponsored by a variety of local businesses.

At 0.9 mile you come to a junction with a path going right. Continue walking straight on the path that hugs the beach. The Ventura Pier is just ahead. Leashed dogs are welcome on the pier and this is a great spot for an open-air snack at one of the two dog-friendly restaurants when you've both worked up an appetite on the way back. For now continue your excursion toward the estuary.

At 1.6 miles bear left on the path passing Surfer Point. The fairgrounds are on the right and the good news is that you are now leaving the state beach park zone, and although you are still on state property, the dog rules are about to get looser and so can your dog's leash. From here to the turnaround point at the estuary, dogs can romp off leash on the beach.

At 1.9 miles you come to a short boardwalk loop spur out to the sand. Leashed pooches are welcome to explore the boardwalk. Save this side jaunt for your return and continue walking on the path to where it veers right at the estuary. At 2.0 miles you reach the estuary, where the Ventura River meets the Pacific. The beach beckons. For your bow-wow, the beach is the equivalent of a pot of gold at the end of the

San Buenaventura State Beach Park to Ventura River Estuary

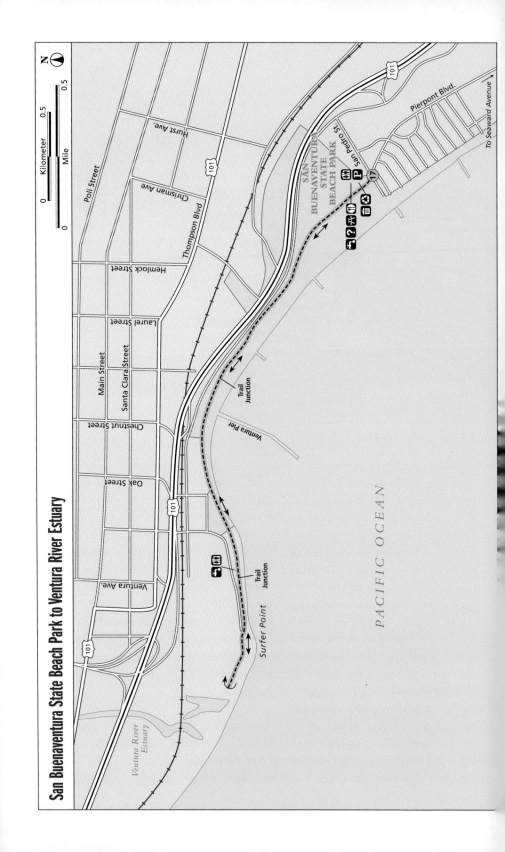

rainbow. Take time to bask in the feel-good negative ions permeating the beach air with your dog before returning to the trailhead the way you came.

Miles and Directions

0.0 Start at the San Buenaventura State Beach Park at the north end of Pierpont Boulevard at San Pedro Street.

0.9 Come to a trail junction. Continue walking straight.

1.0 Walk under the Ventura Pier.

1.6 Bear left and come to Surfer Point.

2.0 Arrive at the Ventura River Estuary and dog-friendly stretch of beach. Enjoy frolicking on the beach before going back to the trailhead the way you came. Elevation: 18 feet. **GPS:** N34 16.48' / W119 18.41'

4.0 Arrive back at the trailhead.

Creature Comforts

Fueling Up

Pizza Man Dan's, 444 E. Santa Clara St., Ventura 93001; (805) 658-6666. Local chain with fresh salad bar.

Beach House Tacos on the Pier, 668 Harbor Blvd., Ventura 93001; (805) 648-3177; beach-house-tacos.com. Good refueling stop with pooch on your hike.

Beach House Fish/The Deck, 668 Harbor Blvd., Ventura 93001; (805) 643-4783; beachhousefish.com. It's a fish market and restaurant. Dog-friendly deck.

Resting Up

Marriott Ventura Beach, 2055 E. Harbor Blvd., Ventura 93001; (805) 643-6000; marriottventurabeach.com. A hotel that prides itself on being "The Pet Friendly Hotel."

Four Points by Sheraton Ventura Harbor Resort, 1050 Schooner Dr., Ventura 93001; (888) 627-8081; www.fourpointsventuraharborresort.com. Scenic location at the entrance to the harbor. Bed and breakfast rates. Rooms have refrigerators. Pet fee. Furry family members welcome on the restaurant patio.

Motel 6 Ventura Beach, 2145 E. Harbor Blvd., Ventura 93001; (805) 643-5100; motel6.com. Great location for small budgets. Free Wi-Fi and pool. The wood laminate floors are a great surface for canine guests with beach paws.

Campgrounds

Ventura Beach RV Resort, 800 Main St., Ventura 93001; (805) 643-9137; venturabeachrvpark.com. It's a great dog-friendly campground with grassy tent sites, full hookup sites, and the conveniences of luxury RV resorts if you don't mind the traffic drone from nearby highways.

Emma Wood State Beach Pacific Coast Highway, 2 miles northwest of downtown Ventura on US 101; (805) 968-1033, (800) 444-7275; parks.ca.gov;

reserveamerica.com. No tent camping; only self-contained vehicles, as there are no amenities and that includes no water and no restrooms. Reservations between mid-May to Labor Day and campground can close due to high tides.

Things to Do with Pooch

The free **Downtown Harbor Trolley,** (805) 827-4444, makes several stops for sightseeing and welcomes furry tourists onboard. If Fido is a fan of courtroom-drama television shows, he might enjoy walking to 21 S. California St., where Erle Stanley Gardner wrote his first Perry Mason novels. Your dog's ears might perk up hearing about "The Case of the Howling Dog" published in 1934 and aired as a TV episode in 1959.

Puppy Paws and Golden Years

From the Buenaventura State Beach, drive 1 mile south on Pierpont Boulevard to the **Marina Park.** The paved pathways and greenbelts welcome pooches on leash. Pooch can get his sand-and-surf fix on the stretch of beach between the two breakwaters. Your leashed four-legged pal doesn't have to be Catholic to enjoy the **Buenaventura Mission** gardens at 225 Main St. on the corner of Figueroa Street in downtown Ventura. But if he's a history buff, he will enjoy soaking up a little of California's Spanish history. The entrance to the garden is through the Mission Museum and shop. There's an admission fee for humans.

The **"Future Home of the Ventura Botanical Gardens"** has a dog-friendly mile-long dirt trail with long, gentle zigzags that offer hikers spectacular views of coastal Ventura, the pier, and the Channel Islands within a couple of switchbacks. The trail begins to the right of City Hall at 501 Poli St. at the top of California Street. There is parking in the rear of City Hall. You need not walk farther than the first 0.6 mile of trail, which is the best-maintained section to enjoy the full panorama. If pooch wants to call it quits sooner, the plateau at about 0.3 mile is a great vista point for you and a planted area for your pal's sniffing pleasure.

Ventura's 0.3-mile-long pier is one of California's longest wooden piers and a favorite stroll for local canines. The pier is lined with interpretive panels about the marine life and Ventura's history.

18 Paradise Falls

Wildwood Park's 1,800 acres are a surprising open-space oasis on the edge of a suburban neighborhood. Views of unusual geologic formations from the cactus-carpeted ridge, a shady creekside canyon, and a year-round waterfall make this relatively short hike's variety a tail-wagging experience.

Start: From the Moonridge Trail at the east end of the Wildwood Park parking lot

Distance: 2.8-mile loop

Hiking time: About 1.5 hours

Difficulty: Easy

Trailhead elevation: 663 feet

Highest point: 663 feet

Best season: Year-round; wildflowers in the spring; can be hot in the summer

Trail surface: Dirt and sand

Other trail users: None

Canine compatibility: On leash

Land status: City and land conservancy

Fees and permits: None

Maps: USGS Newbury Park; Wildwood Park Trail Map

Trail contacts: Conejo Recreation and Park District, 403 W. Hillcrest Dr., Thousand Oaks 91360; (805) 495-6471; conejo-openspace .org

Nearest town: Thousand Oaks

Trail tips: Keep your dog on a short leash at the beginning of the hike. The trail is narrow and flanked by beavertail cacti. There is 1 picnic table and a drinking fountain in the parking lot. The dog-waste bag dispenser is next to the information board at the west end of the parking lot.

Finding the trailhead: From Thousand Oaks on US 101 take the Lynn Road exit 45 and drive 2.5 miles north on Lynn Road to Avenida de Los Arboles. Turn left on Avenida de Los Arboles at the sign for Wildwood Park. Drive 0.8 mile on Avenida de Los Arboles to the road's end. Wildwood Park's large parking lot is on your left.

There is an information board and a map at the west end of the parking lot. Moonridge Trail to Paradise Falls is at the east end (lower end) of the parking lot left of the service road gate and down the wooden steps. **GPS:** N34 13.18' / W118 54.15'

The Hike

The Chumash Indians made this land home for thousands of years before the Spanish settlers arrived. During the early 1800s this expansive swath of land and its various wildlife habitats were part of Rancho El Conejo. The grasslands were prime grazing territory for cattle and sheep through the 20th century. Between the 1930s and 1960s, Wildwood Park was a popular film and television-series set for Hollywood studios. Some of the most iconic films and television series included *Spartacus* and *Gunsmoke*.

The Conejo Recreation and Park District (CRPD) acquired the canyon land in 1967 and expanded the park to include the mesa in 1987. The Conejo Open Space Conservation Agency (COSCA) manages the 1,800 acres under the City of Thousand Oaks and the CRPD.

Prickly pear cacti keep you on the trail.

Although the information panel at the west end of the parking lot is at the most visible trailhead in the park with heavy visitor traffic, the loop hike to Paradise Falls begins at the more discreet trailhead down a set of wooden steps at the opposite end of the parking lot. Turn right onto Moonridge Trail to Paradise Falls at the bottom of the stairs and walk along the narrow dirt trail braced by cascades of beavertail cacti along the exposed ridge with the canyon on your left. You will see a couple of houses perched on the bluffs to the left, but from here on, nature dominates in Wildwood Park.

At about 0.3 mile the cactus slopes give way to toyon berries and scrub oak. Walk across a footbridge over a seasonal creek and a dirt service road another 0.2 mile ahead.

At 0.9 mile bear left at the trail junction. The trail descends toward a large teepee overlooking the canyon. Take a moment to look around the open teepee and continue walking downhill, bearing right at the trail junction for Wildwood Canyon and Paradise Falls. Come to another trail junction 0.2 mile down and turn left onto a narrow dirt trail.

At the next junction just ahead, bear right on the trail and make an immediate left past the picnic tables to walk down the wooden steps to the base of the falls on the north fork of Arroyo Conejo. There are shaded picnic tables to the right at the

Arriving at Paradise Falls

falls. The falls are a highlight in Wildwood Park, and consequently the area can get congested with four-legged hikers and their companions, especially on weekends and holidays.

To continue your loop, walk back 0.1 mile up the wooden stairs to the trail junction and turn right to follow the fence along the narrow trail corridor above the falls. At 1.6 miles there is another picnic area with tables and grills under majestic oaks along the creek. This is a good alternative to the falls picnic tables on a busy day. The canyon floor's cooler riparian woodland is a refreshing and enchanting contrast to the sun-blazed ridge and plateaus above.

You come to another trail junction just past the picnic area. Continue walking straight on Wildwood Canyon Trail until you reach a footbridge on the right. Walk across the footbridge over the creek and follow the sign for Wildwood and Indian Creek Trails. Turn left onto Indian Creek Trail. At 2.3 miles, walk across Indian Creek. At the next trail junction, bear left and walk uphill toward the exposed mesa to Wildwood Park parking lot and the trailhead to complete your loop.

Miles and Directions

0.0 Start at the Moonridge Trailhead.

0.3 Walk across a footbridge over a seasonal creek.

0.5 Walk across a service road.

0.9 Come to a trail junction. Turn left toward the teepee and Paradise Falls.

1.0 Come to a trail junction at the Teepee Overlook. Turn right to Wildwood Canyon and Paradise Falls.

1.2 Come to a trail junction and turn left on the narrow dirt trail.

1.3 Come to a trail junction. Bear right and almost immediately turn left and walk down the wooden stairs to the base of the falls.

1.4 Arrive at Paradise Falls. Elevation: 330 feet. Walk 0.1 mile back to the trail junction to continue walking the loop.

1.6 Come to a picnic area by the creek.

1.7 Come to a trail junction. Continue walking straight on Wildwood Canyon Trail.

1.9 Come to a trail junction. Turn right and walk across the bridge over the creek. Turn left on Indian Creek Trail immediately after the bridge.

2.3 Walk across Indian Creek.

2.5 Come to a trail junction. Bear left and walk uphill to the Wildwood Park parking lot and trailhead.

2.8 Arrive back at the trailhead.

Creature Comforts

Fueling Up

Moorpark Road in the suburb of Thousand Oaks is a commercial area with various businesses and services including fast-food eateries.

Paradise Falls

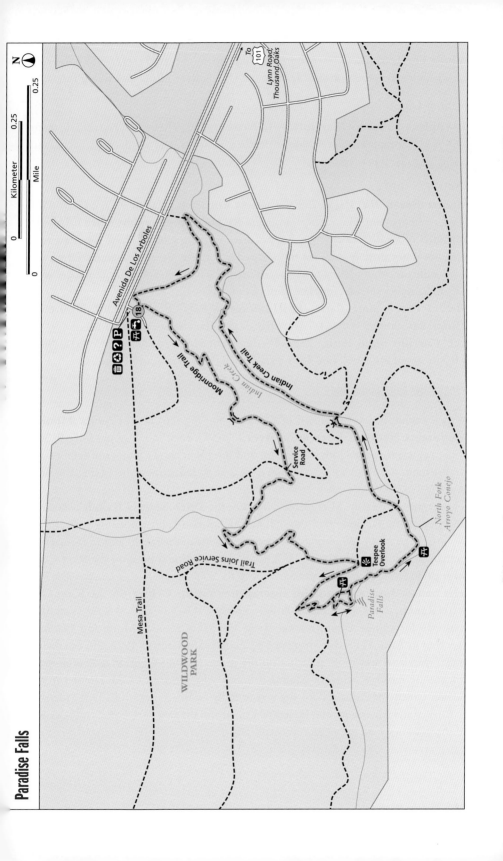

Whole Foods Market, 740 Moorpark Rd., Thousand Oaks 91360; (805) 777-4730. Good choice for provisions and food to go. The outdoor eating area is dog friendly.

Resting Up

Townplace Suites by Marriott, 1712 Newbury Rd., Thousand Oaks 91320; (805) 499-3111. Complimentary breakfast, kitchen in suites, and outdoor barbecue and picnic area; $100 pet fee.

Campgrounds

Malibu Beach RV Park, 25801 Pacific Coast Hwy., Malibu 90265; (310) 456-6052; maliburv.com. This clean, convenient RV park across from the beach has all the amenities of an RV resort and is a short drive to the trailhead. There are a few tent sites, but unfortunately dogs are not allowed at the tent sites. The bonus to this park is a 2-mile canyon trail loop from the private RV park. You and your pooch get your fix of morning exercise complete with coastal views.

Malibu Creek State Park, 1925 Las Virgenes Rd., Calabasas 91302; (818) 880-0367; reservations, (800) 444-7275; parks.ca.gov. Tent, trailer, and RV sites.

Leo Carrillo State Park, 35000 Pacific Coast Hwy., Malibu 90265; (818) 880-0363; reservations, (800) 444-7275; parks.ca.gov. Tent, trailer, and RV sites.

Puppy Paws and Golden Years

Which canine has not dreamed of being on the big screen? The **Santa Monica Mountains National Recreation Area,** 2903 Cornell Rd., Agoura Hills 91301, is the centerpiece for Hollywood films and television shows. Pups and seniors can stroll Paramount Ranch's western town set and fantasize about becoming the next Rin Tin Tin.

Three miles farther up Mulholland Highway, the **Peter Strauss Ranch** welcomes pooches on the 0.5-mile trail through an oak riparian habitat boasting native-plant blooms in the spring. Water dogs will drool at the site of the ranch's historic (currently unmaintained) swimming pool, built in 1940 as the largest pool on the West Coast with a 650,000-gallon water capacity for up to 3,000 people.

The Santa Monica Mountains Interagency Visitor Center on the King Gillette Ranch, 26800 Mulholland Hwy., Calabasas 91302; (805) 370-2301, is another must-see for complete information about the Santa Monica Mountains National Recreation Area. The razor magnate's Spanish estate, built in 1925 and opened as public parkland, welcomes pooches on the grounds along the ADA-accessible trails tracing the meadow where a Chumash Indian village once thrived. Housed in the former Gillette Mansion stables, the eco-friendly visitor center is LEED (Leadership in Energy and Environmental Design) certified and the first "net-zero" visitor center in the National Park Service.

Los Angeles County

The most populous county in the United States boasts mountains and ocean as well as forests and desert. Santa Catalina Island in Los Angeles County is the only privately owned and developed of the eight Channel Islands and is dog friendly, as it is not in the Channel Islands National Park.

More than 10 million residents mill about this county, not to mention the hordes of visitors who flock to Los Angeles, one of the world's most famous cities. It's not a

ISLAND HOP WITH YOUR HOUND

Santa Catalina Island is 22 miles long and 8 miles wide. It can be accessed by foot ferry with your bow-wow from Long Beach, San Pedro, Dana Point, or Newport Beach on a 45- to 75-minute crossing to Avalon, Catalina's 1-square-mile compact tourist hub tucked at the foot of chaparral-covered slopes.

Native Americans called it home for more than 7,000 years before Spanish explorers dropped anchor and named the shores Santa Catalina. William Wrigley of the Wrigley gum empire stepped up Avalon's resort development when he purchased the island from the Banning brothers in 1919.

Catalina sparkled as a star-studded retreat between the 1920s and '50s. Spring brought Wrigley's Chicago Cubs for training alongside vacationing Hollywood idols like Bogart, Monroe, and big-screen sweethearts Robert Wagner and Natalie Wood.

Except for Avalon, most of the island had been private and off limits to visitors. But in 1972 the Wrigley and Offield families founded the Catalina Island Conservancy. An impressive 88 percent of the land has since been protected. The conservancy focuses on habitat rehabilitation for endemic plants and animals, and education in balance with backcountry recreation for hikers, mountain bikers, and campers. There are no car rentals, but the conservancy offers several Jeep Eco-Tours to connect visitors with the island's unspoiled inland vistas.

The steep Sky Summit Trail in Avalon offers fit dogs and their two-legged companions a panoramic loop through the Wrigley Memorial and Botanic Gardens. Less ambitious or energetic visitors enjoy the scenic waterfront promenade.

For more information, visit gotocatalina.com, catalinachamber.com, or catalinaconservancy.org.

surprise to bump up against vehicular and people traffic within miles of "Tinseltown," movie star capital of the universe. But as the second-largest city in the United States after New York City, the "City of Angels" also happens to be surrounded by mountains on three sides with preserved open space and the Angeles National Forest for recreation. Griffith Park, one of the largest urban parks in California and largest city park in the county, showcases a 4,000-acre outdoor haven, where hikers can escape the metropolitan cacophony with their dog. As of June 2016 the Backbone Trail, a project in progress for the last forty years, was completed and connects 67 contiguous miles of trail in the Santa Monica Mountains National Recreation Area, the largest urban national park in the country. The advantage of urban trails is the access to myriad lodging and dining options for those less keen on sleeping in a tent and cooking hot dogs over the campfire.

19 Solstice Canyon Loop

You won't find solitude on this very popular and easily accessible hike. But a year-round creek up a shady canyon for pooch combined with sweeping views of the Pacific along the sundrenched ridge is worth sharing the trail with four-legged locals and their human companions.

Start: From the Tropical Terrace Trail behind the gate at the north end of the parking lot
Distance: 3.2-mile loop
Hiking time: About 2 hours
Difficulty: Moderate
Trailhead elevation: 114 feet
Highest point: 777 feet
Best season: Year-round
Trail surface: Pavement and dirt
Other trail users: None
Canine compatibility: On leash
Land status: National park
Fees and permits: None
Maps: USGS Malibu Beach, Point Dume; National Park Service Solstice Canyon Map;

National Geographic Map Santa Monica Mountains National Recreation Area.
Trail contacts: Santa Monica National Recreation Area, 401 Hillcrest Dr., Thousand Oaks 91360; (805) 370-2301; nps.gov/samo
Nearest town: Malibu
Trail tips: The trailhead has an interpretive panel with a map of the Santa Monica National Recreation Area and information about the ecology of Solstice Canyon and fire safety. There is a sheltered picnic area, trash and recycling containers, a drinking fountain, and a pay phone. Four vault toilets are on the trail just beyond the parking lot along with another drinking fountain.

Finding the trailhead: From Malibu at CA 1/Pacific Coast Highway and Corral Canyon Road, drive 0.1 mile east on Corral Canyon Road to the Solstice Canyon entrance. Continue 0.3 mile to the end of the road and the parking lot. (The first parking spaces on your right as you enter are for overflow. The larger and main parking lot is at the end of the road.) Walk to the far end of the parking lot to the sign for the Tropical Terrace Trail behind the gate. **GPS:** N34 02.26' / W118 44.86'

The Hike

The Santa Monica Mountains National Recreation Area encompasses almost 160,000 acres laced with 500 miles of trails. The National Park Service in cooperation with several other government agencies administers the recreation area. The Chumash Indians inhabited Solstice Canyon long before the arrival of settlers and cattle ranchers. The Santa Monica Mountains Conservancy opened Solstice Canyon as a public park in 1988. The National Park Service now manages the canyon park.

In spring, fall, and winter, the loop trail can be hiked comfortably in both directions. But summers and early fall days can be hot, so plan to hike early if you begin clockwise up the canyon, as the last 2 miles on the ridge are exposed and the midday and afternoon sun can be brutal.

The trail begins on a paved path and alternates between dirt and eroded pavement for the first 1.4 miles as it traces Solstice Creek under canopies of sycamore and bay trees with a couple of creek crossings.

At 0.7 mile you come to an interpretive panel about the original wood cabin that was destroyed by fire and rebuilt with stone for Henry Keller's hunting lodge in the late 1800s. Unfortunately, wood porches and add-ons over the years made the lodge more vulnerable, and when the Corral Fire of 2007 swept through the canyon, it left only the stone walls visible across the creek. You will then pass a bridge on your right and come to an unmarked fork on the trail. The right fork follows a narrower dirt path through a riparian woodland and crosses Solstice Creek twice. But if the creek flow is too swift, bear left at the fork to avoid the creek crossings. The two forks merge 0.15 mile ahead after the second creek crossing.

At 1.3 miles you come to the Tropical Terrace, the stone ruins of a ranch house known for its organic design integrating the natural landscape into the home's interiors. Although the structure was destroyed in the 1982 Dayton Canyon Fire, the

The trail climbs above Tropical Terrace and ranch house ruins.

The loop hike rewards with views of the Pacific.

garden's stone terraces bear the signature of renowned architect Paul R. Williams. Just past the stone terraces, there is a sign for a waterfall to the left. Unfortunately dogs are not allowed to the base of the waterfall about 50 yards away. But all is not lost, as the cascade will soon be visible behind you after you cross Solstice Creek and bear right to climb up a stretch of stone steps on the Rising Sun Trail. The exposed trail, flanked by low sage and coffee berry bush, crests at 1.9 miles, revealing sweeping views down the canyon to the Pacific and Channel Islands. This is a good photo spot and rest stop to offer your dog water. Walk another 0.5 mile to a trail junction and continue on Rising Sun Trail as you begin a gradual descent.

At 2.8 miles you come to a junction with a paved road. Walk across the road to the dirt trail and the trail sign. Bear right on the dirt trail and come to another trail junction. Bear left and follow the sign to the parking lot. You come to another paved road junction just ahead. Continue walking on the dirt trail toward the parking lot and the trailhead. The parking lot will come into view just below on the right.

At 3.2 miles you close the loop at the bottom of the stone steps at the trailhead where you began. Walk left to the parking lot and take the time to share a snack with your furry friend at one of the picnic tables.

Miles and Directions

0.0 Start at the Solstice Canyon Trailhead.

0.2 Come to a trail junction for the picnic area on the left. Continue walking straight on the paved path.

0.3 Walk past the trail junction and walk across Solstice Creek on the bridge. Turn right at the trail junction after the bridge.

0.7 Come to an interpretive panel about Henry Keller's stone hunting lodge across the creek.

0.75 Walk past the bridge on your right and bear right at the fork just past the bridge.

0.8 Walk across Solstice Creek.

0.9 Walk across Solstice Creek and merge onto main trail.

1.3 Come to a trail junction for Sostomo Trail to the left. Continue walking straight past the Tropical Terrace and interpretive panel about the Roberts Ranch House.

1.4 Come to a trail junction for the waterfall to the left and Rising Sun Trail ahead. Cross Solstice Creek and continue uphill on Rising Sun Trail.

1.9 Come to a viewpoint of the Pacific Ocean and the Channel Islands on the western horizon.

2.4 Come to a trail junction. Continue walking on Rising Sun Trail.

2.8 Come to a trail junction at a paved road. Walk across the road to the trail sign and bear right on the dirt trail.

2.9 Come to a trail junction and bear left to the parking lot.

3.0 Walk across the paved road to the dirt path going downhill and follow the sign for the parking lot.

3.2 Complete the loop and arrive back at the trailhead.

Creature Comforts

Fueling Up

Ralph's Supermarket, 23841 Malibu Rd., Malibu 90265; (310) 456-2917. The Malibu Colony Plaza on Malibu Colony Road has a Ralph's Supermarket for provisions, along with dining options and Pacific Coast Pets for supplies and accessories (23705 Malibu Rd., Malibu 90265; 310-317-8600). If your dog is a star hound, this might be the place to shop.

Ollo in the Malibu Colony Plaza, 23750 Pacific Coast Hwy., Malibu 90265; (310) 317-1444; ollomalibu.com. Enjoy "farm to table" breakfast, lunch, and dinner menus with pooch on the outdoor patio.

Malibu Kitchen & Gourmet Country Market, 3900 Cross Creek Rd., Malibu 90265; (310) 456-7845. Sandwiches and salads for every palate with dog-friendly outdoor tables. The staff claims they "like dogs better than people."

Resting Up

Malibu Motel, 22541 Pacific Coast Hwy., Malibu 90265; (310) 456-6169; themmotel.com. First-floor rooms. Pet fee.

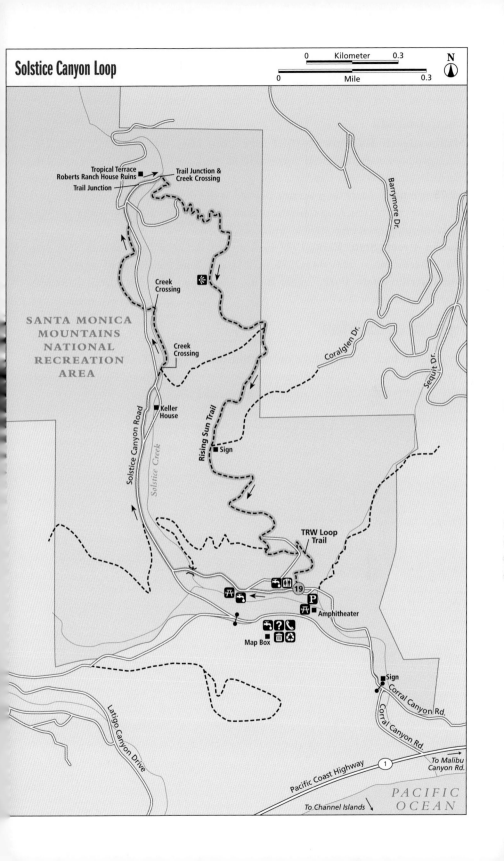

Solstice Canyon Loop

Barrymore Dr.

Tropical Terrace
Roberts Ranch House Ruins

Trail Junction &
Creek Crossing

Trail Junction

Creek
Crossing

Coralglen Dr.

Sequit Dr.

SANTA MONICA
MOUNTAINS
NATIONAL
RECREATION
AREA

Creek
Crossing

Keller
House

Rising Sun Trail

Sign

Solstice Canyon Road

Solstice Creek

TRW Loop
Trail

19

P

Amphitheater

Map Box

Sign

Corral Canyon Rd.

Corral Canyon Rd.

Latigo Canyon Drive

Pacific Coast Highway

1

To Malibu
Canyon Rd.

To Channel Islands

PACIFIC
OCEAN

Malibu Country Inn, 6506 Westward Beach Rd., Malibu 90265; (310) 457-9622; malibucountryinn.com. The rooms have refrigerators to store Fido's goodies and your doggie bag if you happen to have leftovers from your patio dining. Pet fee.

Campgrounds

Malibu Beach RV Park, 25801 Pacific Coast Hwy., Malibu 90265; (310) 456-6052; maliburv.com. This clean, convenient RV park across from the beach has all the amenities of an RV resort and is a short drive to the trailhead. There are a few tent sites, but unfortunately dogs are not allowed at the tent sites. The bonus to this park is a 2-mile canyon trail loop from the private RV park. You and your pooch get your fix of morning exercise complete with coastal views.

Malibu Creek State Park, 1925 Las Virgenes Rd., Calabasas 91302; (818) 880-0367; reservations at (800) 444-7275; parks.ca.gov. Tent, trailer, and RV sites.

Leo Carrillo State Park, 35000 Pacific Coast Hwy., Malibu 90265; (818) 880-0363; reservations at (800) 444-7275; parks.ca.gov. Tent, trailer, and RV sites.

Puppy Paws and Golden Years

An out-and-back 2.6-mile hike on the **Solstice Canyon Trail to the Tropical Terrace** makes an easy, pleasant excursion for less-energetic dogs. The trail is mostly level to this point with lots of shade along the creek.

20 Cold Creek Valley Preserve

This isn't a knock-your-dog's-booties-off spectacular trail. Having said that, access to a shady canyon with a year-round creek and a chaparral meadow exploding with tail-wagging scents just doesn't get any more convenient than this hike within the beautifully diverse Santa Monica Mountains National Recreation Area.

Start: From the Stunt High Trail sign on Stunt Road
Distance: 2.35-mile lollipop
Hiking time: About 1.5 hours
Difficulty: Easy
Trailhead elevation: 1,261 feet
Highest point: 1,261 feet
Best season: Year-round; winter and spring for most water flow; spring for wildflowers
Trail surface: Dirt, rock, and loose dirt
Other trail users: Horses
Canine compatibility: On leash
Land status: National Recreation Area
Fees and permits: None

Maps: USGS Malibu Beach; Santa Monica Mountains National Recreation Area; National Geographic Map Santa Monica Mountains National Recreation Area
Trail contacts: Santa Monica Mountains National Recreational Area Interagency Visitor Center, 26800 Mulholland Hwy., Calabasas 91302; (805) 370-2301; lamountains.com; nps.gov/samo
Nearest town: Calabasas
Trail tips: There is a trashcan, bike rack, dog-waste bag dispenser, and a portable toilet at the trailhead. There is no drinking water on the trail.

Finding the trailhead: From Malibu on CA 1/Pacific Coast Highway (PCH) at Malibu Canyon Road, turn north (inland) on Malibu Canyon Road and drive 6 miles to Mulholland Highway. Turn right on Mulholland Highway and drive 4 miles to Stunt Road. Turn right on Stunt Road and drive 1 mile to the pullout on the right side of the road just past the horse-crossing sign. The trailhead is to the left of the Stunt High Trail sign behind the gate. **GPS:** N34 05.70' / W118 38.91'
From Calabasas on US 101, take exit Las Virgenes/Malibu Canyon and drive 3 miles south on Las Virgenes Road. Turn left onto Mulholland Highway and drive 4 miles to Stunt Road. Turn right on Stunt Road and drive 1 mile to the pullout on the right side of the road just past the horse-crossing sign. The trailhead is to the left of the Stunt High Trail sign behind the gate. **GPS:** N34 05.70' / W118 38.91'

The Hike

The Santa Monica Mountains National Recreation Area was established in 1978 and encompasses almost 160,000 acres laced with 500 miles of trails. The earth's shifting plates along the San Andreas Fault created the 46-mile-long and 8-mile-wide mountain range. Native Americans, Spanish explorers, ranchers, filmmakers, and nature lovers have all made an imprint on this biologically diverse ecosystem.

The Stunt High Trail is right off the shoulder of the Mulholland Highway and immediately leads you down the oak-shaded canyon with sycamore trees showing

Passing a chaparral yucca

off their golden autumn coat. Within 300 feet from the small parking area, the trail crosses a drainage channel. At 0.1 mile you cross Cold Creek. In the fall of 2015, California was struggling through its fourth year of severe drought, and what is typically a year-round flow in Cold Creek was reduced to a trickle. At about 0.25 mile you pass the only bench on the trail on the right-hand side. The trail continues down the rocky swale, tracing the creek-sliced ravine on your right. At 0.5 mile the trail dips across a seasonal creek. Small signs sporadically posted along the trail remind hikers that it is illegal to remove anything from the protected preserve. A keen eye will spot some of the mortar holes ground into the sandstone by the native people, who once lived and foraged in the canyon woodlands.

At 0.6 mile, the trail emerges out of the canyon onto the chaparral plateau covered in sage and buckwheat. Continue walking straight at the unmarked trail junction. The view opens to the mountains flanking the preserve across Stunt Road on the right.

At 0.8 mile you walk across Cold Creek and come to a trail junction at the Cold Creek Valley Preserve sign. This is where the lollipop loop begins and will close after you meander around the chaparral meadow through four trail junctions.

Turn right at the Preserve sign and follow the loose dirt trail on the right of the sign to the next trail junction 0.2 mile ahead. The spur on the right goes to Stunt Road. Bear left at the junction. The trail parallels Stunt Road on the right. The trail veers away from the road another 0.2 mile ahead.

At 1.3 miles you come to another trail junction. Bear left on the trail and away from the house at the edge of the meadow. The meadow is in the process of restoration with native plants. Continue walking along the trail to the next junction at the post and turn left. The trail rises and you come to another unmarked trail junction. Continue walking straight at this junction to close the lollipop's loop just ahead at the Cold Creek Valley Preserve sign. Continue walking straight past the sign and down into the creekside woodland to return to the trailhead the way you came.

Cold Creek Valley Preserve

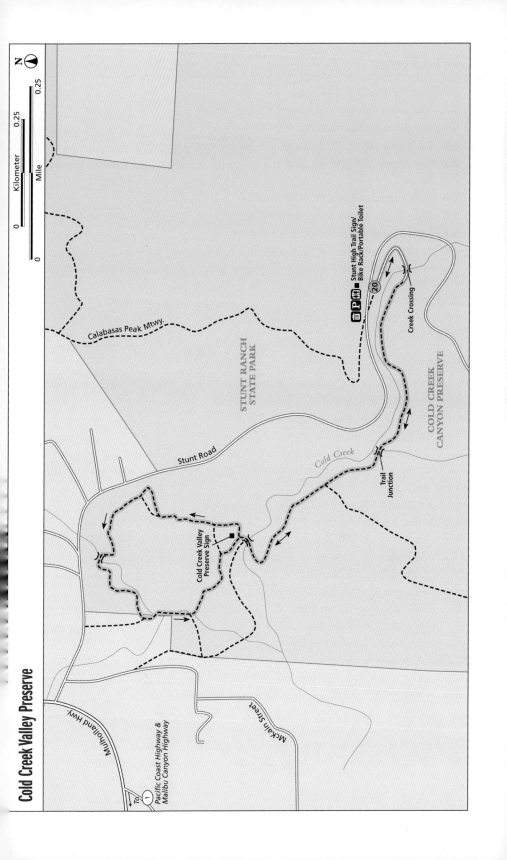

Miles and Directions

0.0 Start at the Stunt High Trail sign.

0.1 Walk across year-round Cold Creek.

0.5 Walk across a seasonal creek.

0.6 Come to an unmarked trail junction and continue walking straight.

0.8 Walk across Cold Creek and come to a trail junction at the Cold Creek Valley Preserve sign. Turn right.

1.0 Come to an unmarked trail junction. Bear left.

1.3 Come to an unmarked trail junction and bear left.

1.4 Come to a trail junction at a post and bear left.

1.5 Come to an unmarked trail junction and bear right. Walk 0.05 mile to the Cold Creek Valley Preserve sign to close the loop of your lollipop. Continue walking straight back the way you came to the trailhead.

2.35 Arrive back at the trailhead.

Creature Comforts

Fueling Up

Pedalers Fork, 23504 Calabasas Rd., Calabasas 91302; (818) 225-8231; pedalersfork .com. The coffee shop and restaurant emphasize locally grown food served in a modern/rustic decor. The deck is dog friendly.

The Old Place Restaurant, 29983 Mulholland Hwy., Agoura Hills 91301; (818) 706-900. This place exudes rustic charm. A convenient place for a bite of breakfast, lunch, or dinner at one of the outdoors picnic tables after a stroll through Peter Strauss Ranch.

Malibu Colony Plaza. Fast food and grocery store.

Ralph's Supermarket, 23841 Malibu Rd., Malibu 90265; (310) 456-2917. The Malibu Colony Plaza on Malibu Colony Road has a Ralph's Supermarket for provisions, along with dining options and Pacific Coast Pets for supplies and accessories (23705 Malibu Rd., Malibu 90265; 310-317-8600). If your dog is a star hound, this might be the place to shop.

Ollo, in the Malibu Colony Plaza, 23750 Pacific Coast Hwy., Malibu 90265; (310) 317-1444; ollomalibu.com. Enjoy "farm to table" breakfast, lunch, and dinner menus with pooch on the outdoor patio.

Malibu Kitchen & Gourmet Country Market, 3900 Cross Creek Rd., Malibu 90265; (310) 456-7845. Sandwiches and salads for every palate with dog-friendly outdoor tables. The staff claims they "like dogs better than people."

Resting Up

The **Anza A Calabasas Hotel,** 23627 Calabasas Rd., Calabasas 91302; (818) 222-5300; theanzahotel.com. The "paws and relax" rooms are designed for furry guest needs on the ground floor with hard-surface flooring. Pooches are treated to their own list of welcome amenities. Pet fee.

Campgrounds

Malibu Beach RV Park, 25801 Pacific Coast Hwy., Malibu 90265; (310) 456-6052; maliburv.com. This clean, convenient RV park across from the beach has all the amenities of an RV resort and is a short drive to the trailhead. There are a few tent sites, but unfortunately dogs are not allowed at the tent sites. The bonus to this park is a 2-mile canyon trail loop from the private RV park. You and your pooch get your fix of morning exercise complete with coastal views.

Malibu Creek State Park, 1925 Las Virgenes Rd., Calabasas 91302; (818) 880-0367; reservations at (800) 444-7275; parks.ca.gov. Tent, trailer, and RV sites.

Leo Carrillo State Park, 35000 Pacific Coast Hwy., Malibu 90265; (818) 880-0363; reservations at (800) 444-7275; parks.ca.gov. Tent, trailer, and RV sites.

Puppy Paws and Golden Years

Which canine has not dreamed of being on the big screen? The **Santa Monica Mountains National Recreation Area,** 2903 Cornell Rd., Agoura Hills 91301, is the centerpiece for Hollywood films and television shows. Pups and seniors can stroll Paramount Ranch's western town set and fantasize about becoming the next Rin Tin Tin.

Three miles farther up Mulholland Highway, the **Peter Strauss Ranch** welcomes pooches on the 0.5-mile trail through an oak riparian habitat boasting native-plant blooms in the spring. Water dogs will drool at the site of the ranch's historic (currently unmaintained) swimming pool, built in 1940 as the largest pool on the West Coast with a 650,000-gallon water capacity for up to 3,000 people.

The **Santa Monica Mountains Interagency Visitor Center on the King Gillette Ranch,** 26800 Mulholland Hwy., Calabasas 91302; (805) 370-2301, is another must-see for complete information about the Santa Monica Mountains National Recreation Area. The razor magnate's Spanish estate, built in 1925 and opened as public parkland, welcomes pooches on the grounds along the ADA-accessible trails tracing the meadow where a Chumash Indian village once thrived. Housed in the former Gillette Mansion stables, the eco-friendly visitor center is LEED (Leadership in Energy and Environmental Design) certified and the first "net-zero" visitor center in the National Park Service.

21 Trail Canyon Falls

A short stretch of graded dirt road in the Angeles National Forest drops you at the head of a scenic riparian canyon flanked by sandstone walls, sage, and chaparral yucca. The trail crosses several seasonal creeks before the mellow climb to a projection overlooking a dramatic seasonal waterfall.

Start: From the Trail Canyon trailhead off Forest Service Road 3N34
Distance: 3.4 miles out and back
Hiking time: About 2 hours
Difficulty: Moderate
Trailhead elevation: 1,794 feet
Highest point: 2,465 feet
Best season: Year-round; summers are hot; water in the creek and falls in the winter and spring; wildflowers in the spring and golden leaves in the fall
Trail surface: Dirt and rock
Other trail users: Horses and mountain bikers
Canine compatibility: Voice control

Land status: National forest
Fees and permits: Adventure Pass
Maps: USGS Sunland; Angeles National Forest map; Tom Harrison Angeles Front Country
Trail contacts: Los Angeles River Ranger District, 12371 N. Little Tujunga Canyon Rd., San Fernando 91342; (818) 899-1900; fs.usda .gov/angeles
Nearest town: Sunland
Trail tips: There are no amenities or potable water at the trailhead. There is a trashcan. It is safest to have your dog on harness along the narrower stretch of trail with the steep dropoff.

Finding the trailhead: From Sunland on I-5, take exit CA 210 and drive 0.7 mile east on CA 210 to Oro Vista Avenue. Drive 5.2 miles on Oro Vista Avenue (Oro Vista becomes Big Tujunga Canyon Road at 0.8 mile) to North Canyon Road/FS Road 3N34and turn left on North Canyon Road/FS Road 3N34. Drive 0.4 mile on the dirt road (3N34) to the parking area. The trailhead is on the left at the information board and gate. **GPS:** N34 18.33' / W118 15.32'

The Hike

The Angeles National Forest rises up above Sunland, one of the older communities north of Los Angeles. One minute you are crossing residential intersections and the next you are driving in the shadow of the San Gabriel Mountains' steep, rocky chaparral slopes. The Angeles National Forest was established in 1892 and covers about 700,000 acres. Elevations range from 1,200 to more than 10,000 feet. Trail Canyon Falls is within the Los Angeles River Ranger District and gives you a glimpse of how steeply sliced the San Gabriel Mountain range can be.

The hike begins at the trail sign next to the sign-in box and around the gate to the right of the information board. The trail follows a dirt road with cabins sprinkled on both sides for the first 0.3 mile until you step on the narrower trail at the sign straight ahead. Even in the dry season you can tell how much water has draped the sandstone walls over time to create that polished gleam.

Fall colors bring the canyon to life.

You come to the first creek crossing at 0.5 mile and another 0.2 mile farther. You will have several more creek crossings after walking down the terraced stone steps. Bear right at the bottom of the steps.

At 1.0 mile there is a picnic table on the left and a recycling can. The trail leaves the wider creek bed and the shade of sycamore and oak trees as you begin to climb uphill on the exposed west side of the canyon. Looking back down the canyon, the views just keep getting more dramatic as you continue to thread along the narrow trail hugging the precipitous slope.

At 1.7 miles the trail comes to an arrow-shaped projection on the right. This is your vista point destination overlooking the falls across the canyon to the left. In a substantially wet winter, you may see water draping another sandstone wall to the right of the main cascade. This is a short hike with minimal exertion for maximum scenic reward. Savor the moment before going back down to the trailhead the way you came.

Miles and Directions

0.0 Start at the gate and information board in the Trail Canyon Falls parking lot.

0.3 Come to a trail junction. Follow the trail sign straight ahead.

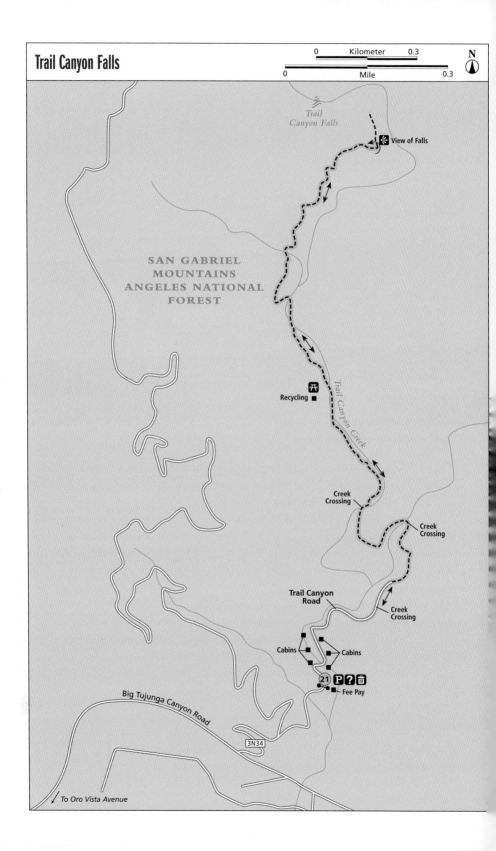

Trail Canyon Falls

0   Kilometer   0.3

0   Mile   0.3

N

Trail
Canyon Falls

View of Falls

SAN GABRIEL
MOUNTAINS
ANGELES NATIONAL
FOREST

Recycling

Trail Canyon Creek

Creek
Crossing

Creek
Crossing

Trail Canyon
Road

Creek
Crossing

Cabins   Cabins

21   P ?

Fee Pay

Big Tujunga Canyon Road

3N34

To Oro Vista Avenue

0.5 Walk across seasonal Trail Canyon Creek.

0.7 Walk across seasonal Trail Canyon Creek.

1.0 Come to a picnic table on the left.

1.7 Come to a projection on the right with view of the falls. Soak in the dramatic setting before going back to the trailhead the way you came. Elevation: 2.465 feet. **GPS:** N34 19.16' / W118 15.21'

3.4 Arrive back at the trailhead.

Creature Comforts

Fueling Up

In-N-Out Burger, 761 First St., Burbank 95102. The bark is out about the "protein style" all beef, no bun burger off the "secret menu."

The **Burbank Airport strip mall** across from the Marriott Hotel on Hollywood Way showcases a couple of fast-food outlets and a Starbucks Coffee.

Viewing the falls from the turnaround point.

George's Greek Cuisine, 2575 N. Hollywood Way, Burbank 95105; (818) 565-0512; georgesgreekcusine.com. For Mediterranean flavors, its George's Greek Cuisine, where you can savor a variety of specialties including baba ghanoush, kebabs, and baklava at the outdoor tables, to go, or delivered to the airport hotel.

Resting Up

Los Angeles Burbank Airport Hotel, 2500 Hollywood Way, Burbank 91505; (818) 843-6000; mariott.com. Dogs wag their tail at the mention of room service after a day's hike. Eat on the hotel patio with food to go from the hotel's Daily Grill restaurant, open 6:30 a.m. to 11 p.m.

Extended Stay America, 2200 Empire Ave., Burbank 91504; (818) 567-0952; extendedstayamerica.com. Some dog-friendly rooms. All have kitchenettes.

Puppy Paws and Golden Years

It's tough to find good patches of nature outside of the Angeles National Forest in this neighborhood, but pooch can soothe his CDD (celebrity deficit disorder) with a stroll around **Beverly Hills** and along **Rodeo Drive.** Urth Caffé, 267 S. Beverly Dr. 90209; (310) 205-9311, is popular with organic coffee and tea lovers and with dogs who like to scan for celebrity sightings.

22 Mount Hollywood

Is there anything that says Southern California more than "Hollywood"? Your four-legged star may not get discovered, but he'll love all the smells on the way up to the summit of Mount Hollywood. The views of the Los Angeles Basin from this trail don't get any better and there's a great vista point to snap a photo of your favorite pooch with the famous Hollywood sign as the backdrop.

Start: From the Mount Hollywood Hiking Trail in the Griffith Observatory parking lot
Distance: 3.0 miles out and back
Hiking time: About 1.5 hours
Difficulty: Easy
Trailhead elevation: 1,129 feet
Highest point: 1,625 feet
Best season: Year-round; summers can be hot
Trail surface: Loose dirt
Other trail users: Horses
Canine compatibility: On leash
Land status: City

Fees and permits: None
Maps: USGS Hollywood, Burbank; Official Map and Guide, Griffith Park
Trail contacts: Griffith Park Visitors Center, 4730 Crystal Springs Dr., Los Angeles 90027; (323) 644-2050; laparks.org
Nearest town: Los Angeles
Trail tips: There is a drinking fountain to the left of the trailhead, but no other water on the trail. There are flush toilet, sinks, and trashcans on the west side of the parking lot.

Finding the trailhead: From Los Angeles on CA 101 take Vermont Avenue exit and drive 4 miles north toward the mountains on Vermont Avenue to the observatory parking lot in Griffith Park. The Mount Hollywood Hiking Trail is at the north end of the parking lot. **GPS:** N34 07.25' / W118 18.02'

The Hike

According to one version, the root of the name *Hollywood* stems from the native toyon plant's close resemblance to holly. As far as the iconic Hollywood sign, it was originally a real estate sign erected in 1923 to advertise a new housing development called Hollywood Land. The sign deteriorated over several decades before it was restored to its present condition as "Hollywood."

The land that is now Griffith Park in the Hollywood Hills in the eastern part of the Santa Monica Mountains was first home to the Gabrieleno Indians. Spanish land grants followed in the late 1700s. In 1882 a controversial gold mine speculator named Colonel Griffith J. Griffith purchased Rancho Los Feliz. He gave 3,000 acres of his estate for parkland as a Christmas present to the people of Los Angeles in 1896. Acquisitions and donations of additional land over the years have created today's 4,511-acre Griffith Park, "one of the largest city parks in North America with an urban wilderness and the largest historic landmark in the city of Los Angeles." It's a popular oasis from the throbbing pulse of the city for Angelenos and visitors.

The Mount Hollywood hike is a small sample of the park's natural chaparral-draped slopes and woodland canyons laced with 56 miles of hiking and equestrian trails. The park boasts rare species of native plants along with a cocktail of ceanothus, chamise, toyon, and sagebrush commonly found in mixed chaparral zones. Several species of birds, native insects, and reptiles along with mammals like coyotes, bobcats, and mountain lions make up the diverse wildlife community of the park.

The hike begins at the Mount Hollywood Hiking Trail sign and commemorative plaque honoring Charlie Turner, who loved and cared for Griffith Park. You immediately begin uphill on the wide, loose dirt trail and quickly pass the Berlin Forest's pine grove and picnic area on the left, named in honor of Berlin, Los Angeles' sister city.

The trail continues its long swirls up to the summit past a couple of spurs and some viewpoints. The entire hike is a panoramic view fest. At 0.7 mile you come to an overlook on the left and the best photo spot for a snapshot of the Hollywood

Griffith Park Observatory and the Los Angeles skyline in the distance

A close-up view of the famous Hollywood sign

sign on Mount Lee with 1,820-foot-high Cahuenga Peak as the backdrop across the canyon.

At the unmarked trail junction 0.3 mile farther up, bear left and continue walking on the trail clockwise past a viewpoint with a bench and a short, narrow spur trail leading to the palm-lined knob on the left. You pass a water tank on the left just before coming to a trail junction at 1.4 miles. There is a picnic area and overlook on the left. Bear right to continue to the summit's picnic tables and survey monument in the ground. The 360-degree mountain and city views with the Pacific on the western horizon will astonish you. Enjoy a snack, snapshots, and water before heading back to the trailhead the way you came.

Miles and Directions

0.0 Start at the Mount Hollywood Hiking Trail sign.

0.1 Come to the Berlin Forest on the left.

0.2 Walk across the land bridge braced by concrete shoulders.

0.7 Come to an overlook toward the Hollywood sign.

1.0 Come to a trail junction. Bear left and walk clockwise.

1.1 Come to a viewpoint above the palm-lined knob.

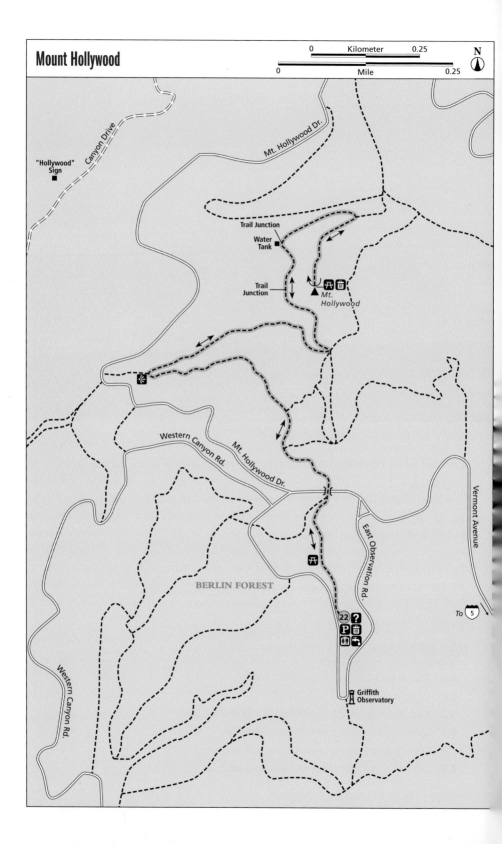

Mount Hollywood

0 Kilometer 0.25
0 Mile 0.25

N

"Hollywood" Sign

Canyon Drive

Mt. Hollywood Dr.

Trail Junction

Water Tank

Trail Junction

Mt. Hollywood

Western Canyon Rd.

Mt. Hollywood Dr.

East Observation Rd.

Vermont Avenue

BERLIN FOREST

22

P

To 5

Western Canyon Rd.

Griffith Observatory

1.2 Walk past a water tank on the left.

1.4 Come to a trail junction. Bear right to the summit.

1.5 Arrive at the top of Mount Hollywood and be wowed by the views. Go back to the trailhead the way you came. Elevation: 1,625 feet. **GPS:** N34 07.69' / W118 18.07'

3.0 Arrive back at the trailhead.

Creature Comforts

Fueling Up

Los Feliz Café, 3207 Los Feliz Blvd., Los Angeles 90039; (323) 661-2355; losfeliz cafe.com. Get a bite next to Griffith Park on the dog-friendly patio. (Patio open in dry weather only.)

Trails Café, 2333 Fern Dell Dr., Los Angeles 90068; (323) 871-2102. The cafe is at the base of Griffith Park and trailheads. Vegan and vegetarian menu except for the all-beef hot dog and the dog treats. The vegan apple pie and seasonal pies are lip-smacking good. Patio is open year-round. Jessica says that the best part of working here is all the dog customers.

Resting Up

Sunset Tower Hotel, 8358 Sunset Blvd., Los Angeles 90069; (323) 654-7100; sunset towerhotel.com. The building is a local landmark of Art Deco style on the famous Sunset Strip. Four-paw guests are treated to a pet dining menu, a bed, bowls, and treats. The adjacent off-leash dog park seals the deal.

Le Parc Suites, 733 N. Knoll Dr. West, Hollywood 90069; (310) 855-8888; leparc-suites.com. The rooftop restaurant welcomes dogs on the patio. Pet fee.

Chateau Marmont, 8221 Sunset Blvd., Hollywood 90046; (323) 656-1010; chateau marmont.com; It's chic and pricey with a Euro cachet. If your bow-wow wants to splurge, he'll be greeted with two dog bowls and access to the restaurant patio as well as the gardens.

Puppy Paws and Golden Years

The **Main Trail** around the **Wilson & Harding Golf Course** is a flat, sandy 3-mile loop that begins by the Griffith Park Visitor Center, 4730 Crystal Springs Dr., Los Angeles. Hounds must share the trail with horses. Well-behaved pooches are welcome in the visitor center for a treat at the front desk. The docents consider their "dog fix" therapeutic.

Orange County

There is no defined urban center or city at the heart of Orange County. It's mostly a densely populated, flashy suburb of new shopping malls, attractive boulevards, and private toll roads stretching from the beach communities across the valley to the Santa Ana Mountains. Disneyland is Orange County's most famous landmark and world-renowned theme park. But nature lovers have the Cleveland National Forest, Irvine Regional Park, and the network of trails around Newport Back Bay's wetlands and ecological reserve for their playground.

23 Horseshoe Loop

In the land of multiple freeway lanes and mega shopping malls, Irvine Regional Park is an unexpected oasis of calming nature for dogs, horses, and their human companions to replenish their spirits. Horseshoe Loop's ridgeline boasts views across the chaparral foothills and over the park's oak- and sycamore-studded greenbelts. The loop's seasonal creek-fed riparian woodlands offer a pleasing contrast to the park's arid plateau.

Start: From the Horseshoe Loop Trail outside the entrance
Distance: 3.6-mile loop
Hiking time: About 2 hours
Difficulty: Easy
Trailhead elevation: 571 feet
Highest point: 821 feet
Best season: Year-round; summers are hot; wildflowers in spring; fall colors
Trail surface: Dirt and some rock
Other trail users: Horses and mountain bikes
Canine compatibility: On leash

Land status: County
Fees and permits: Parking fee
Maps: USGS Black Star Canyon, Orange; Irvine Regional Park Map
Trail contacts: Irvine Regional Park, 1 Irvine Park Rd., Orange 92869; (714) 973-6835; (866) OCPARKS; ocparks.com/irvinepark
Nearest town: Orange
Trail tips: The entrance has flush toilets, drinking fountains, picnic tables, grills, trashcans, pay telephone, information panel, and trail maps.

Finding the trailhead: From Orange on 55 Freeway, take Chapman Avenue exit going east and drive 4.2 miles to Jamboree Road. Turn left on Jamboree Road and drive 0.4 mile to Irvine Park Road and turn right to the park entrance. Enter the park and turn left to Parking Lot 1. Walk back past the park entrance booth. Trailhead is just outside the entrance on the left. **GPS:** N33 47.77' / W117 45.47'

The Hike

Irvine Regional Park's roots go back to Mexican rancho land grants of the 1840s. By the mid 1800s the land was sold to ranchers and German colonists discovered the area's recreational value. The oak grove became known as the "Picnic Grounds," and was a popular site for community festivities. The severe drought of the 1860s cost the cattle ranching industry dearly, and James Irvine was one of several land barons to profit. He purchased the rancho in 1876. Several years after James's death, his son donated the land to the county. In 1897 Orange County Park became the first county park in California. It was renamed Irvine Regional Park in 1928. Over the years, the park was expanded with the acquisition of surrounding property, and a variety of recreational enhancements were made. The park's almost 500 acres of open space invite dogs and horses with their companions, as well as mountain bikers, to enjoy the trails.

The Horseshoe Loop hike begins at the park's entrance with a moderate climb to the highest trail, known as Puma Ridge. The 0.7-mile open ridgeline stretch of the trail offers the best views of the heart of the park's oak and sycamore groves as well as a glimpse of the duck lake, which was added in 1913. Looking south, you can see the outline of the main road and Orange County's expanding urbanization.

The trail descends back to the flatland, where signs continue to direct you along the Horseshoe Loop. The east end of the park becomes more arid and exposed with a mix of chaparral vegetation, eucalyptus trees, cacti, and tumbleweed. At 1.2 miles you cross a rock drainage culvert, where the trail parallels the paved service road. You come to a fork in the road ahead. There is a gate to the right for access by authorized vehicles only. Bear left and follow the paved emergency access road for about 0.4 mile. You share this section of the park road with equestrians and the occasional authorized vehicle.

At 1.8 miles you leave the access road and turn right uphill on a loose dirt trail. Bear right along this plateau trail and come to a junction for Toyon Trail. Continue walking straight along the wider dirt trail as it drops down and meets seasonal Santiago Creek and the riparian woodlands in the ravine. Walk paralleling Santiago Creek on your left to the trail junction at 2.6 miles. Turn left and walk across Santiago

Hiking the ridge in Irvine Regional Park

A view of Duck Lake from Puma Ridge

Creek's wide creek bed to the trail junction ahead. Turn right on Santiago Creek Trail, and Santiago Creek is now on your right.

At 3.0 miles you cross the paved road and follow the sign for Santiago Creek Trail. Just ahead is another trail junction. Road Runner Trail goes right. Continue walking straight and you rejoin Horseshoe Loop for a few steps. Horseshoe Loop Trail heads right. Stay on the left trail. At 3.3 miles you come to a trail junction for Egret Trail to the right. Residential houses are visible on the bluff ahead. Continue walking on Santiago Creek Trail for about 100 feet until you come to the trail junction, where Santiago Creek Trail turns right and Peters Canyon Trail goes uphill to the road. Directly across from Santiago Creek Trail is an unmarked single-track dirt trail at the foot of the hill. Turn left and walk on the narrow dirt trail corridor between the lodge-pole fence on the left and the park's entrance road on the right above. The trail traces the park's greenbelt picnic grounds. Follow the trail back to your trailhead at the entrance. The park's sycamore and oak grove sprinkled with picnic tables is a delightful place for you and pooch to end your excursion. Your pal is sure to luxuriate, lounging and rolling on Mother Nature's cool green carpet.

Miles and Directions

0.0 Start at the Horseshoe Loop Trail just outside the entrance to Irvine Regional Park and walk 250 feet to the trail junction for Horseshoe Loop Trail on the right uphill.

Horseshoe Loop

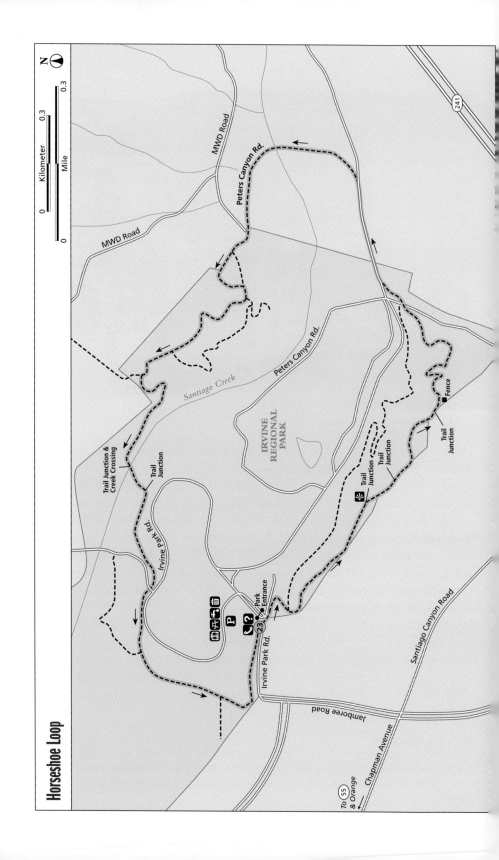

0.1 Come to a trail junction for Horseshoe Loop Trail. Walk straight uphill past the junction to the unmarked Puma Ridge Trail bearing left.

0.4 Come to a viewpoint overlooking the heart of Irvine Regional Park.

0.7 Trail descends. Bear left at the unmarked trail junction and fence.

1.1 Come to a paved service road. Walk across the road to the dirt trail.

1.4 Walk straight across the parking area and follow the signs for Horseshoe Loop Trail. Bear left at the fork in the paved road.

1.8 Come to a trail junction. Leave the paved road and turn right uphill on the loose dirt trail.

1.9 Come to a fork. Continue walking counterclockwise uphill on this short mesa loop.

2.0 Close the loop and bear right.

2.2 Come to a trail junction for Toyon Trail going left. Continue walking straight.

2.6 Come to a trail junction. Turn left on Horseshoe Loop Trail and walk across seasonal Santiago Creek.

2.7 Come to a trail junction. Turn right on Santiago Creek Trail.

3.0 Walk across the paved road and follow the sign for Santiago Creek Trail.

3.1 Come to a trail junction for Roadrunner Loop Trail on the right. Continue walking straight and bear left.

3.3 Come to a trail junction for Egret Trail to the right. Continue walking straight on Santiago Creek Trail to the next junction 100 feet ahead. Turn left onto the single-track dirt trail across from the Santiago Creek Trail sign. Follow the dirt trail to the entrance and trailhead to complete your loop.

3.6 Arrive back at the trailhead.

Creature Comforts

Fueling Up

Rutabeborz, 264 N. Glassell St., Orange 92866; (714) 633-3260. This place caters to everyone's palate, including vegetarians and gluten-free fans. Enjoy a taste of Old Town Orange with pooch on the dog-friendly patio.

In-N-Out Burger, 3501 E. Chapman St., Orange 92869. Your furry friend can join you in a protein fix with the all-beef patty without the bun.

Irvine Regional Park Food Concession, 1 Irvine Park Rd., Orange 92869; (714) 973-6835. There are outdoor tables for pooch to enjoy his kibbles at your side.

Resting Up

Ayres Inn, 3737 W. Chapman Ave., Orange 92868; (714) 978-9168. Pet fee.

Puppy Paws and Golden Years

Irvine Regional Park is laced with greenbelts and flat, level trails for leisurely strolls. Hop on the **Irvine Park Railroad** so your four-legged pal can enjoy a tour of the park's village area aboard the open-air cars past duck ponds.

24 Holy Jim Falls

There are three good reasons why this hike is worth the 4.5-mile jostle on an unpaved road. This is a creekside trail up a picturesque box canyon to a 20-foot waterfall that still had some water after four years of drought. From a historical point of view, you and pooch get to hike the canyon where the last grizzly bear in Southern California was tracked and killed in 1907. On a future note, Holy Jim Falls happens to be in the heart of the proposed Grizzly Bear National Monument.

Start: From the Holy Jim Trail sign in the Forest Service parking area just past the fire station on Trabuco Creek Road
Distance: 3.4 miles out and back
Hiking time: About 1.5 hours
Difficulty: Easy
Trailhead elevation: 1,763 feet
Highest point: 2,413 feet
Best season: Year-round; summers are hot; road to trailhead not recommended after a heavy rain
Trail surface: Dirt and rock
Other trail users: Horses and mountain bikes

Canine compatibility: On leash
Land status: National forest
Fees and permits: Adventure Pass fee
Maps: USGS Santiago Peak; Cleveland National Forest
Trail contacts: Cleveland National Forest Trabuco Ranger District, 1147 E. Sixth St., Corona 92879; (951) 736-1811; fs.fed.us/r5/cleveland
Nearest town: Laguna Hills
Trail tips: There is a portable toilet in the trailhead parking lot, a picnic table, and a trashcan. There is no water at the trailhead.

Finding the trailhead: From Laguna Hills on I-5 take exit #91/El Toro Road and drive 7.2 miles east on El Toro Road to Live Oaks Canyon. Turn right on Live Oaks Canyon at the sign for the O'Neil Regional Park and Wilderness Area. Drive 4.2 miles on Live Oaks Canyon, which becomes Trabuco Canyon, and turn left on the unmarked Trabuco Creek dirt road 1 mile past O'Neil Regional Park just beyond Rose Canyon Road on the left and after the bridge. Drive 4.5 miles on the unmarked gravel road, which is a county road for the first couple of miles and becomes a national forest road for the last couple of miles. The last 2 miles are a rougher dirt stretch. Park in the forest service parking area past the fire station. There is a picnic table on the left and the Holy Jim Trail sign and arrow is across the parking lot at the intersection of a dirt road heading uphill to the left. **GPS:** N33 40.62' / W117 31.03'

The Hike

The canyon was named for James T. Smith, known as "old cussin' Jim" for his colorful and extensive blasphemous vocabulary. Government surveyors referred to him as "Holy Jim" when they named the canyon. During the late 1890s Smith's beehives and others in Trabuco Canyon were irresistible to a local grizzly nicknamed the "honey thief." The grizzly's last raid in 1907 proved fatal. He escaped a trap set by local ranchers, who eventually tracked and killed the last grizzly bear in the Santa Ana Mountains.

Fig trees create shaded corridors along the trail.

The trail begins in the forest service parking lot. The first of three small interpretive boards about Holy Jim and the history of the canyon are on a post at the lower end of the lot. The trailhead is across the parking lot by the information board and map. The trail follows the forest service road heading left uphill. You cross Holy Jim Creek twice as you pass cabins on both sides of the road. Prickly pear cacti, chaparral yucca, and enormous agave plants guard the roadside. At 0.5 mile you come to a stunning rustic stone cabin on the left just before the Cleveland National Forest sign and the hiker trail to Holy Jim Falls at the gate. Walk through the gate and across the creek. The trail leaves the dirt road and transitions to a narrow path climbing a mellow grade over rocks and lacing across the creek several times.

At 1.2 miles you come to a stone "check dam" designed to slow the creek flow. The third small interpretive board is to the left of the check dam. The narrow canyon is lush with sycamore and alder trees interrupted by fig trees' leafy arches. At 1.5 miles you come to a trail junction. Bear right at the sign for the "Falls." The well-worn trail crisscrosses the creek, requiring some cautious footwork over wet rocks. You arrive at the base of the falls and the head of the box canyon at 1.7 miles. Take the time to snap a few shots and enjoy the setting before going back the way you came. Keep your eye out for an inviting boulder to sit and snack with pooch along the way back to the trailhead.

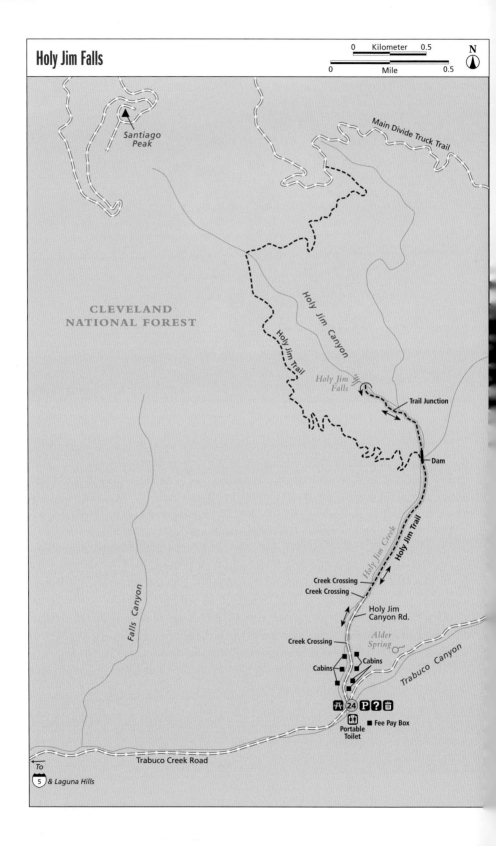

Holy Jim Falls

0   Kilometer   0.5

0   Mile   0.5

N

Santiago Peak

Main Divide Truck Trail

CLEVELAND NATIONAL FOREST

Holy Jim Canyon

Holy Jim Trail

Holy Jim Falls

Trail Junction

Dam

Holy Jim Creek

Holy Jim Trail

Creek Crossing

Creek Crossing

Holy Jim Canyon Rd.

Alder Spring

Creek Crossing

Cabins

Cabins

Falls Canyon

Trabuco Canyon

24   **P**   ?

Portable Toilet

■ Fee Pay Box

Trabuco Creek Road

To

5 & Laguna Hills

Miles and Directions

0.0 Start at the Holy Jim Trailhead in the parking lot just past the fire station.

0.3 Walk across Holy Jim Creek and bear right.

0.5 Walk across Holy Jim Creek at the stone cabin.

0.6 Come to the Cleveland National Forest sign, a walk-in gate, and sign for Holy Jim Trail. Walk across the creek.

1.2 Come to the rock "check dam" and interpretive panel #3.

1.5 Come to a trail junction. Turn right to the falls at the sign.

1.7 Arrive at the falls. Turn around and go back the way you came. Elevation: 2,413 feet. **GPS:** N33 41.66' / W117 30.95'

3.4 Arrive back at the trailhead.

Creature Comforts

Fueling Up

Trabuco Oaks General Store, 31021 Trabuco Canyon Blvd., Trabuco Canyon 92679; (949) 858-1711. Quaint country store in horse country; quick snacks and picnic tables.

Resting Up

The Hills Hotel, 25205 La Paz Rd., Laguna Hills 92653; (949) 586-5000; choicehotels.com. The Hills Hotel Café has a dog-friendly patio area.

Campgrounds

O'Neil Regional Park, 30892 Trabuco Canyon Rd., Trabuco Canyon 92678; (949) 923-2260 or 923-2256; ocparks.com; (800) 600-1600 for reservations. Tents and RVs (no hookups).

Holy Jim Falls trickles during dry seasons.

Puppy Paws and Golden Years

The **Mesa Trail in O'Neil Regional Park** and campground allows dogs on this mostly level 2-mile trail.

25 San Juan Loop

The Cleveland National Forest is largely chaparral country. This short trail offers a contrast, with interesting sandstone topography, unobstructed views of the surrounding hills, and a seasonal creek with a waterfall.

Start: From the San Juan Loop Trailhead parking lot off Ortega Highway/CA 74
Distance: 2.2 miles
Hiking time: About 1 hour
Difficulty: Easy
Trailhead elevation: 1,982 feet
Highest point: 2,013 feet
Best season: Year-round; summers are hot; winter and spring for water in the creek and the falls; autumn has pleasant temperatures and fall colors in the sycamores
Trail surface: Dirt and sandstone rock
Other trail users: Horses and mountain bikes
Canine compatibility: On leash
Land status: National forest

Fees and permits: Adventure Pass fee
Maps: USGS Sitton Peak; Cleveland National Forest
Trail contacts: Cleveland National Forest Trabucco Ranger District, 1147 E. Sixth St., Corona 92879; (951) 736-1811. Fire Station and Ranger Visitor Center on Ortega Highway 74, fs.fed.us/r5/cleveland.
Nearest town: San Juan Capistrano and Lake Elsinore
Trail tips: There are 2 vault toilets in the parking lot, water, 2 picnic tables, and trashcan. The map board at the trailhead has educational information about mountain lion and rattlesnake habitat.

Finding the trailhead: From San Juan Capistrano on I-5 take exit 82 Ortega Highway/CA 74 and drive 19 miles east on Ortega Highway/CA 74. Turn left into the parking lot at the sign for the San Juan Loop, Bear Canyon Trailhead. The San Juan Loop Trailhead is to the left of the information and map board. **GPS:** N33 36.81' / W117 25.63'
From Lake Elsinore drive 9 miles on Ortega Highway/CA 74 west and turn right into the parking lot at the sign for the San Juan Loop, Bear Canyon Trailhead. The San Juan Loop Trailhead is to the left of the information and map board. **GPS:** N33 36.81' / W117 25.63'

The Hike

The Cleveland National Forest, created under President Theodore Roosevelt and named after former president Grover Cleveland, is the southernmost national forest in California. Therefore it is not surprising that the 425,000-acre landscape is largely chaparral. Safeguarding the watershed was the primary engine behind preserving this natural resource when the Cleveland National Forest was first established. Today, although the watershed of the Cleveland National Forest still plays a role in San Diego's water supply to the south, recreation plays a much more dominant role.

The San Juan Loop Trail is a little gem that jams maximum natural beauty into minimal distance. The hike combines easy access from a main road, views of sandstone-dappled ridges, several seasonal creeks to feed the riparian oak woodland, and a scenic, sculpted gorge with a seasonal waterfall.

The trail is well maintained with only three well-marked junctions for an easy, straightforward excursion. If not for the noise that intrudes from the nearby twisty mountain road close to the trailhead, this hike would deserve a five-paw rating.

You begin on a narrow, loose dirt path with views immediately opening northward across the rounded mountain ridges. The trail transitions to exposed sandstone with the gorge on your right. At 0.3 mile you come to a trail junction and a bench. The spur on the right leads to the creek and the top of the seasonal

Leaping along the trail

cascade plunging down the gorge after a wet winter. In the drier season, this spur leads to numerous boulders that make perfect perches for a snack break with pooch. If your dog likes to dawdle, you won't mind indulging him here.

To continue on the loop, bear left on the trail at the bench and continue walking with the gorge on your right. The sandstone boulders sprinkled on the slopes across the canyon add visual interest to the chaparral landscape. Watch your step down the trail as you negotiate the large rocks. Keep your dog on a short leash to avoid tripping if he lunges.

At 1.0 mile you reach the creek bottom. Even after four years of drought, the canyon floor flourished with green grasses beneath the oak woodland's leafy canopy. Just ahead you come to a trail junction for Chiquito to the right. Continue walking straight. At 1.3 miles, Ortega Highway/CA 74 is visible across the canyon. In the fall, even the whizzing sound of speeding cars along the curvy road is not enough to distract you from the soft touch of sunlight casting its amber glow behind the sycamore leaves.

At 1.7 miles you come to the trail junction for the Upper San Juan Campground to the right. Although the campground sign with an arrow may still be there, as of December 2015, this campground was still listed as permanently closed according to the Trabucco Ranger District station. Your dog would enjoy the pleasant, short, scent-filled meander around this small creekside pocket before continuing straight with the seasonal creek on your right. At 2.2 miles the trail emerges at the trailhead parking lot to the left of the vault toilet. Walk across the parking lot back to the trailhead at the information board to complete the loop.

San Juan Loop

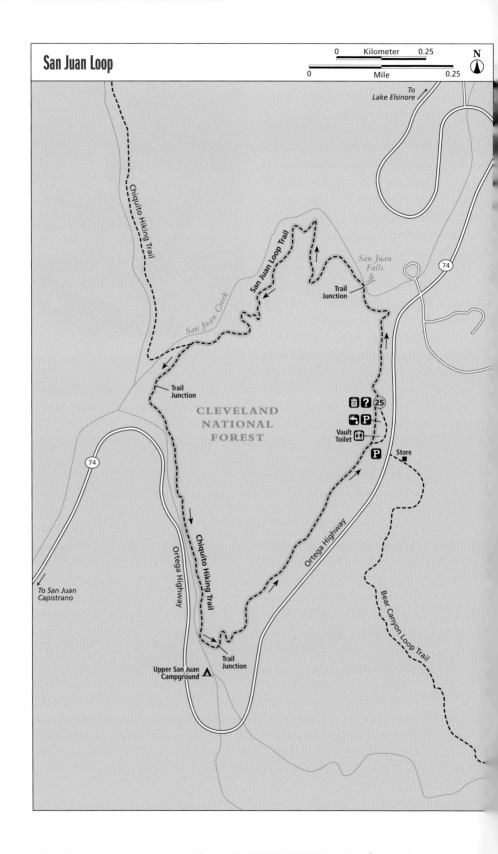

To
Lake Elsinore

Chiquito Hiking Trail

San Juan Loop Trail

San Juan Creek

San Juan Falls

74

Trail Junction

Trail Junction

CLEVELAND
NATIONAL
FOREST

25

Vault Toilet

P

P

Store

74

Ortega Highway

Ortega Highway

Chiquito Hiking Trail

To San Juan Capistrano

Bear Canyon Loop Trail

Trail Junction

Upper San Juan Campground

Miles and Directions

0.0 Start at the San Juan Loop Trailhead sign.
0.3 Come to an unmarked trail junction. Bear left past the bench.
1.0 Reach the bottom of the creek bed.
1.1 Come to a trail junction at the bench. Continue walking straight.
1.7 Come to a trail junction for the campground on the right. Continue walking straight.
2.2 Arrive back at the parking lot. Trailhead is just across the parking lot ahead.

Creature Comforts

Fueling Up

Ortega Oaks Candy Store and Goods, 34950 Ortega Hwy., Lake Elsinore 92530; (951) 678-5406; the74candystore.com. Shannon, a dog mom of three rescues, is the owner, cook, baker, and operator of this store across the road from the trailhead. Pooches are welcome at the shaded picnic tables. The eatery is open 363 days a year for your refueling pleasure after the hike.

Resting Up

Best Western Capistrano Inn, 27174 Ortega Hwy., San Juan Capistrano 92675; (949) 493-5661; bestwest ern.com. Conveniently located, rooms have refrigerators and microwaves and complimentary continental breakfast. Reliable pet-friendly hotel chain.

Residence Inn Dana Point, San Juan Capistrano 92675; (949) 443-3600; marriott.com. Kitchenettes for whipping up Fido's gourmet meals. Pleasant location near Doheny State Beach, where dogs can only sniff the beach from the campground roads. Barbeque and picnic area on hotel grounds.

Shaded switchbacks along the trail

Best Western Plus Lake Elsinore Inn & Suites, 31781 Casino Dr., Lake Elsinore 92530; (951) 674-3131; bestwestern.com. In-room refrigerators make it handy to store fresh snacks for you and your pooch.

Campgrounds

Blue Jay National Forest Campground, off CA 74 on North Main Divide Road, is about 5 miles past San Juan Loop trailhead, 6 miles from Lake Elsinore, and 23 miles from San Juan Capistrano; fs.usda.gov. Vault toilets, water; first-come, first-served.

Puppy Paws and Golden Years

Lake Elsinore, lake-elsinore.org, is the largest freshwater lake in Southern California. Dogs on leash on the public beaches.

26 Rancho San Clemente Ridgeline Trail

In Southern California's densely populated communities, where open space is at a premium, this 3-mile paved horseshoe service road along a panoramic ridge is a favorite romp with locals. The wide dirt shoulder is a cornucopia of scents for pooches, while their companions inhale the mountain and ocean views.

Start: From the San Clemente Ranch Ridgeline Trailhead
Distance: 5.8 miles out and back
Hiking time: About 2.5 hours
Difficulty: Moderate
Trailhead elevation: 780 feet
Highest point: 873 feet
Best season: Year-round; summers are hot; late fall, winter, and spring for cooler temperatures; winter and spring for greener landscape
Trail surface: Pavement and dirt
Other trail users: Bicycles

Canine compatibility: On leash
Land status: City
Fees and permits: None
Maps: USGS San Clemente
Trail contacts: City of San Clemente, 100 Avenida Presidio, San Clemente 92673; (949) 361-8264; san-clemente.org
Nearest town: San Clemente
Trail tips: There are no services or amenities along the trail. Make sure you have lots of water for your dog on this exposed sun-drenched trail.

Finding the trailhead: From San Clemente on I-5, take exit 74/El Camino Real. Turn north on El Camino Real and drive 0.5 mile to Avenida Presidio. Avenida Presidio briefly becomes Avenue La Esperanza. Make a right on Avenida Presidio (second street) uphill into a residential neighborhood. Drive 0.7 mile on Avenida Presidio to Avenida Salvador. Drive 0.5 mile on Avenida Salvador. The trailhead is on the left. **GPS:** N33 25.88' / W117 35.95'

The Hike

In suburban Southern California's "fancyland," characterized by meticulously manicured lawns and tropical landscaped shopping malls, it's a treat to discover a hiking route that's mostly "au naturel." "Natural" in this part of California is predominately a dry chaparral landscape. The hike begins around a discreet gate tucked between houses in a spiffy residential neighborhood. The San Clemente Ranch Ridgeline Trail sign lists the various trail rules, users, and customary warnings about hiking through wildlife habitat.

You begin to climb immediately up the paved service road past a water tank and communication towers on your right. The chamise and chaparral grasses typical of these arid parts have been cut to provide a wide dirt shoulder on either side of the narrow paved road. What the hike lacks in lush and vegetative variety it makes up for with unobstructed 360-degree views across the urban sprawl to the Pacific Coast and the Santa Ana Mountains. The horseshoe-shaped route is straightforward as it rolls up and down with a couple of steeper stretches past designated viewpoints and trailheads with maps and dog-waste bag dispensers and trashcans.

At 0.9 mile you pass the first designated viewpoint with a picnic table on a knoll to the left. Continue walking on the main path. At 1.3 miles you come to a trail junction with a spur connecting the ridgeline trail to a residential neighborhood and a dirt trail up to a communication tower on the left. Continue walking on the main path past the spur. Just ahead you come to another trail junction with a right spur connecting the ridgeline trail to Steed Park. The green ballfields are visible to the right below the trail. You climb a short, steep stretch of about 0.2 mile and emerge on a eucalyptus-framed saddle. This is a good spot to offer your furry pal water and enjoy the shade from the wispy-leafed trees.

At 1.7 miles you come to another viewpoint with a picnic table and a map of the ridgeline trail. The trail descends to meet a trailhead at Calle del Cerro Street. Turn right on Calle del Cerro and walk 150 feet to the signed pedestrian crosswalk. Walk across Calle del Cerro and rejoin the ridgeline trail. The trail continues to be flanked

Soaking up the views above San Clemente to the Pacific

by a eucalyptus grove. Judging by how much tail-wagging and sniffing goes on with every pooch that walks by, this grove is definitely doggie scent-o-rama.

At 2.4 miles the trail leaves the shade of the eucalyptus trees and drops down to meet a service road. Walk across the service road and climb up the steep, exposed dirt slope to the unmarked Knob Hill at the two benches and the one small tree on the left. The expansive views toward the Pacific Coast provide a spectacular end to the trail. Look to the left and you will see the water tank and communication towers, where you began across the canyon. The horseshoe shape of your route is evident from this vantage point.

Soak in the views and share a snack and water with your companion before going back to the trailhead the way you came.

Miles and Directions

0.0 Start at the San Clemente Ranch Ridgeline Trailhead on Avenida Salvador.
0.9 Walk past a viewpoint and picnic table on the left.
1.3 Come to a trail junction. Continue walking on main trail.
1.4 Come to a trail junction. Continue walking on main path.
1.7 Come to a viewpoint with picnic table and map of Ridgeline Trail.
1.9 Come to Calle del Cerro Street trailhead and Ridgeline Trail map. Turn right and walk 150 feet to the pedestrian-crossing sign and walk across the street to rejoin the trail.
2.4 Walk across the service road.
2.9 Arrive at the top of unmarked Knob Hill and end of trail at benches. Go back to the trailhead the way you came. Elevation: 489 feet. **GPS: N33 26.77' / W117 36.50'**
5.8 Arrive back at the trailhead.

Creature Comforts

Fueling Up

Italian Cravings, 105 S. Ola Vista, San Clemente 92672; (949) 492-2777; italiancravingsmenu.com. Dog-friendly patio and to-go menu.
Pierside Restaurant and Bar, 610 Avenida Victoria, San Clemente 92672; (949) 218-0980; piersidesc.com. Local produce and a dog-friendly patio; first-come, first-served.
The Laid Back Shack, 1700 Avenida Estacion, San Clemente 92672. At the north end of the San Clemente Beach Trail.
Ruby's Shake Shack, 7703 E. Coast Hwy., Newport Coast 92657; (949) 464-0100; rubys.com. A diner with a view and dog-friendly outdoor patio near Moro Campground.

Resting Up

Sea Horse Resort, 602 Avenida Victoria, San Clemente 92672; (949) 492-1720; seahorseresort.com. Pet fee.

Rancho San Clemente Ridgeline Trail

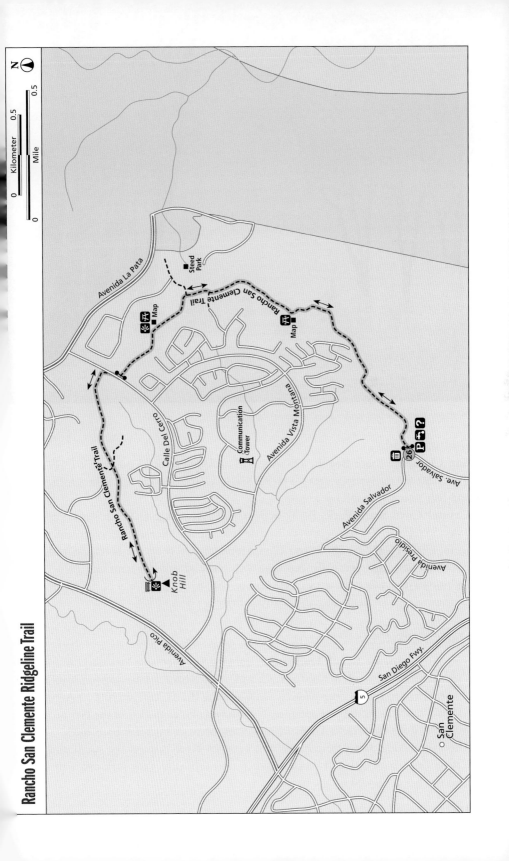

A shady stretch of trail under the eucalyptus canopy

Campgrounds

San Clemente State Beach, 225 Avenida Calafia Ave., San Clemente 92672; (949) 492-3156; for reservations, (800) 444-7275; reserveamerica.com. Campsites for tents and RVs (some with full hookups).

Crystal Cove State Park, 8471 Pacific Coast Hwy., Laguna Beach 92651; (949) 494-3539, (949) 494-9143; crystalcovestatepark.org; for reservations, reserveamerica .com; (800) 444-7275. The Moro Campground across from the beach opened in 2011 and sits on a spectacular location with terraced sites for tents and RVs. The bathrooms have token showers. Luv 2 Camp, (888) 898-2267, is one of the approved concessionaires for delivering an RV to a campsite.

Puppy Paws and Golden Years

The **San Clemente Beach Trail** section from the San Clemente Pier at 611 Avenida Victoria stretching south to Calafia Beach parking area is a 1.3-mile dogs-on-leash flat sand trail tracing the no-dogs-allowed San Clemente Beach. You can park on Avenida Victoria and walk to the pier entrance. The sandy trail is to the left of the pier on the west side of the train tracks. There are public restrooms and water at both ends.

The 3-mile-long paved recreational trail between Reef Point at the south end of Crystal Cove State Park and Pelican Point at the north end of the park makes up for dogs not being allowed on the beach.

27 The Beach Trail

There are no waterfalls or mountain views to wow you on this hike. But ironically, this is one of Southern California's best gifts to dogs of all ages and fitness levels. Dogs are not allowed on San Clemente State Beach, but the hard-packed sand trail tracing the beach combines a front-row view of the surfers catching waves with a coastal nature experience.

Start: From the San Clemente Beach Trail in the Avenida Estacion parking lot
Distance: 4.6 miles out and back
Hiking time: About 2.5 hours
Difficulty: Easy
Trailhead elevation: 27 feet
Highest point: 40 feet
Best season: Year-round
Trail surface: Sand
Other trail users: Bicycles
Canine compatibility: On leash

Land status: City
Fees and permits: Parking fee
Maps: USGS San Clemente, Dana Point
Trail contacts: City of San Clemente, 100 Avenida Presidio, San Clemente 92673; (949) 361-8264; san-clemente.org
Nearest town: San Clemente
Trail tips: There are amenities at the trailhead, the pier, and the turnaround point: restrooms, showers, drinking fountains, snack bars, trash, recycling, dog-waste bag dispensers.

Finding the trailhead: From San Clemente on I-5 take exit 76/Avenida Pico. Turn west on Avenida Pico and drive 0.6 mile to El Camino Real. Turn right on El Camino Real and drive 0.1 mile to Avenida Estacion. Turn left on Avenida Estacion and drive 0.1 mile to the parking lot and trailhead at the far end of the parking lot. **GPS:** N33 25.85' / W117 37.88'

The Hike

Beachfront trails are typically paved and multi-use in Southern California. But San Clemente Beach Trail's sandy surface sets the tone for a more natural experience suitable for beach cruisers rather than inline skates and road cycles. The trail parallels the beach between North Beach at one end and Calafia Beach at the south end. An Amtrak rail line also happens to parallel the beach, and the trail occasionally alternates from the inland side to the ocean side of the tracks and beach. At first, the idea of a hiking trail anywhere near train tracks seems less than desirable, but there's nothing off-putting about the San Clemente Beach Trail. The tracks disappear as your eyes dance along the endless stretch of wide, light sand to the right, highlighted by trailside rows of blooming agave plants and palm trees beneath sandstone bluffs. Surprisingly, even the occasional whistle of an approaching passenger train adds a romantic touch to the jaunt.

The parking areas at both ends have developed amenities with bathrooms, showers, drinking fountains, dog-waste bag dispensers, and trash and recycling. Some of the benches along the trail are works of art boasting elaborate tile work. Make sure

Lush vegetation along the trail

you offer your dog water frequently, as the hike can be warm any time of year on a cloudless day.

At 0.4 mile the trail transitions to a raised boardwalk for about 1,000 feet before dropping back down to the sand. The trail comes to several junctions along the way with spurs going left to streets and neighborhoods and beach access by path or tunnel.

At 0.9 mile the trail crosses the tracks so you are now between the tracks and the beach. The San Clemente Pier is just ahead on the right. There is a snack bar and restrooms on the left across from the pier in the paved service road area. Bear left past the pier and rejoin the sandy trail lined with palm trees on the right.

At 1.3 miles walk under the raised pedestrian walkway and continue walking 0.2 mile to where you cross the tracks once again. Bear right and continue walking on the trail with the railroad tracks and beach on your right along the base of the sandstone cliffs.

At 1.9 miles you come to a junction with stairs heading up to the street on the left and a path to the beach on the right. The south end of the trail is quiet and undeveloped with dunes on the ocean side and sandstone bluffs inland with a few residences perched above. Pooch will be busy sniffing the wilder side of San Clemente Beach Trail while you soak up some solitude.

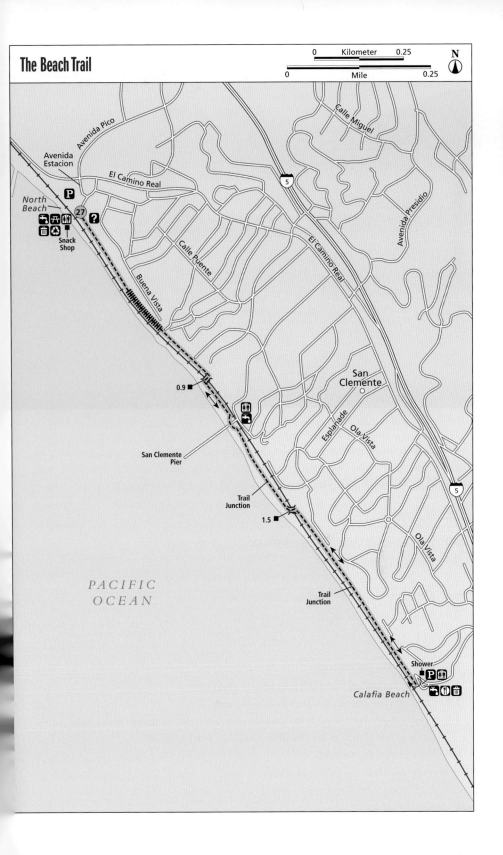

The Beach Trail

0 Kilometer 0.25
0 Mile 0.25

N

Calle Miguel

Avenida Pico

Avenida Estacion

El Camino Real

5

El Camino Real

Avenida Presidio

North Beach

27

Snack Shop

Calle Puente

Buena Vista

San Clemente

0.9

Esplanade

Ola Vista

San Clemente Pier

Trail Junction

1.5

5

Ola Vista

PACIFIC OCEAN

Trail Junction

Shower

Calafia Beach

Watching the surfers ride waves

You arrive at the end of the trail in the Calafia Beach parking lot at 2.3 miles. The snack bar is open every day during the summer and on weekends the rest of the year. Enjoy a snack before going back to the trailhead the way you came.

Miles and Directions

0.0 Start at the San Clemente Beach Trail sign.

0.4 Come to a raised boardwalk.

0.6 Come to end of boardwalk and trail junction. Continue walking on sandy trail.

0.8 Come to a trail junction. Continue on sandy trail.

0.9 Walk across railroad tracks.

1.0 Come to the pier on the right. Walk past the pier and bear left to continue on the sandy trail.

1.3 Walk under raised walkway.

1.5 Walk across railroad tracks and bear right on sandy trail.

1.9 Come to a trail junction. Continue walking on sandy trail.

2.3 Arrive at the end of the trail in the Calafia Beach parking lot. Go back to the trailhead the way you came. Elevation: 19 feet. **GPS:** N33 24.32' / W117 36.39'

4.6 Arrive back at the trailhead.

Creature Comforts

Fueling Up

Italian Cravings, 105 S. Ola Vista, San Clemente 92672; (949) 492-2777; italian-cravingsmenu.com. Dog-friendly patio and to-go menu.

Pierside Restaurant and Bar, 610 Avenida Victoria, San Clemente 92672; (949) 218-0980; piersidesc.com. Local produce and a dog-friendly patio; first-come, first-served.

The Laid Back Shack, 1700 Avenida Estacion, San Clemente 92672, at the north end of San Clemente Beach Trail.

Ruby's Shake Shack, 7703 E. Coast Hwy., Newport Coast 92657; (949) 464-0100; rubys.com. A diner with a view and dog-friendly outdoor patio near Moro Campground.

Resting Up

Sea Horse Resort, 602 Avenida Victoria, San Clemente 92672; (949) 492-1720; seahorseresort.com. Pet fee.

Campgrounds

San Clemente State Beach, 225 Avenida Calafia Ave., San Clemente 92672; (949) 492-3156; for reservations, (800) 444-7275; reserveamerica.com. Campsites for tents and RVs (some with full hookups).

Crystal Cove State Park, 8471 Pacific Coast Hwy., Laguna Beach 92651; (949) 494-3539, (949) 494-9143; crystalcovestatepark.org; for campground reservations, reserveamerica.com. The Moro Campground across from the beach opened in 2011 and sits on a spectacular location with terraced sites for tents and RVs. The bathrooms have token showers. Luv 2 Camp, (888) 898-2267, is one of the approved concessionaires for delivering an RV to a campsite.

Puppy Paws and Golden Years

The 3-mile-long paved recreational trail between Reef Point at the south end of Crystal Cove State Park and Pelican Point at the north end of the park makes up for dogs not being allowed on the beach.

San Diego County

The southwesternmost county in the lower 48 states is tucked between Orange County and the Mexican border. Seventy miles of coastline and its arid Mediterranean climate make it a desirable place for sun worshippers to live and a popular snowbird destination. Hikers enjoy scenic coastal trails and the contrast of the more arid to desert landscape to the east. The mountains and canyons of the Cleveland National Forest are close by, but it would be more apt to call it Cleveland National Chaparral given the predominant vegetation. It beats all other California counties with a backcountry of more than a million acres of chaparral.

Closer to the urban bustle, hikers are fortunate to have the expansive parklands around Mission Bay and the fabulous Mission Trails Regional Park. Old Town San Diego in the heart of the city is a rare opportunity for canines to have the privilege of sampling culture and history with their human in a state historic park.

146

28 Bernardo Mountain

This hike is an opportunity to sample the Coast to Crest Trail that will eventually stretch 70 miles from Del Mar to the Volcan Mountains overlooking Anza-Borrego Desert. If you can go to your Zen place just long enough to get beyond the intrusive freeway noise at the start of the hike, the payoff is a jaunt past expansive cactus habitat, across a year-round creek in a palm canyon culminating with 360-degree views from the summit of Bernardo Mountain.

Start: From the Coast to Crest Trailhead in San Dieguito River Park
Distance: 7.4 miles out and back
Hiking time: About 3.5 hours
Difficulty: Strenuous
Trailhead elevation: 332 feet
Highest point: 1,150 feet
Best season: Year-round; summers are hot
Trail surface: Concrete, dirt, rock
Other trail users: Horses and mountain bikes
Canine compatibility: On leash
Land status: City and conservancy

Fees and permits: None
Maps: USGS Escondido; Coast to Crest Trail Map-Lake Hodges
Trail contacts: San Dieguito River Park Office, 18372 Sycamore Creek Rd., Escondido 92025; (858) 674-2270; sdrp.org
Nearest town: Escondido
Trail tips: There are no amenities at the trailhead except a trashcan and maps. There is a portable toilet across the cul-de-sac at the Sikes Adobe farmhouse in San Dieguito River Park.

Finding the trailhead: From I-15 in Escondido take exit 27/Via Rancho Parkway. Drive 0.1 mile east on Via Rancho Parkway to Sunset Drive. Turn right on Sunset Drive and drive 0.2 mile to the cul-de-sac into the parking lot for the San Dieguito River Park Staging Area. The Coast to Crest Trailhead is at the south end of the parking lot. **GPS:** N33 03.97' / W117 04.10'

The Hike

Like they have for much of the open space in densely populated areas, citizen activists spared Bernardo Mountain from development. San Diguieto River Park and San Diguieto River Valley Conservancy purchased the land in 2004. San Diguieto River Park was established in 1989 and encompasses more than 90,000 acres. The Bernardo Mountain hike begins along the Coast to Crest Trail on a paved multi-use corridor between I-15 and a pocket of Lake Hodges reservoir. The reservoir's water level fluctuates with seasons and rainfall. In the winter of 2015 the east end of Lake Hodges was dry.

At 0.5 mile, the trail passes under the freeway and you start to leave the sound of the urban speedway behind you at the trail junction just ahead. Turn left at the junction and the bench and begin to put some distance between yourself and I-15 as you head toward Bernardo Mountain. Lake Hodges with or without water is on your left. The hillsides are a typical Southern California chaparral mix of coast sage

Taking a break on the top of Bernardo Mountain

scrub, toyon, and buckwheat. The sandstone outcrops give the arid landscape added character. The trail picks up along a section of the historic Highway 395 and its gravel shoulder for about 0.3 mile until you reach a trail junction with interpretive panels about Lake Hodges. There is a portable toilet on the right and a bicycle pedestrian bridge on the left spanning across Lake Hodges. The 990-foot-long David Kreitzer Bridge, built in 2009, links the north and south shores of the reservoir. Its claim to fame is that it is the "longest stress ribbon structure in the world."

Continue walking straight past the bridge to Bernardo Mountain Summit Trail. From here on, the trail alternates between loose dirt and rock. There is a lone picnic table on the left and a prickly pear cactus field under restoration to support the coastal cactus wren. On the bluff to the right, private property and houses overlooking Lake Hodges hem in the parkland.

At 1.6 miles you come to a shady picnic table on the banks of Felicita Creek on the left just before the wooden footbridge in the palm canyon. This riparian oasis is one of the trail's highlights and is a perfect destination on a hot day or if neither you nor your dog is inspired to hike 800 feet over the next 2 miles to the summit.

To continue to the top of Bernardo Mountain, walk across the footbridge and turn right to the Bernardo Mountain Summit at the next trail junction just 0.2 mile ahead. This is where you leave the Coast to Crest Trail. The summit trail begins with switchbacks bordered by sections of lodge-pole fencing. Bear left uphill at the

Crossing Felicita Creek

unmarked trail junction. The dirt trail on the right along Felicita Creek's sycamore and eucalyptus woodland with lush carpet below is popular with mountain bikers.

At 2.7 miles you pass an unmarked trail junction on the right and come to the trail sign on the left for Summit Mountain Trail. The trail becomes rockier and steeper for the next 0.3 mile. Make sure you offer your dog water frequently on this more exposed slope.

At 3.3 miles you pass a water tank on the right and continue the climb on rocky surface. It's a pleasant surprise to see water at the west end of the reservoir as you approach the summit. Panoramic views and a sandstone slab perch welcome you at 3.7 miles. Enjoy a snack as you soak up the views where golden eagles once nested. Snap a photo of your furry pal as king of the mountain for his Facebook friends before going back to the trailhead the way you came.

Miles and Directions

0.0   Start at the Coast to Crest Trailhead in San Dieguito River Park.

0.5   Walk under I-15.

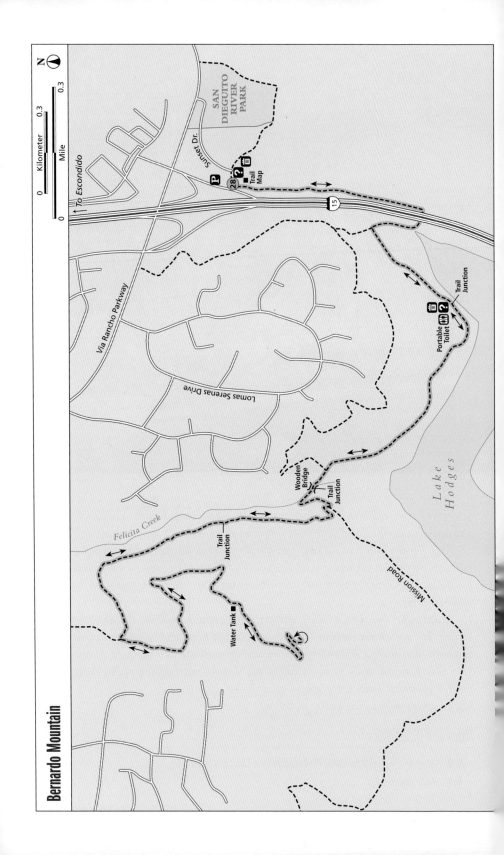

Bernardo Mountain

0.6 Come to a trail junction. Turn left away from I-15.

0.9 Come to a trail junction and interpretive panels. Continue walking straight to Bernardo Mountain Summit Trail past the pedestrian and bicycle bridge on the left.

1.6 Come to a picnic table on the left and walk across Felicita Creek on a wooden footbridge.

1.8 Come to a trail junction and turn right on Bernardo Mountain Summit Trail.

2.1 Come to an unmarked trail junction. Bear left uphill.

2.7 Come to a trail sign for Summit Mountain Trail.

3.3 Walk past the water tank on the right.

3.7 Arrive at the summit and take time to inhale the panoramic view before going back to the trailhead the way you came. Elevation: 1,150 feet. **GPS:** N33 03.84' / W117 05.27'

7.4 Arrive back at the trailhead.

Creature Comforts

Fueling Up

Vincent's, 113 W. Grand Ave., Escondido 92025; (760) 745-3835. Enjoy French classics of onion soup and escargot on the dog-friendly patio.

Vinz Wine Bar, 201 E. Grand Ave., Escondido 92025; (760) 743-8466; vinzwinebar .net. Sip your pinot grigio on the dog-friendly patio with a light bite or a full-course meal. You might have to share the Maine lobster watermelon salad with Fido.

Charlie's Family Restaurant, 210 North Ivy St., Escondido 92026; (760) 738-1545. charliesescondidorestaurant.com. No-frills comfort food served for breakfast, lunch, and dinner in a family-owned and -operated restaurant with dog-friendly patio.

Resting Up

Best Western Escondido Hotel, 1700 Seven Oakes Rd., Escondido 92026; (760) 740-1700; bwescondido.com. The recently renovated hotel has pet-friendly rooms and some rooms have refrigerators. Pet fee. As a Best Western guest, your furry friend can romp at the private Escondido RV Dog Park (directions available at the front desk).

Campgrounds

Escondido RV Resort, 1740 Seven Oakes Rd., Escondido 92026; (760) 740-5000; escondidorvresort.com. Full hookups for RVs and trailers. A 1/3-acre fenced dog park opened in 2013 for the safe off-leash pleasure of the four-legged guests.

Puppy Paws and Golden Years

Take a short stroll across the street from the Coast to Crest Trailhead along the trail to the historic **Sikes Adobe Farmstead.**

29 Blue Sky Ecological Reserve

A dirt service road leads you along a lush creek before snaking up a riparian canyon with boulder slopes on the way to Ramona Dam. The hike combines a shady creek bed, exposed hillsides, and views of the surrounding chaparral-covered hills flanking the reservoir.

Start: From the Blue Sky Ecological Reserve parking lot
Distance: 5 miles out and back
Hiking time: About 2.5 hours
Difficulty: Moderate
Trailhead elevation: 705 feet
Highest point: 1,350 feet
Best season: Year-round; early morning in the summer to avoid heat; winter and spring for creek flow and a thriving riparian habitat
Trail surface: Dirt and pavement
Other trail users: Horses on some trails
Canine compatibility: On leash
Land status: City
Fees and permits: None

Maps: USGS Escondido, San Pasqual; Blue Sky Ecological Reserve map at the trailhead
Trail contacts: Blue Sky Ecological Reserve, (858) 668-4781; poway.org/bluesky
Nearest town: Poway
Trail tips: There are several interpretive panels in the parking lot along with trash and recycling. There is a covered shelter with 2 benches on the east side of the parking lot and a portable toilet. The water fountain is on the west side. The exposed sections of the trail as you approach the reservoir can get dangerously hot in the summer. Be sure to bring plenty of water for you and pooch when hiking this trail on a sunny day anytime of year.

Finding the trailhead: From I-15 in Rancho Bernardo take exit 24/Rancho Bernardo Road and drive 3.2 miles east on Rancho Bernardo Road (Rancho Bernardo Road becomes Espola Road at the Poway City line). Turn left into the Blue Sky Ecological Reserve parking lot. The trailhead is at the southern end of the parking lot. **GPS:** N33 00.96' / W117 01.42'

The Hike

Blue Sky Ecological Reserve protects 700 acres of riparian woodland and chaparral-covered hills in the shadow of Ramona Dam. The reservoir project initiated by the Ramona Municipal Water District was approved in 1981 and the dam was dedicated in 1988. The City of Poway, California Department of Fish and Wildlife, and County of San Diego Department of Parks and Recreation own Blue Sky Ecological Reserve.

The hike to the reservoir begins at the south end of the Blue Sky Ecological Reserve parking lot. The trail sign directs you along a lodge-pole fence corridor dropping you on Green Valley Truck Trail, which is a dirt service road. The trail begins with a gentle descent into the creekside oak woodland. There are several plant identification signs along the way describing the various vegetation, including toyon and laurel sumac bushes, chaparral yucca, western sycamore, and California wild rose.

Arriving at Ramona Dam above the reservoir

At 0.2 mile you come to a trail junction for the Creekside Trail on the left. Although the narrower shady trail looks very inviting, dogs are not allowed on this trail. Continue walking straight on the wider Green Valley Truck Trail. Creekside Trail rejoins Green Valley Truck Trail from the left 0.4 mile ahead.

At 1.0 mile you come to another trail junction. Lake Poway is to the right and Lake Ramona is straight. Lake Poway is part of the Lake Poway Recreational Area. Continue walking toward Lake Ramona. Just ahead on the right are a portable toilet and a no-fluff picnic area in a clearing with a few picnic tables.

At 1.25 miles you come to a trail junction. Authorized vehicles only straight ahead to the pumping station. Turn left to Ramona Dam. At this point you can see part of the face of the dam in the V of the canyon above. The trail begins its sweeping serpentine climb to the dam for about a mile. The sandstone boulders on the left side are very picturesque, and in a wet winter and spring the canyon on the right comes to life, feeding the riparian ravine highlighted by a couple of palm trees. Depending on the temperatures and your dog's stamina, this is also a good turnaround point if pooch was only in the mood for the cooler woodland excursion.

At 2.1 miles, the trail transitions to pavement at the sign outlining the reservoir rules. The grade is noticeably stiffer as you and pooch make a cardio push for 0.4 mile to the top, where the trail plateaus at the reservoir. Enjoy the views from this perch and notice Poway Lake and the recreation area's greener picnic areas to the south.

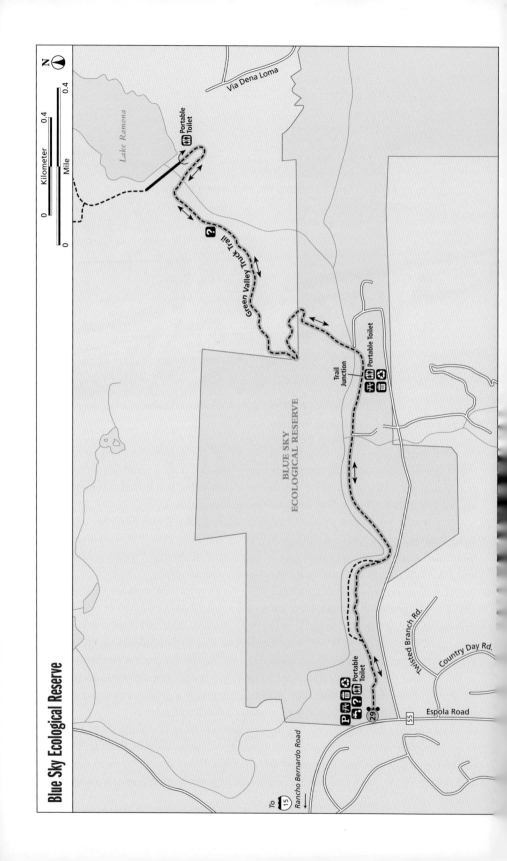

Blue Sky Ecological Reserve

You won't find anything this inviting at Ramona Dam. But when you return to the trailhead parking lot the way you came, you can easily drive about 0.5 mile south on Espola Road to Poway Lake Recreation Area on the left and treat your four-legged pal to a picnic lunch on cool, green grass.

Miles and Directions

0.0 Start at the south end of the Blue Sky Ecological Reserve parking lot.

0.2 Come to a trail junction for Creekside Trail left. Continue straight.

0.6 Come to a trail junction, where Creekside Trail rejoins main trail from the left. Continue walking straight.

1.0 Come to a trail junction for Lake Poway to the right. Continue walking straight to Lake Ramona.

1.2 Come to a portable toilet on the right and a few picnic tables.

1.25 Come to a trail junction. Turn left uphill to Lake Ramona.

2.1 The trail transitions from dirt to pavement.

2.5 Arrive at Lake Ramona reservoir. Go back to the trailhead the way you came. Elevation: 1,350 feet. **GPS:** N33 01.39' / W116 59.81'

5.0 Arrive back at the trailhead.

Creature Comforts

Fueling Up

Company Pub & Kitchen, 13670 Poway Rd., Poway City Center, Poway 92064; (858) 668-3365; companypubandkitchen.com. Dog-friendly patio complete with a menu for Bowser.

Resting Up

Best Western Plus/Poway, 13845 Poway Rd., Poway 92064; (858) 748-6320; best western.com. Pet fee.

Dos Picos County Park, 17953 Dos Picos Park Rd., Ramona 92065; (760) 789-2220; reservations, (858) 694-3049; sdparks.org. Campsites for tents and RVs with partial hookups.

30 Cowles Mountain

One of San Diego's most accessible cardio hikes to the highest point in the City of San Diego almost immediately rewards hikers with views of surrounding mountains and the Pacific. The south-facing trail has almost zero shade, but on a cool day if your four-legged pal likes to socialize on his workouts, this is the jaunt for him.

Start: From the Cowles Mountain trailhead in Mission Trails Regional Park
Distance: 3 miles out and back
Hiking time: About 1.5 hours
Difficulty: Moderate
Trailhead elevation: 669 feet
Highest point: 1,591 feet
Best season: Year-round; summers can be too hot
Trail surface: Dirt and sandstone
Other trail users: None
Canine compatibility: On leash
Land status: City and county
Fees and permits: None
Maps: USGS La Mesa; Mission Trails Regional Park trail map

Trail contacts: Mission Trails Visitor Center and Interpretive Center, 1 Junipero Serra Trail, San Diego 92119; (619) 668-3275; (619) 668-3281; mtrp.org
Nearest town: San Diego
Trail tips: There are flush toilets, a drinking fountain, benches, vending machine with water and sport drinks, trash and recycling, a bike rack, and a map board at the trailhead. Bring plenty of water for your dog. Hike in the early morning on warm days. Watch your dog for signs of overheating and do not hesitate to turn around if your dog seems lethargic. Heat stroke can be fatal.

Finding the trailhead: From the intersection of I-5 and I-8 in San Diego take the I-8 East/El Centro exit and drive 8 miles on I-8. Take exit 10/College Avenue and bear left to follow the signs for College Avenue North. Drive 1.2 miles north on College Avenue to Navajo Road. Turn right on Navajo Road, drive 2 miles to Golfcrest Drive, and turn left on Golfcrest Drive. Immediately turn right into the Mission Trails Regional Park parking lot or park on the street if lot is full. **GPS:** N32 48.28' / W117 02.23'

The Hike

The 1,600-foot mound protruding above the San Diego skyline is protected within Mission Trails Regional Park's approximately 6,000 acres. The seed for Mission Trails Regional Park grew from community concern about the rapid spread of new development during the 1960s. Over the next 35 years, the park acquired more land and a stunning visitor center opened to the public in 1995. Cowles Mountain, named after George A. Cowles, a rancher and businessman in San Diego County in the late 1800s, was originally part of the Rancho Mission San Diego Spanish land grants. Cowles Mountain had been slated for development when it was acquired in 1974.

Cowles Mountain is a cardio workout for dogs and their humans.

The hike to the summit of the chaparral and sandstone mountain is a straightforward, exposed trek following a zigzag trail bordered by sections of lodge-pole fence. Although you can see the ocean from the trail as you climb, this hike is inland and the sun can sizzle any time of the year, hence the several advisories posted at the trailhead about protecting your dog from heat stroke and the warnings about hiking to the summit on hot days.

The trail begins on loose sand and alternates between loose sand, terraced steps over sandstone, and uneven rock terrain, which calls for trail etiquette when passing other hikers and dogs around the narrower bends.

Apart from the occasional unmarked spur to a vista point along the way, the only trail junction is at 0.9 mile. Barker Way Trail is to the right, and you bear left to continue on the main trail up to the summit. There's a communication tower on the left just below the summit and a dirt service road coming up the backside. There is a plaque dedicated to George A. Cowles marking the summit and two interpretive panels identifying the mountains that can be seen from the summit. Soak up the panoramic views across San Diego County before finding a cool spot to sit in the shadow of one of the many boulders. Offer your dog water and a snack before heading back down to the trailhead the way you came.

Miles and Directions

0.0 Start at the Cowles Mountain trailhead in Mission Trails Regional Park.

0.9 Come to a trail junction for Barker Way Trail. Bear left and continue walking uphill to the summit.

1.5 Arrive at the summit. Elevation: 1,591 feet. **GPS:** N32 48.77' / W117 01.91'. Go back to the trailhead the way you came.

3.0 Arrive back at the trailhead.

Creature Comforts

Fueling Up

Whole Foods Market, 711 University Ave., San Diego 92103;(619) 294-2800. If your dog likes you to shop organic, this is a convenient downtown location.

Casa de Reyes Mexican Cantina in Old Town San Diego State Historic Park, 2754 Calhoun St., San Diego 92110; (619) 220-5040; fiestadereyes.com. Enjoy the dog-friendly garden seating and a unique opportunity to step back in time surrounded by a Mex-Cal atmosphere of the early 1800s.

Bar Vie in the Residence Inn San Diego, Downtown Gaslamp Quarter, 356 6th Ave., San Diego 92101; (619) 487-1200. If Fido is more of city slicker than a suburbanite, but prefers "historic" over "nouveau," he'll enjoy the outdoor patio dining and the vibe of this Victorian charm.

Resting Up

There are several dog-friendly hotel/motel chains in San Diego and around the bay, including Best Western, La Quinta, and Sheraton.

Old Town Inn, 4444 Pacific Hwy., San Diego 92110; (619) 260-8024; oldtown-inn .com. This motel is walking distance to Old Town. Some rooms have microwaves, refrigerators, and kitchenettes if Fido prefers home cooking. Pet fee.

Best Western Plus Hacienda Hotel Old Town, 4041 Hamey St. (Old Town Avenue exit 19 off the I-5), San Diego 92110; (619) 298-4707; bestwestern.com. Steps away from the State Historic Park. Some rooms are designated for the furry guests. Check on their "crate" rules. Pet fee.

Residence Inn San Diego Downtown Gaslamp Quarter, 356 6th Ave., San Diego 92101; (619) 487-1200; marriott.com. Modern architecture in a convenient historic district. Hot breakfast buffet included. Rooms have kitchenettes for easy dine-in evenings with your four-legged pal.

Westin Gaslamp San Diego Gaslamp Quarter, 910 Broadway Circle, San Diego 92101; (619) 239-2200; westingaslamp.com. The location has a historic vibe and with the famous Horton Plaza steps away, this outdoor mall satisfies pooches who like to shop for sport. Canine guests are treated to an amenity bag upon check-in, including their own Heavenly Bed.

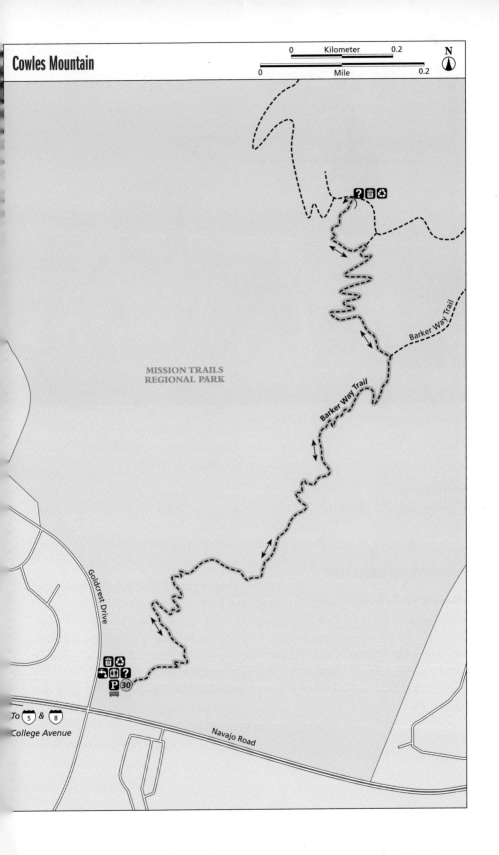

Cowles Mountain

MISSION TRAILS
REGIONAL PARK

Barker Way Trail

Barker Way Trail

Goldcrest Drive

Navajo Road

To 5 & 8
College Avenue

Standing on 1,591-foot-high Cowles Mountain

The Sofia Hotel, 150 W. Broadway, San Diego 92101; (619) 234-9200; historic hotels.org. The desk clerks confess to being "obsessed with dogs."

Campgrounds

Mission Bay RV Resort, 2727 De Anza Rd., San Diego 92109; (858) 270-4300; missionbayrvresort.com. The waterfront sites for RVs and trailers are quiet with good duck-watching for pooch entertainment adjacent to a bayside paved trail for strolls.

Puppy Paws and Golden Years

Mission Trails Visitor and Interpretive Center, 1 Father Junipero Serra Trail, San Diego 92119; (619) 668-3275; mtrp.org. Although dogs are not allowed inside the visitor center, this stunning facility at the mouth of the Mission Gorge is a must-see. Four-legged visitors think the perimeter walk with the outdoor nature exhibits complete with wildlife sound effects is a tail-wagging experience.

Stroll around the historic buildings nestled in **Old Town San Diego**'s 230-acre state historic park.

31 Cabrillo National Monument

This is a rare occasion within the National Park Service, when dogs are more welcome on a natural dirt trail than on the paved paths. Don't miss the opportunity to sample a national historic landmark and enjoy a hike along a rugged bluff, with tide pools and coastal views, in the company of your four-legged pal. This hike is about quality over quantity.

Start: From the Tidepool Trailhead in Cabrillo National Monument
Distance: 1.2 miles out and back
Hiking time: About 1 hour
Difficulty: Easy
Trailhead elevation: 50 feet
Highest point: 103 feet
Best season: Year-round
Trail surface: Dirt and sandstone
Other trail users: None
Canine compatibility: On leash
Land status: National Park
Fees and permits: Entrance fee

Maps: USGS Point Loma
Trail contacts: Cabrillo National Monument, 1800 Cabrillo Memorial Dr., San Diego 92106; (619) 557-5450; nps.gov/cabr
Nearest town: San Diego
Trail tips: There are 2 vault toilets at the trailhead. No drinking water. There are flush toilets and water at the main visitor center at the top of the hill. Sandstone cliffs are unstable and can be hazardous, so be sure to keep your dog on a short leash where the trail skirts closest to the edge. This is an example of a hike where a harness is safer than a collar.

Finding the trailhead: From San Diego on I-5 southbound, take Rosecrans exit/CA 209 and drive 3 miles on Rosecrans Street to Canon Street. Turn right on Canon Street and drive 1.2 miles to Catalina Boulevard. Turn left on Catalina Boulevard (Catalina Boulevard becomes Cabrillo Memorial Drive) and drive 3 miles to the entrance of Cabrillo National Monument. Turn right downhill on Cabrillo Road following the sign for Tidepool. Drive 0.8 mile to the parking lot on your left. The trailhead for this hike begins at the Tidepool Trail. **GPS:** N32 40.10' / W117 14.66'
  From San Diego on I-5 northbound, take Pacific Highway exit, drive 1 mile to Barnett Avenue, and turn left on Barnett Avenue. Drive 0.7 mile to Rosecrans Street. Turn left on Rosecrans Street and drive 3 miles to Canon Street. Turn right on Canon Street and drive 1.2 miles to Catalina Boulevard. Turn left on Catalina Boulevard (Catalina Boulevard becomes Cabrillo Memorial Drive) and drive 3 miles to the entrance of Cabrillo National Monument. Turn right downhill on Cabrillo Road, following the sign for Tidepool. Drive 0.8 mile to the parking lot on your left. The trailhead for this hike begins at the Tidepool Trail. **GPS:** N32 40.10' / W117 14.66'

The Hike

Juan Rodriguez Cabrillo set out to claim more land for Spain, and landed in present-day San Diego in 1542. He is believed to be the first European to explore San Diego Bay and what is now the West Coast of the United States. He described "a very good port" as his flotilla entered the harbor, where the Kumeyaay Indians met him.

The Pacific surf sculpts the sandstone bluffs.

Cabrillo named the area San Miguel in honor of the saint whose feast was celebrated the following day. Cabrillo's notes are the first written accounts of the vegetation, climate, and culture of coastal California.

Cabrillo National Monument on Point Loma strategically sits on a sandstone peninsula, which acts as a natural barrier at the entrance to San Diego Bay. The 422-foot-high rampart was designated a military reserve in 1822. The monument was established in 1913 to commemorate Cabrillo's 1542 voyage to the area.

Dogs are not allowed in the visitor center or around the old Point Loma Lighthouse. The good news is that dogs don't care, because some fluke allows them on the cliff trail above the tide pools, which is an adventure in the most pristine and scenic part of the monument. The trail begins in the first parking lot at the bottom of Cabrillo Road to the right of the visitor information station. The station is a small trailer with the National Park logo, where volunteers offer tide pool information and exhibits.

Follow the trail along the bluff and be sure to observe the warning signs about staying back from the unstable cliff edge. The trail meanders across sandstone shelves and up wooden stairways. At 0.1 mile you come to the tide-pool access on the left around the end of the rope and post fence. The monument boasts one of the best-preserved intertidal areas open to the public on the Southern California coast. Note that the tide pools are subject to the tides, as the name implies. There is a vast difference between tide levels and you should not risk stepping down to the tide pools unless you are there at low tide. Tide-pool rocks are slippery and the barnacles can slice your dogs' pads.

If you cannot access the tide pools safely, continue following the trail along the cliffs heading up the coast. The views are superb and the ruggedness of the surf-sculpted

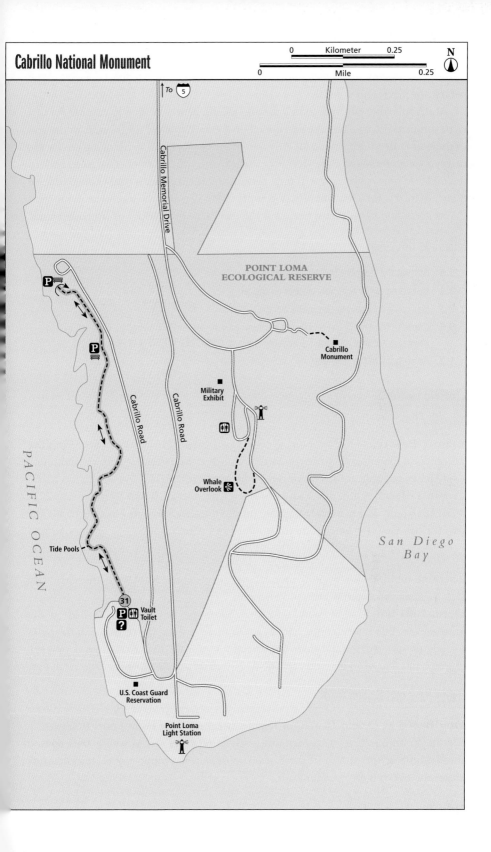

Cabrillo National Monument

POINT LOMA
ECOLOGICAL RESERVE

Cabrillo
Monument

Military
Exhibit

Whale
Overlook

Tide Pools

31

Vault
Toilet

U.S. Coast Guard
Reservation

Point Loma
Light Station

PACIFIC OCEAN

San Diego
Bay

Cabrillo Memorial Drive

Cabrillo Road

Cabrillo Road

To 5

N

0   Kilometer   0.25

0   Mile   0.25

bluffs interrupted by southern maritime chaparral is almost primeval in some sections. The monument protects more than 140 acres of this Mediterranean ecotype habitat for plants and wildlife.

At 0.5 mile the trail emerges at a parking lot and bench. Erosion has caused the trail to be rerouted briefly along the paved road on a gravel shoulder for 0.1 mile to the end of the trail in the third parking lot. Any one of the two benches overlooking the Pacific makes a great spot to savor the view over a snack with your bowser before going back to the trailhead the way you came. If time permits and the weather is cool enough to leave pooch in the car for a few minutes, stop at the visitor center at the top of the monument for commanding views of San Diego's skyline and across to Mexico's Coronado Islands.

Miles and Directions

0.0 Start at the Tidepool Trail off Cabrillo Road.

0.1 You come to the tide-pool access on the left.

0.5 You come to a parking lot and a bench.

0.6 Come to the end of the trail in the northern parking lot and two benches. Go back to the trailhead the way you came. Elevation: 94 feet. **GPS:** N32 40.50' / W117 14.77'

1.2 Arrive back at the trailhead.

Creature Comforts

Fueling Up

Azucar Bakery, 4820 Newport Ave., Ocean Beach 92107; (619) 523-2020; ilove azucar.com. French-style patisserie with a Cuban twist. Breakfast goodies and lunch sandwiches available at the two dog-friendly outdoor tables.
Tower 2 Beach Café, 5083 Santa Monica Ave., Ocean Beach 92107; (619) 223-4059; t2ob.com. Enjoy breakfast all day on the dog-friendly patio or stop by for the popular fish tacos for lunch. Call for summer and winter hours.

Resting Up

There are multiple dog-friendly motel/hotel chains in the San Diego area, including Best Western, Marriott, Westin, and Sheraton.
Ocean Villa Inn, 5142 W. Point Loma Blvd., San Diego 92107; (619) 224-3481; ocean villainn.com. Life is a beach for canines at this motel at Dog Beach. Some of the perks include tile-floored, ground-floor dog-friendly rooms for easy access to a communal dog run and fenced-in grassy space. The dog-wash area makes keeping Fido clean easy.

Puppy Paws and Golden Years

Dog Beach at Ocean Beach on Voltaire Street off West Point Loma Boulevard is San Diego canines' favorite playground, with an off-leash area as well as trails around the wetlands at the mouth of the San Diego River. The multi-use recreational trail above the beach is for dogs on leash.

Central Valley

The largest city in Central Valley is Fresno, almost the bull's-eye center of the state of California. The Central Valley covers one of the most productive agricultural regions in the state, up to 60 miles wide and 450 miles long. Once upon a time the Central Valley was a much different landscape, lush with grasslands, savannas, wetlands, and woodlands providing habitat for pronghorn antelope and tule elk. Exploring this landscape would have been an experience of unparalleled beauty against snow-draped peaks of the Sierra to the east along the banks of a voluminous San Joaquin River.

These days, dogs and their owners are grateful for the existence and protection of open space along Fresno's San Joaquin River Parkway and within Woodward Park's nature oasis.

32 Lewis S. Eaton Trail

This is a perfect example of a relatively flat urban hike combining the paved multi-use section of the San Joaquin River Parkway and its dirt shoulder with the natural setting of the Tom MacMichael Sr. Trail. The outline of the snowcapped Sierra Nevada to the east is an added visual treat.

Start: From the trailhead across from the Welcome Pavilion
Distance: 8.5-mile lollipop
Hiking time: About 4 hours
Difficulty: Moderate
Trailhead elevation: 293 feet
Highest point: 361 feet
Best season: Year-round; summers can be very hot and shade is scarce
Trail surface: Pavement and dirt
Other trail users: Horses and bicycles

Canine compatibility: On leash
Land status: City
Fees and permits: None
Maps: USGS Fresno North, Lanes Bridge
Trail contacts: San Joaquin River Parkway and Conservation Trust, (559) 248-8480; riverpark way.org
Nearest town: Fresno
Trail tips: There are flush toilets, drinking water, trash and recycling, dog-waste bag dispenser, and picnic tables across from the trailhead.

Finding the trailhead: From Fresno on CA 41, take Friant Road exit and drive 3.2 miles north on Friant Road. Turn left on Old Friant Road just before the traffic signal. Drive 1 mile on Old Friant Road and turn left into the Coke Hallowell Center for River Studies and at the sign for San Joaquin River Parkway and Conservation Trust Inc. at 11605 Old Friant Road. Park in the spaces in front of the Leon and Pete Peters Welcome Pavilion. The trailhead is across from the pavilion. **GPS:** N36 54.39' / W119 45.41'

The Hike

The hike begins on the Coke Hallowell Center for River Studies' 20-acre patch of land above the San Joaquin River, the primary water source serving San Joaquin Valley cities and farmland. The property showcases a historic 1890s ranch house, River Studies and Conservation Trust buildings, gardens, a vineyard, a picnic area, and a gift shop. Majestic palm trees line the entrance to the grounds.

The collaboration between the River Parkway Trust and other local and land management agencies will eventually result in lacing 22 miles of trail for public recreational access between Highway 145 and Millerton Lake.

This pleasant urban hike lets you sample the most scenic section of the recreation trail between the Center for River Studies and Woodward Park before dropping down closer to the banks of the San Joaquin.

The first 3 miles trace the bluff on a paved section of the multi-use trail overlooking the San Joaquin River floodplain. There are several benches along the way for enjoying the views. Interpretive panels describe the ecology and geology of the area.

A shady corridor leading to the San Joaquin River floodplain

This is a particularly pretty setting in the fall when the temperatures are cooler and buckwheat brush bursts into deep maroon as trees change their leaf colors from green to burnt amber in the warm glow of the autumn light.

At 3.3 miles you come to an unmarked trail junction to the right. The paved trail continues straight into Woodward Park, the largest regional park in the Central Valley. Turn right at the wood fence and bear left downhill on the dirt trail. At 3.5 miles you come to an unmarked trail junction. This will be the close of your lollipop when you complete your loop along the unmarked Tom MacMichael Sr. Trail. Continue walking downhill to the double dirt trail in the flats of the floodplain. Turn right on the flat double dirt trail to begin the loop.

At 4.3 miles you come to an unmarked trail junction with a paved trail. Turn left to continue your loop on the paved trail. The dirt equestrian trail parallels the paved trail on the other side of the wood post fence. Just ahead are two vault toilets, bike racks, a drinking fountain, and picnic tables. This is a perfect spot to enjoy a snack with pooch. The bank of the San Joaquin River is just beyond the picnic area camouflaged by lush vegetation.

At 4.9 miles you come to an unmarked trail junction with a paved spur going uphill on the right. Bear left on the dirt trail past the bench and walk uphill on the spur trail 0.1 mile up to the unmarked trail junction to close the loop of your lollipop. From here you continue walking back up to the main trail and return to the trailhead the way you came. The outline of the Sierra peaks on the eastern horizon is the highlight of the return to the trailhead.

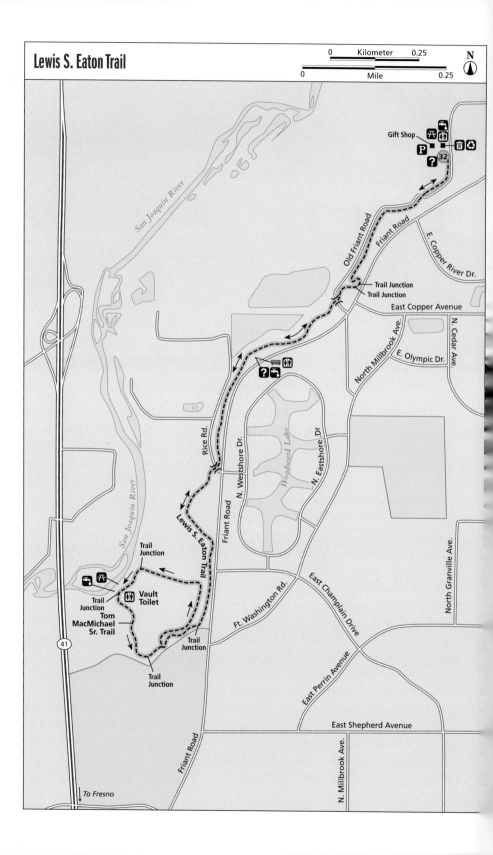

Lewis S. Eaton Trail

0 Kilometer 0.25

0 Mile 0.25

N

San Joaquin River

Gift Shop

32

Old Friant Road

Friant Road

E. Copper River Dr.

Trail Junction
Trail Junction

East Copper Avenue

North Millbrook Ave.

N. Cedar Ave.

E. Olympic Dr.

San Joaquin River

Rice Rd.

N. Westshore Dr.

Woodward Lake

N. Eastshore Dr.

Friant Road

Lewis S. Eaton Trail

East Champlain Drive

North Granville Ave.

Trail Junction

Trail Junction
Tom MacMichael Sr. Trail

Vault Toilet

Trail Junction

Trail Junction

Ft. Washington Rd.

East Perrin Avenue

41

East Shepherd Avenue

N. Millbrook Ave.

Friant Road

To Fresno

Miles and Directions

0.0 Start at the trailhead across from the Leon and Pete Peters Welcome Pavilion.

0.3 Walk across Friant Road.

1.0 Come to a spur trail on the left. Continue walking on the main trail.

1.05 Come to a spur trail on the left, a sculpture, and a young stand of trees. Continue walking on the main trail.

1.2 Come to a spur trail on the left and walk across the Cappie Barrett footbridge on the main trail.

1.8 Come to an interpretive panel, commemorative plaque dedicated to Lewis S. Eaton, restroom with a vault toilet, drinking fountain, and bench.

2.3 Come to a spur trail on the left and walk across the footbridge to continue walking on the main trail.

3.3 Come to an unmarked trail junction at the wood fence. Turn right and walk downhill on the left fork.

3.5 Come to an unmarked trail junction and continue walking downhill to the dirt double track ahead and turn right to begin your loop along the unmarked Tom MacMichael Sr. Trail. This junction will be the close of the loop in your lollipop.

4.3 Come to an unmarked trail junction and turn left on the paved trail.

4.4 Come to a picnic area with tables, bike rack, two vault toilets, and drinking water.

4.9 Come to an unmarked trail junction with a paved spur trail heading uphill to the right. Turn left past the bench and walk 0.1 mile uphill on the spur trail to the unmarked junction to close the loop of your lollipop. Continue walking back to the trailhead the way you came.

8.5 Arrive back at the trailhead.

Creature Comforts

Fueling Up

Riverpark Shopping Centre, 220 El Paseo Del Centro, Fresno 93720; (559) 437-4855. This outdoor mall has several of the most popular fast-food chains and coffee bars as well as some casual dining restaurants. **Macaroni Grill,** (559) 436-6690, offers Italian favorites, to-go menu, and dog-friendly outdoor seating.

Resting Up

La Quinta Inn & Suites Fresno Riverpark, 330 E. Fir Ave.; (559) 449-0928; laquintariverparkfresno.com. No fee. Guests sign the Pet Policy agreement at check-in.

Puppy Paws and Golden Years

Dogs of all ages and fitness levels will find their stride along any section of the **San Joaquin River Parkway.** The closest parking to the **Tom MacMichael Sr. Trail** and the southeast end of the **Lewis B. Eaton Trail** is in Woodward Park, 7775 N. Friant Rd., Fresno 93720.

Southern Sierra Nevada

The Sierra Nevada Mountain Range extends from the Cascade Range in the north, 400 miles south to the Transverse Range. This book uses Oakhurst on the west side of Yosemite National Park in the Sierra National Forest as the northern boundary for the western Southern Sierra Nevada. Bishop and the Inyo National Forest mark the northern boundary for the eastern Southern Sierra Nevada.

The western slopes are heavily forested and rise gently from California's Central Valley. By fall of 2015 much of the state of California was in the fourth year of drought. According to Dave Smith, a silviculturist for the United States National Forest, drought conditions in the Central Sierra were classified as Exceptional (the worst drought condition classification) for the entire summer of 2015. Snowpack measurements for the winter of 2014–2015 were recorded at 5 percent of normal and were considered to be the lowest snowpack in at least the past 500 years. This lack of precipitation was accompanied by warmer than normal temperatures.

The combination of above-normal temperatures, lack of rainfall and snowmelt, and an increase in bark beetle activity has resulted in substantial mortality in many tree species. Significant mortality has been noted in a number of tree species, including gray pine, ponderosa pine, sugar pine, incense cedar, white fir, and several oak species. To date, the hardest-hit areas appear to be below 5,000 feet.

This devastation seemed much more pronounced on the west side, where the slopes displayed large swaths of dry, rust-colored pine trees among the green healthier trees.

The El Niño that brought rain in late 2015 and into the beginning of 2016 will help the snowpack and quench some of the landscape's thirst, but unfortunately Dave Smith predicts that the "severity of the drought causing this increased level of mortality can be expected to continue for several more years, even following several winters of normal or above precipitation."

The less-forested east side of the Sierra drops off abruptly, revealing a dramatic canvas of granitic escarpments, peaks, and palisades cradling crystalline lakes in narrow, stream-fed canyons.

The Sierra has more than 200 warm, sunny days a year, golden autumns, and snowstorm winters in the higher elevations. Population centers and agricultural land in the lower valleys depend on the snowpack and gradual spring melt in the rivers and streams to fill the reservoirs for the rest of the year, since "it never rains in California," as the song goes, except during the winter months.

The Southern Sierra Nevada hikes in this book include trails in the Sierra National Forest, Inyo National Forest, Sequoia National Forest, John Muir Wilderness, and

Golden Trout Wilderness. The Sierra Nevada is a kingdom of pristine lakes, streams, and wildflower-cloaked meadows that attracts hikers, fishers, and nature contemplators from all over the world.

Within the Southern Sierra are Mt. Whitney, 14,495 feet, the highest mountain in the lower 48 states, and precious groves of giant sequoias.

Like most of California's mountain ranges, the Sierra Nevada's rich resources supported native tribes for thousands of years because they learned to live in harmony with the rhythm of the seasons and respect the indomitable. Many an explorer, fur trader, pioneer, and fortuneseeker underestimated the power of Mother Nature and perished trying to conquer the colossal mountain barrier. Many of the hiking trails and developed recreation sites you enjoy with your dog today were established along ancient paths traveled by Native Americans and historic routes blazed by early emigrants.

33 Lewis Creek National Scenic Trail

This is a great opportunity to enjoy a dog-friendly historic trail just outside of not so dog-compatible Yosemite National Park. Following a normal snowpack winter season, this narrow canyon trail delivers a lively creek with log-rail footbridges and two small waterfalls over the 3 uphill miles between the Cedar Valley Drive trailhead and your turnaround point at Red Rock Falls. The good news is that even when Mother Nature is less generous with white and wet, as was the case for the fourth year in a row in 2015, this is still a great little cedar-scented trail with shade for pooch, a boulder-strewn creek bed, ferns, and some flow into early summer. In a drier year, the creek's flow is most limpid in the springtime until it wanes to a trickle in late summer and early fall.

Start: From the National Forest Trail sign on the left-hand side of the road 1 mile down Cedar Valley Drive

Distance: 6.4 miles out and back

Hiking time: About 4 hours

Difficulty: Strenuous with some steep uphill sections

Trailhead elevation: 3,396 feet

Highest point: 4,238 feet

Best season: Spring for most vigorous creek flow and delicate dogwood blooms

Trail surface: Dirt and some narrow stretches around large rocks and boulders

Other trail users: Horses are allowed but discouraged from traveling on the lower section of the trail

Canine compatibility: Voice control

Land status: National forest

Fees and permits: None for day hikes; campfire permit for dispersed camping

Maps: USGS White Chief Mountain, Fish Camp; USFS Sierra National Forest; National Geographic Shaver Lake Trail Map

Trail contacts: Sierra National Forest, Bass Lake Ranger District, 57003 Road 25, North Fork 93643; (559) 877-2218; 40343 CA 41, Oakhurst 93644; (559) 658-7588; fs.usda .gov/sierra

Nearest town: Oakhurst

Trail tips: There are no toilets or water at the trailhead. If you have an exuberant dog that can't resist jumping in anything wet, it is safer to leash your dog on the sections where the trail meets the creek, especially when the spring and early summer flow is at its most vigorous.

Finding the trailhead: From Oakhurst at the intersection of CA 41 and CA 49, drive 5 miles north on CA 41 to Cedar Valley Drive. Turn right on Cedar Valley Drive and drive 1 mile. There is a dirt parking area on both sides of the street just before the bridge and the 25 mph speed limit sign on the right. The discreet National Forest Trail sign and a mountain lion information board mark the beginning of the trail. There is no official Lewis Creek National Recreation Trail sign at this trailhead. There is a signed parking lot off CA 41 at the trail's midpoint 1.9 miles north from the Cedar Valley Drive turnoff. Many hikers choose to park there for a shorter out-and-back hike in either direction. **GPS:** N37 24.22' / W119 37.55'

The Hike

Most of the Lewis Creek Trail traces the route of the old Madera–Sugar Pine Lumber Company flume. Sawed boards were floated down a V-shaped flume from the mill south to the railroad. This peaceful stretch of trail was designated as part of the National Recreation System in 1982.

The easy access off the main road is another plus for this pleasant, straightforward shady trail with refreshing pools for water-loving dogs. Don't let the sight of dying, rust-discolored pines on the surrounding mountain slopes as you drive CA 41 alarm you. The four-year drought has weakened many trees, making them more vulnerable to the bark beetle infestation, which is taking its toll on the forest. But shortly after stepping on the trail, you are in a healthier forest (for now) of mostly cedar and manzanita.

At the start, the trail is rather nondescript and more of an old dirt road. This early section is dry and the creek is not yet visible. At mile 0.2 you come to a wooden trail

Lewis Creek treats dogs to swimming holes.

sign with an arrow directing you to bear right. The dirt road becomes a mostly level single track. At mile 0.6, your trail meets the creek and begins to climb. You come to the first swimming hole at 1.0 mile and continue uphill to a platform overlooking unmarked Corlieu Falls cascade. Anyone with an artistic soul will find this view inspiring, even when the water is more of a veil than a drape over the boulders' smooth, organic forms. Just ahead you and pooch will pant up thirty-three rock steps leading to the midway trailhead parking lot on CA 41. The trail levels off and you come to a trail junction at almost 1.5 miles. The Lewis Creek Trail 21E06 sign has an arrow pointing right. Hikers who have parked above on CA 41 come to this junction with a choice of hiking left or right even if the sign only has an arrow pointing right in the direction you came from and passing Corlieu Falls.

If you are hiking to Red Rock Falls, you will go left, and Lewis Creek will be on your right. Cross Lewis Creek on tree stumps at 1.5 miles. Lewis Creek is now on your left. The grade mellows as the trail traces the slope higher above Lewis Creek. The trail parallels CA 41, and that is the intermittent sound of traffic you hear across the creek above.

You will cross four more seasonal streams on wooden footbridges before coming to the trail junction at 3.1 miles with a sign for Red Rock Falls left, Sugar Pine ahead 0.8 mile, Corlieu Falls 1.7 miles behind you, and Cedar Valley 3.2 miles. Cedar Valley is your trailhead. The trail continues to Sugar Pine Christian Camp, where it ends without fanfare for those who are curious or eager for a longer excursion.

Red Rock Falls is the destination on this hike. Leash your dog and turn left down the short, steep spur to view Red Rock Falls. Be aware that there is no guardrail at Red Rock Falls and although these are not towering, precipitous falls, the rocks can be slippery on this shelf, especially if you are lucky enough to be here when the water is flushing through with froth. Pick a granite slab perch for a picnic lunch with pooch before going back to the trailhead the way you came.

Miles and Directions

0.0 Start at the National Forest trail sign and mountain lion information board on the left-hand side of Cedar Valley Drive.

0.2 Come to a wooden trail sign with arrow pointing right. Bear right in the direction of the arrow.

0.6 Come to Lewis Creek on your right.

1.0 Come to a swimming hole.

1.1 Come to a platform overlooking Corlieu Falls.

1.2 Walk up the stone steps.

1.45 Come to a trail junction and sign for Lewis Creek Trail 21E06 and arrow pointing right. Turn left. The CA 41 parking lot is above.

1.5 Walk across Lewis Creek on tree stumps.

1.7 Walk across a seasonal stream on wooden footbridge.

2.2 Walk across a seasonal stream on wooden footbridge.

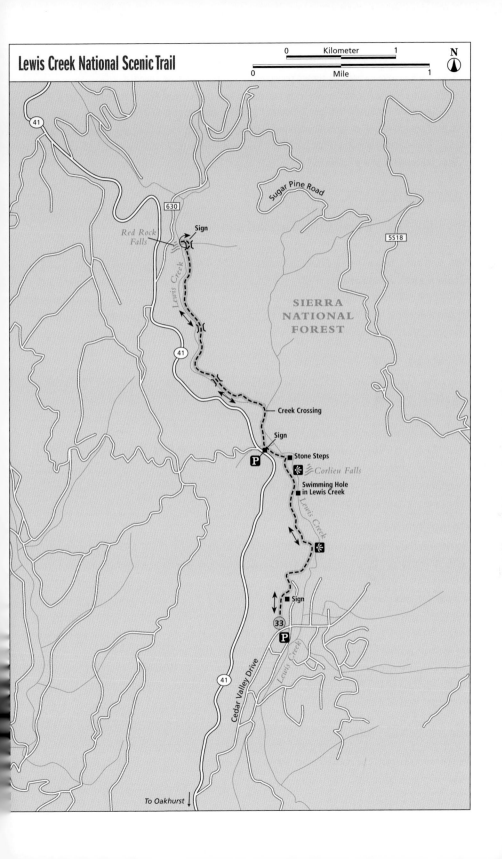

Lewis Creek National Scenic Trail

0 ___ Kilometer ___ 1
0 ___ Mile ___ 1

N

41

Sugar Pine Road

630

Sign

Red Rock Falls

Lewis Creek

5518

41

SIERRA NATIONAL FOREST

Creek Crossing

Sign

P

Stone Steps

Corlieu Falls

Swimming Hole in Lewis Creek

Lewis Creek

Sign

33

P

41

Cedar Valley Drive

Lewis Creek

To Oakhurst

2.5 Walk across a seasonal stream on wooden footbridge with log railing.

3.1 Walk across a seasonal stream on wooden footbridge with log railing.

3.15 Come to a trail junction with a sign for Sugar Pine 0.8, Corlieu Falls 1.7, Cedar Valley 3.2, and Red Rock Falls left. Turn left down the short, steep spur to Red Rock Falls.

3.2 Come to Red Rock Falls. Reward yourself and pooch with snacks before going back to the trailhead the way you came. Elevation: 4,179 feet. **GPS:** N37 26.02' / W119 38.17'

6.4 Arrive back at the trailhead.

Creature Comforts

Yosemite Sierra Visitors Bureau, (559) 683-4636.

Fueling Up

You will find major services in Oakhurst off CA 41, including Safeway.

Crab Cakes Restaurant, 49271 Golden Oak Loop, Oakhurst 93644; (559) 641-7667; crabcakesrestaurant.com. Outdoor patio to enjoy seafood and more with pooch.

Pizza Factory, 40120 CA 41, Oakhurst 93644; (559) 683-2700; pizzafactory.com. The place to satisfy cravings for hand-tossed pizza with 100 percent real mozzarella cheese.

Resting Up

Narrow Gauge Inn, 48571 CA 41, Fish Camp 93623; (559) 683-7720; narrow gaugeinn.com. Its rustic cozy charm roots go back to the original Swiss owners' vision when the inn was first built in the 1950s. The rooms and restaurant were upgraded by the current owners in 2000.

Best Western Plus–Yosemite Gateway Inn, 40530 CA 41, Oakhurst 93644; (559) 683-2378; yosemitegatewayinn.com. It's a relatively luxurious stay for a mountain town. The outdoor pool and indoor pool are unexpected bonuses. The onsite restaurant patio is dog-friendly.

Campgrounds

Summerdale Campground, CA 41, Fish Camp 93623; (559) 642-3212; recreation .gov. Most convenient to Lewis Creek and at a comfortable elevation for camping during hotter summer months.

There are other Forest Service campgrounds off CA 41. Visit fs.usda.gov/sierra and use the "quick link" menu on the right to route to the list of campgrounds in the Sierra National Forest south of Yosemite National Park. Reservations can be made at recreation.gov (877-444-6777) for campgrounds that accept reservations.

Wawona Campground in Yosemite National Park, Wawona 95389; (209) 375-9535; (877) 444-6777; nps.gov; recreation.gov; yosemite.com. The closest Yosemite National Park campground to Lewis Creek Trailhead.

Things to Do with Pooch

Narrow Gauge Railroad Train Ride; well-behaved dogs on leash are welcome to ride on the 4-mile historic route.

34 Indian Pools

This "one hike fits all" trail is easy, delightful, and easily accessed from a paved road at the back of China Peak Mountain Resort. Maps may still show this ski area as "Sierra Summit," as the property changed hands and was renamed about five years ago. Big Creek serves a series of idyllic pools along a mostly level to gentle-grade trail where pooches of all ages and energy levels can sniff, saunter, and swim.

Start: From the back of China Peak Mountain Resort gravel parking lot
Distance: 2.0 miles out and back
Hiking time: About 1.5 hours
Difficulty: Easy
Trailhead elevation: 7,073 feet
Highest point: 7,240 feet
Best season: Summer to fall
Trail surface: Dirt, rock, and granite slabs
Other trail users: Hikers only
Canine compatibility: Voice control
Land status: National forest
Fees and permits: None for hiking or camping, but permit required to use camping stoves; campfires prohibited. Check with ranger station for current and changing regulations regarding campfires and camping equipment with a flame.

Maps: USGS Huntington Lake; USFS Sierra National Forest; National Geographic Shaver Lake Trail Map
Trail contacts: Sierra National Forest, High Sierra Ranger District, 29688 Auberry Rd., Prather 93651; P.O. Box 559, Prather 93651; (559) 855-5355
Nearest town: Fresno is the closest full-service large city. Shaver Lake's mountain village services include a couple of gas stations, food, lodging, and campgrounds. Huntington Lake's smaller community is the closest to the trail with general store, gas station, restaurant, cabins, and campground.
Trail tips: The trailhead is identified with a wooden post and an information board for China Peak Ski Area. There are no toilets at the trailhead and no sign with the name of the trail. There is a recycling bin and a trashcan by the unmarked wooden post.

Finding the trailhead: From Fresno, drive 70 miles east on CA 168 to Huntington Lake. This is the Sierra Heritage Scenic Byway. Turn right at the China Peak Ski Area and drive 1 mile to the far end of the parking lot past the employee trailer housing and park in the gravel parking lot. A wooden post with a trashcan and a recycle bin identifies the unmarked trailhead. There's an information board with bulletins about China Peak resort to the left of the trailhead post. **GPS:** N37 14.05' / W119 09.00'

The Hike

This hidden gem begins on a forested trail and by 0.1 mile the trail opens up to the first of several inviting pools along the mile of trail you will travel. The trail is mostly flat, interrupted by short stretches of gentle uphill, threading around boulders and over granite slabs alongside Big Creek. You come to a flat area and the largest of the

Taking time to reflect at one of the Indian Pools

pools at 0.4 mile. The granite bench is so inviting, you might be tempted to call it a hike right there. Any dog would be happy to spend the rest of the day sniffing and scrambling around here.

The open landscape ahead is like walking through a rock and boulder garden sprinkled with ferns, pines, and coneflowers that remind you of mini sunflowers (green bushes).

Even on an early August afternoon in the fourth year of drought, Big Creek flowed enough to fill her pools and treat hikers to a few light cascades. It's as if Indian Pools is one of Mother Nature's secret stashes of wet beauty revealed as a treat while waiting out the dry cycle.

Athletic dogs will wag their way along the creek as you continue along this agility course. At 0.8 mile you come to a 10-foot waterfall and one of many perfect picnic spots. Just ahead, a granite slab interrupts the more visible creekside path and you have to traverse the large, sloping slab higher above the creek to drop back down to the shore of the long, narrow pool. At 1.0 mile you come to a rock peninsula that sits between the creek and a back pond. The rocky wedge is an ideal photo spot and snack-break roost before going back to the trailhead the way you came.

Miles and Directions

0.0 Start at the unmarked wooden post and China Peak information board at the far end of the gravel parking lot at China Peak Mountain Resort.

0.8 Come to a small, narrow waterfall where Big Creek drops 10 feet into a pool.

1.0 Come to a rock peninsula jutting out between the hidden back pond and far end of the long, narrow pool. The rocky peninsula makes a great perch for admiring the surrounding views in solitude with your canine pal. Go back to the trailhead the way you came. Elevation: 7,240 feet. **GPS:** N37 13.96' / W119 08.41'

2.0 Arrive back at the trailhead.

Creature Comforts

Fueling Up

Bob's Market, 41781 Tollhouse Rd., Shaver Lake 93664; (559) 841-7104. Grocery stop for your and your canine pal's favorite snacks.

Cressman's General Store, 36088 Tollhouse Rd., Shaver Lake 93664; (559) 841-2923; cressmans.org. Sandwiches, pizza, and prepared meals to go.

Hungry Hut, 42008 Tollhouse Rd., Shaver Lake 93664; (559) 841-3586. Come with an appetite and your dog.

Shaver Lake Pizza, 41820 Tollhouse Rd., Shaver Lake 939664; (559) 841-7249. Get a pizza to go if you and pooch are camping nearby.

China Peak Day Lodge, 59265 CA 168, Lakeshore (on Huntington Lake) 93634; (559) 233-2500; skichinapeak.com. At this time the ski resort offers summer food services on weekends only. The Day Lodge serves breakfast and lunch. Outdoor patio is dog friendly.

The Inn at China Peak Restaurant, (559) 233-1200. Only open for dinner on summer weekends, and dogs are welcome on the outdoor patio.

Resting Up

Shaver Lake Village Hotel, 42135 Tollhouse Rd., Shaver Lake 93664; (559) 841-8289; shaverlakevillagehotel.com. For pooches and their companions who prefer rooms to tents.

Campgrounds

There are several Forest Service campgrounds at Huntington Lake and nearby Shaver Lake; fs.usda.gov/sierra. Reservations can be made at recreation.gov, (877) 444-6777, for campgrounds that accept reservations. **Deer Creek Campground** is one of the most pleasant locations.

Camp Edison, Tollhouse Road, Shaver Lake 93664; (559) 841-3134; sce.com/campedison for reservations. The Southern California Electric Company has developed this 252-site campground, which has 43 sites with full hookups for trailers and RVs, cable TV, showers, flush toilets, Laundromat, general store, and boat rentals.

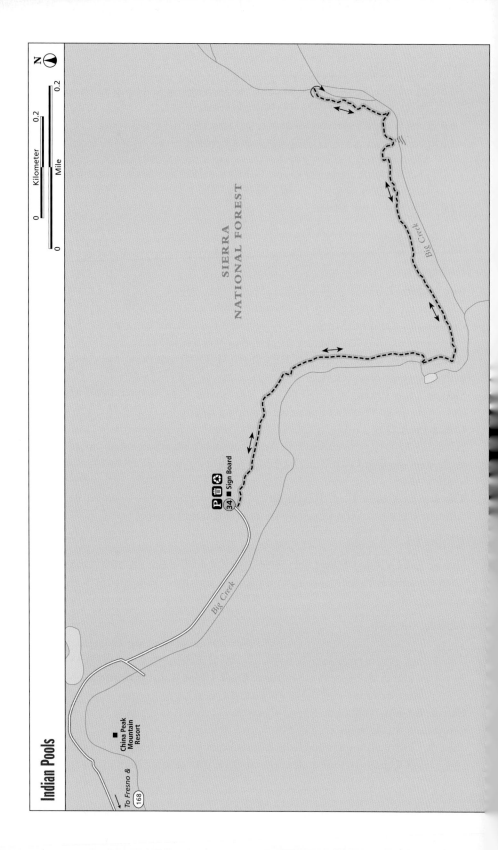

Big Creek cascades into the Indian Pools.

Puppy Paws and Golden Years

There is a lakeshore trail from several of the campgrounds on Huntington Lake as well as a day-use area with access to the lakeshore trail just past the Deer Creek Campground at Bear Cove.

Rancheria Falls National Recreation Trail is a short hike (under 2 miles round-trip with slight elevation change) that rewards you with a 150-foot waterfall. The turnoff for the falls is 1.5 miles past China Peak Ski Area on the right, and it's a 1-mile drive on a part dirt/part paved road from the turnoff to the parking area. The trailhead is to the right just beyond the vault toilet.

35 Hume Lake Loop

This is a level trail for dogs of all ages and stamina, with lots of forest scents and a lake for cooling paws. The hike can be completed as a loop, or pooped-out dogs can turn around and make it an out-and-back at any point. A necklace of interpretive signs about the area's natural and cultural history, wood benches, footbridges, and a couple of viewing decks enhance the excursion for humans tagging along. This easily accessed hike in Sequoia National Monument is extra special because of its proximity to Kings Canyon and Sequoia National Parks.

Start: From the Hume Lake Access parking lot between the toilet and the information board
Distance: 2.8-mile loop
Hiking time: About 1.5 hours
Difficulty: Easy
Trailhead elevation: 5,230 feet
Highest point: 5,241 feet
Best season: Spring, summer, and late fall
Trail surface: Dirt and pavement
Other trail users: Hikers only
Canine compatibility: On leash
Land status: National monument; national forest
Fees and permits: None
Maps: USGS Hume; Sequoia National Forest; Tom Harrison Sequoia and Kings Canyon National Parks Recreation Maps

Trail contacts: Giant Sequoia National Monument; Hume Lake Ranger District; 35860 E. Kings Canyon Rd., Dunlap 93621; (559) 338-2251
Nearest town: Fresno is the largest city; Grant Grove Village in Kings Canyon National Park has a market and restaurant.
Trail tips: There is a vault toilet, trash, and recycling bins in the parking area. Although this is in a national forest, the lake area is a popular recreation site in the summer and dogs must be on leash on the trail. They can dip in the lake, but on leash as well. Dogs are not allowed at the swimming beach at Sandy Cove.

Finding the trailhead: From Fresno drive 55 miles east on CA 180 to the Big Stump Entrance to Kings Canyon National Park. Drive 1.5 miles into the park and bear left toward Grant Grove Village. Drive 5.5 miles past Grant Grove Village to the Hume Lake turnoff on your right. Turn right to Hume Lake and drive 3 miles down the paved road to the fork and sign for Hume Lake Campground ¼ mile, Hume Lake Christian Camps 1¼ mile, Sandy Cove-Hume Lake 3 miles, Generals Highway 12. Bear left toward Hume Lake Campground. At the next sign, the campground is on the right. Bear left downhill for the lake access and parking. **GPS:** N36 47.54' / W118 54.39'

The Hike

Giant Sequoia National Monument's almost 330,00 acres are a relatively new monument designated by President Bill Clinton in 2000. The world's largest tree grows naturally on a 60-mile strip of the Western Sierra. This national monument also has the distinction of being adjacent to Kings Canyon National Park.

Enjoying Hume Lake's scenic setting

Hume Lake area was the site of commercial logging from the late 1800s into the early 1900s. What is now a popular recreation area was originally created as an 87-acre log-holding pond and a flume to carry logs down to the lumberyards in the San Joaquin Valley. One of the engineering attractions on this hike is the twelve-arch dam built in 1908 at the head of the lake.

Since this hike is a loop, you can walk in either direction from the lakeshore. This hike describes the trail walking in a counter-clockwise direction with the lake on your left. From the parking lot you walk down to the dirt trail, tracing the shoreline along a forested path where you come to the first of several interpretive signs along the way. This one describes the building of the dam.

At 0.6 mile you come to a picnic area with tables, grills, toilet, recycling, and trash bins. The Christian Camps compound is just ahead. You pass the Boathouse and snack shop on your right. There's a general store set back beyond the Boathouse. The Hume Lake Christian Camps has lodging and services open to the public. The deck at the Boathouse Snack Shop is dog friendly.

Continue following the lakeshore and come to your first footbridge. Looking eastward up the lake from here, you'll be surprised with a view of the Kings Canyon Park peaks in the distance. You rejoin the trail at 0.8 mile with the lake always on your left.

At about 1 mile the trail rises gently on a bouldered bench above the lake. You will come to your first viewing deck at 1.4 miles before rounding the lake at Sandy Cove on a boardwalk and raised footbridge above Tenmile Creek. Note that dogs are not allowed in the lake or the swimming beach area at Sandy Cove. Shortly after Sandy Cove the trail drops back down to the beach. You come to the dam at 2.3 miles and the trail continues across the lake below the dam just ahead on a raised footbridge above the outflow.

At 2.7 miles you will cross a seasonal stream on a wooden footbridge, and your loop ends 0.1 mile ahead. At the time of this hike in the summer of 2015, California was in its fourth season of drought and Lake Hume, like many bodies of fresh water in the state, was lower, exposing more shoreline as beach. Water-loving dogs will want you to indulge them with a dip before heading back up the trailhead to parking.

Miles and Directions

0.0 Start at the Hume Lake Access Parking Area between the vault toilet and the information board. Walk downhill to the lakeshore and turn right on the dirt trail.

0.6 Come to a picnic area. The Hume Lake Christian Camps compound is just ahead. Follow the shoreline through the Christian Camps.

0.7 Walk across one of the lake's inflowing seasonal streams on a footbridge. The mountain peaks rise on the eastern horizon.

0.8 You come to the Hume Lake Trail sign where you re-enter the forested trail with the lake on your left.

1.4 Come to a viewing deck overlooking the lake.

1.6 Come to Sandy Cove and the boardwalk with raised footbridge across Tenmile Creek.

2.3 Come to the dam and a lookout point.

2.4 Walk across the raised footbridge above the lake's outflow.

2.6 Walk across a seasonal stream on a wooden footbridge.

2.8 Come to the end of your loop and walk uphill to the trailhead.

Creature Comforts

Fueling Up

Grant Grove Village in Kings Canyon National Park has a well-supplied market to stop and pick up snacks and last-minute essentials.

Hume Lake Christian Camps is off CA 180 at Hume Lake. Drive 5.5 miles past Grant Grove Village and turn right for Hume Lake. Drive 3 miles down the road to Hume Lake and follow the sign for the Christian Camps. The general store and Boathouse Snack Bar are open to the public. The outdoor patio at the Boathouse Snack Bar is dog friendly. You walk through the Christian Camps property on your hike, and these food-refueling stations are on the right of the trail.

Hume Lake Loop

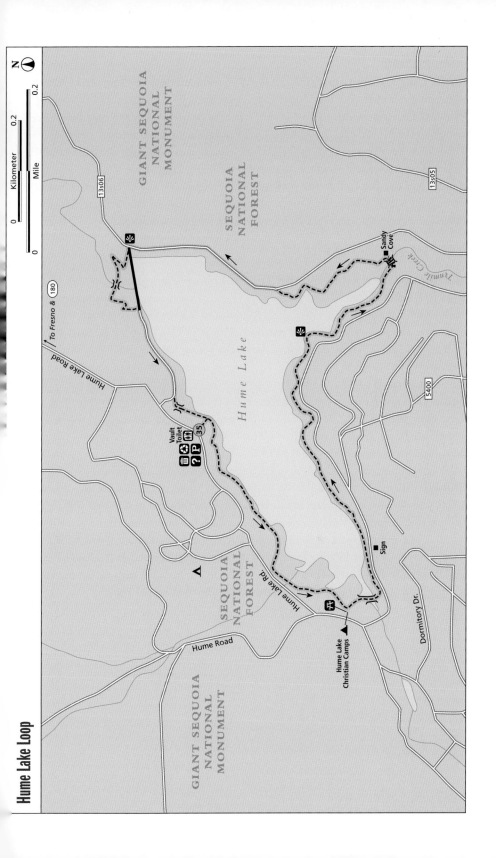

Campgrounds

Hume Lake Campground, (877) 444-6777; recreation.gov, at Hume Lake off CA 180 is on the doorstep of the Hume Lake Loop hike.

Princess Campground, (877) 444-6777; recreation.gov, is only 0.5 mile before the turnoff to the Hume Lake Loop hike. Quiet and pleasant forest setting.

There are other campgrounds in the Grant Grove area of the Kings Canyon National Park within reasonable distance to the Hume Lake Loop hike. Visit fs.usda.gov/sequoia and use the "quick link" menu on the right to route to the list of campgrounds in Sequoia National Forest by region. Reservations can be made at (877) 444-6777 or recreation.gov for campgrounds that accept reservations.

Puppy Paws and Golden Years

Indian Basin Grove Interpretive Trail in Princess Campground off CA 180, 5 miles past Grant Grove Village. Follow the signs for the trailhead on the paved spur road straight ahead as you enter the campground. There is room for about three vehicles in the parking area by the restroom. This is an easy, flat, paved 0.5-mile loop with an optional 0.5-mile dirt loop through the young sequoia grove past some historic giant sequoia ghost stumps. The open views across Indian Basin Meadow are an added visual treat.

Boole Tree is a 2-mile loop and a chance for your bow-wow to leave his mark on the trail of the largest (270-foot-tall) of the sequoia trees in the national forest. The turnoff for Boole Tree is 4 miles past Grant Grove Village in Kings Canyon National Park. Turn left on Forest Service Road 13S55 at the sign for Boole Tree and drive 2.5 miles on a bumpy dirt road, following the signs to the trailhead parking.

Chicago Stump is a sad sight for humans who understand that cutting down a 3,200-year-old tree to impress crowds at the 1878 World's Fair in Chicago was a tragedy and not an exploit. But to your pooch, this short 0.5-mile jaunt to the gargantuan stump is just another feast of scent ecstasy. Drive 3 miles past Grant Grove Village in Kings Canyon National Park and turn left on eroded dirt Forest Service Road 13S03 for 1.8 miles to FR 13S66. Turn right and drive 0.1 mile to the turnout on the right and park. The trailhead is about 100 yards down the road on the right.

36 Trail of 100 Giants

There are three good reasons to hike this paved, ADA–accessible loop trail: It's easy enough for hikers and dogs of any age. It's a rare opportunity to hike with Fido in a national monument. You will be humbled while your dog will be in scent heaven in this rich sequoia cathedral of magnificent giants.

Start: From the Trail of 100 Giants trailhead on the Western Divide Highway/M107
Distance: 1.5-mile loop
Hiking time: About 1 hour
Difficulty: Easy
Trailhead elevation: 6,200 feet
Highest point: 6,244 feet
Best season: Spring, summer, and fall (road closed Oct 15 to May 15 depending on snow)
Trail surface: Dirt
Other trail users: None
Canine compatibility: On leash
Land status: National monument
Fees and permits: Parking fee

Maps: USGS Johnsondale; Sequoia National Forest/Monument Guide to Trail of 100 Giants
Trail contacts: Sequoia National Forest Western Divide Ranger District, 32588 CA 190, Springville 93265; (559) 539-2607; fs.usda.gov/sequoia
Nearest town: Kernville to the south and Springville to the north.
Trail tips: The parking area is on the east side of the road and is a day-use area with 2 vault toilets, picnic tables, and trash containers. There is no water in the parking lot or on the trail.

Finding the trailhead: From Kernville at the intersection of Kernville Road and Sierra Way/M99, drive 30 miles north on Sierra Way/M99 (it becomes M50) to the intersection of Western Divide Highway/M107. Turn right on Western Divide Highway/M107 and follow the sign to Trail of 100 Giants. Drive 2 miles on Western Divide Highway/M107. The trail sign is on your left, but the day-use parking lot is on your right just before the Redwood Campground. No parking on the road shoulders allowed. Walk across the road from the parking lot in the crosswalk to the trailhead sign for the Trail of 100 Giants. **GPS:** N35 58.61' / W118 35.77'
    From Springville on CA 190, drive 36 miles north (CA 190 becomes M107) to the Trail of 100 Giants sign on your right just past the Redwood Campground. The day-use parking lot is on your left. No parking on the road shoulders allowed. Walk across the road from the parking lot in the crosswalk to the trailhead sign for the Trail of 100 Giants. **GPS:** N35 58.61' / W118 35.77'

The Hike

President Bill Clinton protected the giant wonders by establishing the Giant Sequoia National Monument in 2000. Sequoias are considered the largest trees in the world and only grow on a narrow corridor of the western slopes of California's Sierra Nevada Range between 5,000- and 7,500-foot elevations. The monument comprises almost 330,000 acres, and the Trail of 100 Giants in the Long Meadow Grove is located in the southern portion.

The paved trail meanders through this protected grove for close-up views of these majestic sentinels. Several wooden footbridges and strategically placed "meditation" benches along the path add to the aura of magic in this pocket of the Sequoia National Forest.

The best way to savor this hike and see the most impressive of these towering specimens is to bear left on the multi-loop path as you follow the numbered interpretive signs from 1 to 20.

Gazing at a recent fallen giant

At 0.1 mile you come to a trail junction for the campground across the road to the right and the Trail of 100 Giants continuing straight. Follow the arrow straight on the Trail of 100 Giants.

At 0.4 mile and number 9 of the interpretive signs, you come to the fallen twin sequoias. The 1,500-year-old twins attached at the roots toppled, blocking off access to parts of the path, in 2011. This is one of the most dramatic points of interest where you can stand in the shadow of the 17-foot root base in awe as you look down the massive length of this casualty of time. Visitors get a unique opportunity to examine this ancient gem from tip to toe, while pooch's nose goes into overdrive with the rich bouquet of disturbed soil and duff. A boardwalk is being constructed parallel to the fallen sequoias to restore complete access to everyone on the path. A German tourist captured a few seconds of video as the trees were falling (see YouTube for 2011 falling sequoias on Trail of 100 Giants).

At 1.2 miles you come to a trail junction for the campground to the left across the road. This is the only place on the trail where you will bear right rather than left to complete the loop. Points of interest and interpretive signs 18, 19, and 20 are ahead. Follow the signs to the parking lot to return to the trailhead when you rejoin the main path after number 20.

Miles and Directions

0.0 Start at the trailhead sign for Trail of 100 Giants on the west side of Great Western Divide Highway across from the day-use parking lot.

Trail of 100 Giants

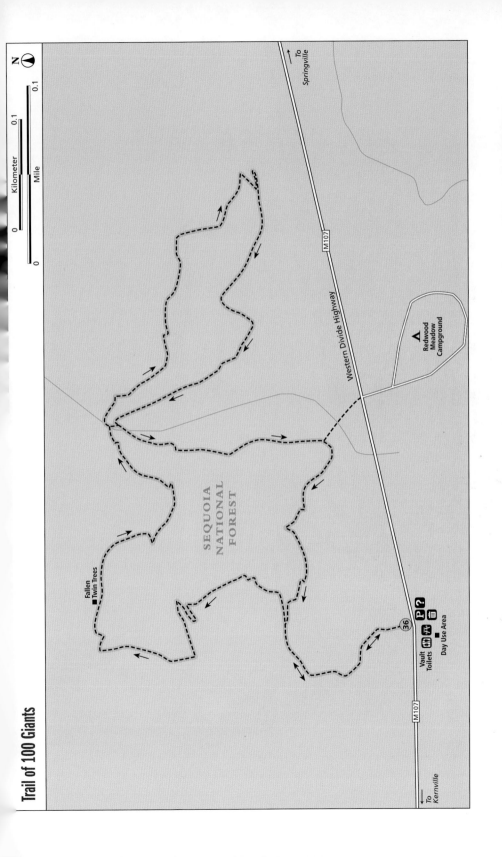

Resting on a giant's shoulder

0.1 Come to a trail junction for the campground to the right and Trail of 100 Giants straight. This is where you will close your loop from the right when you complete the hike. Continue walking straight and bear left at all trail junctions.

0.4 Come to the fallen twin sequoias of 2011 across the trail.

1.2 Come to a trail junction for the campground left. Bear right to close your loop and rejoin the main path back to the trailhead and parking lot.

1.5 Arrive back at the trailhead and walk in the crosswalk to cross the road to the parking lot and day-use area.

Creature Comforts

Fueling Up

The Ponderosa Lodge, 56692 Aspen Dr., Springville 93265; (559) 542-2579; brewersponderosalodge.com. General store for supplies. Well-behaved canine diners welcome on the restaurant deck.

Resting Up

The Ponderosa Lodge, 56692 Aspen Dr., Springville 93265; (559) 542-2579; brewersponderosalodge.com. Owner Mary and Bailey, her 4-year-old min pin (miniature Doberman pinscher) welcome sociable pooches that travel with good manners and responsible owners. Refundable deposit.

Campgrounds

Redwood Meadow Campground off Western Divide Highway, 0.25 mile west of Trail of 100 Giants day-use parking lot; Western Divide Ranger District, (559) 539-2607; (877) 444-6777; recreation.gov. There was no water available in this campground in 2015, so best to call the ranger district for current water status.

Puppy Paws and Golden Years

There's a beautiful meadow for strolling with your pooch at the back of the Trail of 100 Giants day-use area.

37 Whiskey Flat Trail

This is an easy 2-mile hike in the Upper Kern River Canyon, conveniently accessible from the quaint town of Kernville. This is a chance to enjoy some Southern Sierra views and for your dog to soak his paws and maybe take a dip in the snow-fed Wild and Scenic Kern River.

Start: From Whiskey Flat Trailhead at the end of Burlando Road
Distance: 2.2 miles out and back
Hiking time: About 1.5 hours
Difficulty: Easy
Trailhead elevation: 2,731 feet
Highest point: 2,751 feet
Best season: Year-round. Spring boasts wildflowers, while fall and winter bring solitude. Summers can be beastly hot.
Trail surface: Dirt and rock
Other trail users: Horses and bicycles
Canine compatibility: Voice control
Land status: National forest
Fees and permits: None

Maps: USGS Kernville; Sequoia National Forest
Trail contacts: Sequoia National Forest Kern River Ranger District, 105 Whitney Rd., Kernville 93238; (760) 376-3781; fs.fed.us/R5/sequoia/contactus
Nearest town: Kernville
Trail tips: There are no day-use amenities at the trailhead and no water. In a normal snowpack year, unlike the drought years of 2011–2015, the Kern River is as wild as it is scenic, so a leash is safer for dogs that go bonkers around water. The swift flow along some stretches where recreational visitors have taken to the water too casually without proper safety gear has earned it the nickname "killer Kern."

Finding the trailhead: From Kernville at the intersection of Kernville Road and Burlando Road, turn north on Burlando Road in the direction of the Forest Service Station indicated by the sign at the corner of Burlando Road. Drive 2 miles to the end of Burlando Road to the dirt parking area. The Whiskey Flat trailhead is to the right of the white fence and gate. **GPS:** N35 46.58' / W118 26.72'

The Hike

The Kern River, and to a lesser extent Kernville, are the highlights of this short, easy excursion above and along the banks of the Kern River. The Kern River was named by explorer John C. Frémont in honor of Edward Kern, the topographer on Frémont's 1845 expedition, when they came to the fork of two rivers where man-made Lake Isabella now sits.

The headwaters of the Kern are in the high Sierra region of Mount Whitney where snowmelt feeds the river along its almost 200-mile journey through canyons in the Southern Sierra Mountains. The Kern is the only major Sierra Nevada river to drain south. It is part of the Golden Trout Complex, home to the rare and beautiful California freshwater state fish. The Kern River once flowed freely, transforming California's Central Valley into wetlands and seasonal lakes. The Kern River Canyon is

Looking across the Kern River at Yellow Jacket Peak

geologically active and the dam system that sits on a fault below Kernville at Lake Isabella is slated for significant seismic retrofitting and safety upgrades to be completed over the next several years.

Kernville was first founded as Rogersville during the 1858 Gold Rush. It was renamed Williamsburg and eventually was known as Whiskey Flats until it was renamed Kernville in 1864. In 1948 the Isabella Dam project forced Kernville's relocation upstream, where the town now stands at the picturesque tip of the northeast fork of Lake Isabella and recreational area.

The small town retains its charming frontier look and tourist appeal. Although whitewater rafting is the primary visitor attraction, camping is popular and riverside hikes like the trail from Whiskey Flats enhance visits to Kernville. In springtime, mild weather and wildflower blooms make the 1-mile stretch of trail from the Whiskey Flats trailhead especially pleasant.

In fall 2015 at the time we traveled this trail, a four-year drought had taken its toll on the riparian habitats along the river and in the dry creek tributaries, making the scars of the 2010 Bull Fire more evident. Nevertheless, the Kern River was flowing with surprising volume, enhancing the surrounding rugged mountain scenery.

The well-worn trail begins in a high desert meadow corridor of buckwheat brush and fragrant purple-flower poodle-dog brush braced by private land on either side. The beginning of the trail is partially on a stretch of land described by Sequoia National Forest's assistant recreational officer as a "handshake" easement until the deal is finalized with completion of the NEPA report (National Environmental Protection Act). The river is hidden from sight by deciduous vegetation, burned gray pine and scrub oak woodland, and a sprinkling of houses along the dirt county road on your right. After 0.4 mile the rural residential neighborhood is behind you, but you can hear occasional traffic on Highway M-99/Sierra Way threading up the canyon on the opposite bank of the Kern River. The piping going up the mountain across the canyon is part of a turbine electricity-generating plant.

At 0.6 mile you will see a spur coming in from your right and a rustic footbridge ahead with an assist rope overhead. In 2015 Bull Creek dried up for the first time in locals' memory and you could walk across the dry creek bed. But during average years of snowpack, the bridge is the only way across and the creek may be seasonally impassable at the height of snowmelt.

Walk across the creek bed or the bridge and bear right. The landscape opens up with brush, boulders, and expansive views of the mountains and some jagged granite peaks.

You begin to hear the river after .05 mile and the river comes into view at 1 mile. This is the first appropriate access for dogs to cool their paws. Depending on the flow, keep your dog safe on leash and/or with a life jacket.

Walk 0.1 mile farther up the trail for an unobstructed view of the rapids and Yellow Jacket Peak to the east. This is a superb viewpoint and a perfect picnic perch before going back the way you came. The steeper boulder slope prevents safe access to the river at this spot.

If you decide to extend your hike farther, the trail continues up the canyon but veers away from the river, tracing the base of the slope on your left uphill. The landscape is rather stark from here on.

Miles and Directions

0.0 Start at the Whiskey Flat Trailhead at the end of Burlando Road.

0.6 Come to a spur coming in from the right and a rustic wooden footbridge ahead. Walk across Bull Run Creek on the footbridge and bear right on the trail.

1.0 The Kern River comes into view with access to the shore on your right.

1.1 Come to an expansive clearing above the Kern River with views across the canyon to Yellow Jacket Peak. Enjoy the rush of the river and the views with a snack and a drink of water for you and pooch. Go back to the trailhead the way you came. Elevation: 2,751 feet. **GPS:** N35 47.42' / W118 27.02'

2.2 Arrive back at the trailhead.

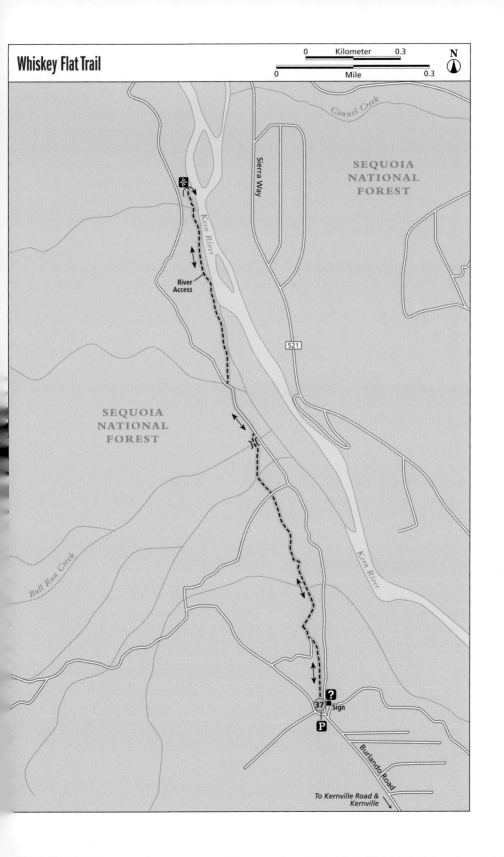

Creature Comforts

Fueling Up

The Sierra Gateway Market, 13432 Sierra Way, Kernville 93238; (760) 376-2424. It's a well-stocked grocery store with a deli and basic camping supplies.

That's Italian Restaurant, 9 Big Blue Rd., Kernville 93238; (760) 376-6020. This is traditional Italian cuisine with red-checkered tablecloths and soft dinner music. It doesn't get more romantic than that for patio dining with your four-legged date.

Pizza Barn, 11401 Kernville Rd., Kernville 93238; (760) 376-1856; pizzabarn.com. The water bowl on the deck is a nice welcoming touch for furry customers.

Resting Up

The Kern Lodge, 67 Valley View Dr., Kernville 93238; (760) 376-2223; thekern lodge.com. Two dog-friendly rooms. Rocky and Rollie are your canine hosts and Tiger Lilly and Lukie are the feline mascots.

Riverview Lodge, 2 Sirretta St., Kernville 93238; (760) 376-6019; riverviewlodge .net. This dog-friendly historic lodge is a piece of western history. Built in the early 1900s in Old Kernville as The Mountain Inn, it was relocated upstream in the 1950s when Lake Isabella was created by the dam.

Pinecone Inn, 86 Valley View Dr., Kernville 93238; (760) 376-6669; pinecone-inn .com. Roberta, the inn's proprietor, and her German shepherd, Fritzky, welcome well-mannered canine guests.

Campgrounds

Camp James, 13801 Sierra Way, Kernville 93238; (760) 376-6119; campjames.net. Tent and RV sites. There are restrictions on certain dog breeds.

Sequoia National Forest Campground near Kernville; (760) 376-3781; fs.usda .gov/sequoia. Reservations can be made at recreation.gov (877-444-6777) for campgrounds that accept reservations.

Puppy Paws and Golden Years

Take a riverside stroll on the paved path in **Kernville's Riverside Park** on Kernville Road. There are flush toilets, picnic tables, and a grassy area to relax with a leashed pooch. There's even a seasonal beach depending on the Kern River flow.

East Side of Southern Sierra Nevada

38 Treasure Lakes

This hike, which feels like it is set in a rugged granite amphitheater, is an up-and-down-and-up-again trail with a moderate grade. Hardy pooches and their human companions are rewarded with stupendous scenery, multiple seasonal streams for cool-off splashes, and wildflowers on the way to two lovely Treasure Lakes guarded by granite sentries.

Start: From Bishop Pass Trailhead at South Lake parking lot
Distance: 6.2 miles out and back
Hiking time: About 4 hours
Difficulty: Strenuous
Trailhead elevation: 9,828 feet
Highest point: 10,680 feet
Best season: Summer to fall
Trail surface: Dirt, rock, granite, and tree roots
Other trail users: Horses
Canine compatibility: Voice control
Land status: National forest
Fees and permits: Permits for overnight camping in the wilderness (Wilderness Permit Office, 760-873-2483, recreation.gov). Check with ranger station about the status of campfire permits and restrictions, which vary by season, trail, and elevation.

Maps: USGS Mount Thompson; Inyo National Forest; John Muir Wilderness; National Geographic Mammoth Lakes and Mono Divide Trail Map; Tom Harrison Bishop Pass
Trail contacts: Inyo National Forest, White Mountain Ranger Station, 798 N. Main St., Bishop 93914; (760) 873-2500 (this number has an excellent menu of information options); fs.usda.gov/inyo
Nearest town: Bishop
Trail tips: There are 2 vault toilets, trash dumpster, recycling bins, and bear-proof food storage lockers in the parking lot. There are 2 day-use parking lots and 1 upper overnight parking lot. Soft-padded pooches will need booties for the rockier stretches and chafing granite slabs. Treasure Lakes is a good overnight destination for beginner backpackers and their canine companions.

Finding the trailhead: From Bishop, at the intersection of US 395 and CA 168/West Line Road turn west on CA 168/West Line Road toward the Sierra mountain range. The high desert landscape alive with sage will transition to pine and aspen forest as you climb into the granite basin. Drive 14.7 miles and turn left at the South Lake turnoff. Drive 7 miles, paralleling the South Fork Bishop Creek, along the paved South Lake Road. South Lake Road ends at the South Lake boat launch facility where bait, tackle, and snack foods are sold. The trailhead is to the left of the vault toilets and the information board in the upper overnight parking lot. **GPS:** N37 10.16' / W118 33.95'

The Hike

Looking up from US 395 in Bishop across the high desert plain to the stark Sierra range that walls the Pacific Coast from the eastern deserts, it's difficult to imagine that the long, winding journey up West Line Road will pass pleasant campgrounds and a couple of inviting cabin resorts on the aspen-lined South Fork Bishop Creek before dropping you at the foot of an alpine paradise. But it does. The South Lake Basin is your portal to the John Muir Wilderness and the shores of two lovely Treasure Lakes.

The trail begins with about twenty-one stone steps down, followed by a gentle 0.5-mile climb above the exposed north shore of South Lake before veering east into a pine forest and soon entering the John Muir Wilderness.

At 0.8 mile you come to the trail junction for Bishop Pass to the left and Treasure Lakes to the right. At 1.0 you cross your first seasonal creek on a wooden footbridge. In the summer, this creek bed is a bouquet of purple monkshood flowers. The trail continues on its gently rising course for another 0.2 mile. You arrive at a rise with grand views of the peaks and the veins of pines highlighting the granite faces before beginning a descent on the side of the hill along a crushed granite path.

South Fork Bishop Creek splits into two forks just above at 1.5 miles where you cross South Fork Bishop creek on a footbridge, with the next crossing of South Fork Bishop Creek on rocks and tree limbs just 0.05 mile ahead. You come to an unmarked stream (outflow of Treasure Lakes) where it meanders through an inviting meadow at 1.9 miles. The bench meadow with its murmuring creek is a very pleasing destination for a picnic and romp before returning to the trailhead the way you came if you and pooch aren't up to the final mile of switchbacks to Treasure Lakes.

Up until now there has been some shade through the sparse forest, but the last mile of switchbacks to the lakes is a stiffer grade across exposed granite slabs where the trail is visible but less defined. Follow the ribbons of dirt where boots have worn

BEST BOW WOW BREAKS ALONG US 395

Puppy Paws and Golden Years

Your best bets for pups and seniors to get a whiff of the great outdoors at their pace (on leash) on the east side of the Southern Sierra, if you are traveling south on US 395 from the north, are in the town of Mammoth Lakes, 40 miles north of Bishop. The recreational trail along gurgling Mammoth Creek begins in the community park on Old Mammoth Road with parking on both the east and west sides of the road. Flat Snowcreek Meadow trail on the west side of Median Boulevard behind Snowcreek Condominiums is a delight for dogs of all ages.

If you are traveling north on the east side of the Southern Sierra from the south on US 395, expect long, scenic but isolated stretches. Fossil Falls, 1.1 miles off US 395 on a well-graded gravel road, is 45 miles south of Lone Pine.

Huffing past South Lake

a narrow path. At 2.2 miles, catch your breath while delighting in the expansive view of South Lake below. The grade mellows a little farther ahead and the water washes the granite slab above where you cross the outflow of Treasure Lakes on a double log. Continue walking uphill to the shore of the first and larger of the two Treasure Lakes embraced by a granite cirque. Follow the unmarked spur to the left to 3.1 miles and arrive at the second Treasure Lake, a smaller, shallower gem where your dog can frolic in the shadow of Hurd Peak's granite sentry. Find a sun-warmed rock to share a well-deserved snack with your furry friend before going back to the trailhead the way you came.

Miles and Directions

0.0 Start at the Bishop Pass trailhead at the south end of the South Lake parking lot. The trail sign is to the left of the information boards. Follow the trail climbing above the north shore of South Lake.

0.6 The trail veers eastward away from South Lake.

0.7 Enter John Muir Wilderness at the posted sign.

0.8 Come to a trail junction for Treasure Lakes to the right and Bishop Pass to the left. Turn right to Treasure Lakes.

1.0 Walk across a seasonal stream on a wooden footbridge.

1.5 Walk across South Fork Bishop Creek on a wooden footbridge.

1.55 Walk across South Fork Bishop Creek on rocks and tree limbs.

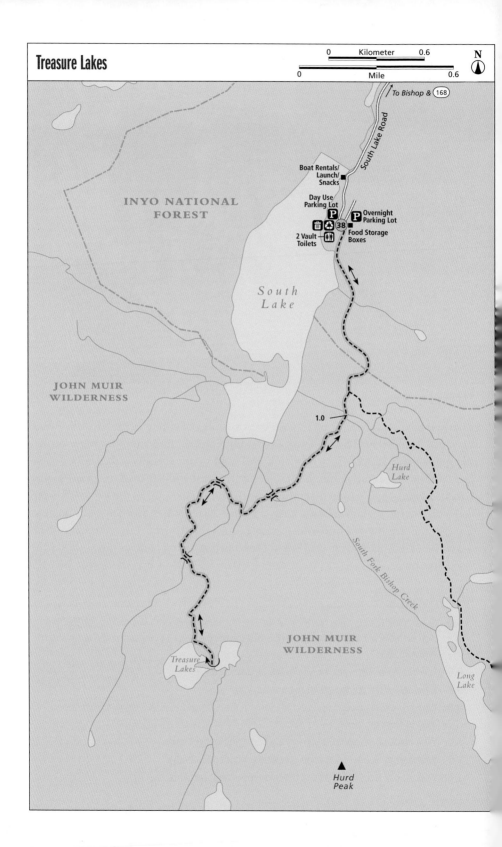

Treasure Lakes

0   Kilometer   0.6

0   Mile   0.6

N

To Bishop & 168

South Lake Road

Boat Rentals/
Launch/
Snacks

Day Use
Parking Lot

P

P   Overnight
Parking Lot

38   Food Storage
Boxes

2 Vault
Toilets

INYO NATIONAL
FOREST

South
Lake

JOHN MUIR
WILDERNESS

1.0

Hurd
Lake

South Fork Bishop Creek

JOHN MUIR
WILDERNESS

Treasure
Lakes

Long
Lake

Hurd
Peak

1.9 Walk across the stream flowing out of Treasure Lakes, on a double log footbridge. This small bench meadow and the sinewy stream is a perfect destination for pooped-out pooches and their human companions, who don't care for more uphill to the Treasure Lakes.

2.4 Walk across the outflow of Treasure Lakes on a double log footbridge.

2.9 Come to the first and larger of the two Treasure Lakes on your right. Bear left on the unmarked spur ahead to go to the second Treasure Lake.

3.1 Arrive at the second and smallest of the two Treasure Lakes on your left. Enjoy the solitude and scenery with your furry friend before going back to the trailhead the way you came. Elevation: 10,672 feet. **GPS:** N37 08.72' / W118 34.52'

6.2 Arrive back at the trailhead.

Creature Comforts

Fueling Up

Hing's Donuts, 905 N. Main St., Bishop 93514; (760) 872-4369. For a trail-size crunchy apple fritter.

Schat's Bakery, 763 N. Main St., Bishop 93514; (760) 873-7156; erikschatsbakery .com. Great spot to pick up picnic goodies, from "Natural California Turkey" for oven-roasted turkey sandwiches on fresh-baked breads to an array of sweet treats. The small outdoor dog-friendly patio has umbrellas for shade and fills up fast at peak hours. The bakery is known for its "Original Sheepherder Bread" brought to the Owen's Valley during the Gold Rush by Basque sheepherders.

Burger Barn, 2675 W. Line St., Bishop 93514; (760) 920-6567; bishopburgerbarn .com. Bishop's best-kept secret is a funky roadside joint committed to "fresh and locally grown." They deliver a quality burger and other freshly grilled options at a bargain. Their homemade ice cream sandwiched between two oatmeal chocolate-chip cookies hits the sweet-tooth spot. Outside tables with cooling overhead misters let you comfortably dine outdoors with bowser.

Bishop Creek Lodge, 2100 S. Lake Rd., Bishop 93514; (760) 873-4484; info@ bishopcreeklodge.com and on Facebook. Store with staples and a cafe. Picnic table outside for dining with pooch. Delicious fresh-baked pies daily.

Parchers Resort, 5001 S. Lake Rd., Bishop 93514; (760) 873-4177; parchersresort .net. Snack shop and cafe, weekday breakfast, and weekend brunches. Dog-friendly deck.

Cardinal Village, 321 Cardinal Rd., Bishop 93514; (760) 873-4789; cardinalvillage resort.com. (Off CA168/Sabrina Lake Road in Aspendell residential community). Among other grill items, it's the best grilled-cheese sandwich in the Eastern Sierra, and a dog-friendly deck.

Farmers' Market, on Church St. off US 395, behind City Hall; Sue Chudy, (760) 937-6768. Saturday 9:00 a.m. to 12:00 noon. Seasonal schedule determined by beginning and end of growing season, weather dependent.

Resting Up

There are several pet-friendly motels in Bishop, including some brand names like Best Western, Holiday Inn Express, Travelodge, and other chains. Bringfido.com is a good resource for dog-friendly lodging. The pet fee and house rules vary per establishment.

Parcher's Resort, 5001 S. Lake Rd., Bishop 93514; (760) 873-4177; parchersresort .net. Dog-friendly housekeeping cabins and hiker cabins with kitchenettes for backpackers who want to acclimate before setting off to higher elevation.

Bishop Creek Lodge, 2100 S. Lake Rd., Bishop 93514; (760) 873-4484; info@ bishopcreeklodge.com. Dog-friendly housekeeping cabins and hiker cabins with kitchenettes for backpackers wishing to acclimate before setting off to higher elevation.

Campgrounds

Creekside RV, 1949 S. Lake Rd., Bishop 93514; (760) 873-4483; bishopcreeksiderv .com. It's dusty and crowded, but a fallback option if you want hookups for your trailer or RV.

Parchers Resort, 5001 S. Lake Rd., Bishop 93514; (760) 873-4177; parchersresort .net. There are three RV sites with hookups.

There are several National Forest Service campgrounds along CA 168 and South Lake Road. Visit fs.usda.gov/inyo and use the "quick link" menu on the right to route to the list of campgrounds in Inyo National Forest by region. Reservations can be made at recreation.gov (877-444-6777) for campgrounds that accept reservations.

Puppy Paws and Golden Years

Bishop Dog Park, at the east end of the Bishop City Park off North Main Street between Yaney and Bruce Streets; bishopdogpark.org, is a good place for some safe off-leash romp time. The dog park has water, benches, a couple of trees for shade, and separate fenced areas for small and large hounds. The dog park was set up as a nonprofit corporation and accepts donations.

Approximately 4 miles up South Lake Road from the South Lake turnoff of CA 168/ West Line Road, watch for a parking area on the right shoulder with a picnic table set in the meadow, where the **South Fork Bishop Creek** makes a gentle run on its course downhill. South Fork Bishop Creek is popular with anglers and this pocket is perfect for a leisurely stroll with less-youthful dogs or pups too young for the high country.

Your best bets for pups and seniors to get a whiff of the great outdoors at their pace (on leash) when traveling along US 395 in the Eastern Sierra are in the town of **Mammoth Lakes.** The recreational trail along gurgling Mammoth Creek begins in the community park on Old Mammoth Road with parking on both the east and west sides of the road. Flat Snowcreek Meadow Trail on the west side of Median Boulevard behind Snowcreek condominiums is a delight for dogs of all ages.

39 Long Lake

For those who have had a couple of days to acclimate to the altitude, lovely Long Lake in the John Muir Wilderness is a moderate hike with an extremely scenic gradual ascent above angler-dotted South Lake. Less-acclimated hikers should make it a cooler morning jaunt with more time for "catch your breath" stops on the shadier stretches. Your dog will love bounding across the occasional seasonal streams up to the lakeside meadow where you can enjoy his antics from the shoreline boulders. The scenery and not the altitude will take your breath away at Long Lake.

Start: From Bishop Pass Trailhead at South Lake parking lot
Distance: 4.4 miles out and back
Hiking time: About 2.5 hours
Difficulty: Moderate
Trailhead elevation: 9,828 feet
Highest point: 10,752 feet
Best season: Summer to fall
Trail surface: Dirt and rock
Other trail users: Horses
Canine compatibility: Voice control
Land status: National forest; wilderness
Fees and permits: Permits for overnight camping in the wilderness (Wilderness Permit Office, 760-873-2483, recreation.gov). Check with ranger station about the status of campfire permits and restrictions, which vary by season, trail, and elevation.

Maps: USGS Mount Thompson; USFS Inyo National Forest; John Muir Wilderness; National Geographic Mammoth Lakes and Mono Divide Trail Map; Tom Harrison Bishop Pass
Trail contacts: Inyo National Forest, White Mountain Ranger Station, 798 N. Main St., Bishop 93914; (760) 873-2500 (this number has an excellent menu of information options); fs.usda.gov/inyo
Nearest town: Bishop
Trail tips: There are 2 vault toilets, trash dumpster, recycling bins, and bear-proof food storage lockers in the parking lot. There are 2 day-use parking lots and one upper overnight parking lot. Soft-padded pooches may need booties on the rockier stretches.

Finding the trailhead: From Bishop, at the intersection of US 395 and CA 168/West Line Road turn west on CA168/West Line Road toward the Sierra mountain range. The high desert landscape alive with sage will transition to pine and aspen forest as you climb into the granite basin. Drive 14.7 miles and turn left at the South Lake turnoff. Drive 7 miles paralleling the South Fork Bishop Creek along the paved South Lake Road. South Lake Road ends at the South Lake boat launch area where bait, tackle, and snack foods are sold. The trailhead is to the left of the vault toilets and the information board in the upper overnight parking lot. **GPS:** N37 10.16' / W118 33.95'

The Hike

Looking up from US 395 in Bishop across the high desert plain to the stark Sierra range that walls the Pacific Coast from the eastern deserts, it's difficult to imagine that the long winding journey up West Line Road will pass pleasant campgrounds and a

Taking time to goof around at Long Lake

couple of inviting cabin resorts on the aspen-lined South Fork Bishop Creek before dropping you at the foot of an alpine paradise. But it does. The South Lake Basin is your portal to the John Muir Wilderness and the shores of postcard-perfect Long Lake.

The trail begins with about twenty-one stone steps down, followed by a gentle 0.5-mile climb above the exposed north shore of South Lake before veering east into a pine forest. Along the way, you will cross two footbridges at seasonal streams. These refreshing stops for your pooch give you time to enjoy the summer display of deep pink shooting stars, white ranger buttons, and purple lupine.

The trail is well traveled, with only two junctions and one unmarked fork. The first junction is shortly after entering the John Muir Wilderness. This is the junction for Treasure Lakes to the right and Bishop Pass to the left. You will bear left toward Bishop Pass.

At 1.4 miles you come to a trail junction for Marie Louise Lakes to the left. Continue walking straight. Your second and last footbridge is at 1.5 miles. A few gradual switchbacks mark the last huff and puff before reaching an unmarked fork in the trail. Bear right at the fork. The trail ends with a slight incline before the plateau as you approach the head of Long Lake and its lush meadow on the left below Chocolate Peak. You can call it a day at any time and lay out the snacks on granite boulders or explore the lake's long, flat shoreline while gawking at the Inconsolable Range on the left and 12,237-foot Hurd Peak on your right.

Miles and Directions

0.0 Start at the Bishop Pass trailhead at the south end of the South Lake parking lot. The trail sign is to the left of the information boards. Follow the trail climbing above the north shore of South Lake.

0.6 The trail veers eastward away from South Lake.

0.7 Enter John Muir Wilderness at the posted sign.

0.8 Come to a trail junction for Treasure Lakes to the right and Bishop Pass to the left. Bear left toward Bishop Pass.

1.0 Walk across a seasonal stream on a footbridge.

1.4 Come to a trail junction for Marie Louise Lakes on the left. Continue walking straight.

1.5 Walk across a seasonal stream on a footbridge.

1.9 Come to an unmarked fork on the trail. Bear right and continue walking uphill.

2.2 Long Lake is your destination. Enjoy the scenery, a snack, and water, and watching pooch romp, before going back the way you came. Elevation: 10,752. **GPS:** N37 08.93' / W118 33.46'

4.4 Arrive back at the trailhead.

Creature Comforts

Fueling Up

Hing's Donuts, 905 N. Main St., Bishop 93514; (760) 872-4369. Trail-size crunchy apple fritters.

Schat's Bakery, 763 N. Main St., Bishop 93514; (760) 873-7156; erikschatsbakery .com. Great spot to pick up picnic goodies, from "Natural California Turkey" for oven-roasted turkey sandwiches on fresh-baked breads to an array of sweet treats. The small, outdoor dog-friendly patio has umbrellas for shade and fills up fast at peak hours. The bakery is known for its "Original Sheepherder Bread" brought to the Owen's Valley during the Gold Rush by Basque Sheepherders.

Burger Barn, 2675 W. Line St., Bishop 93514; (760) 920-6567; bishopburgerbarn .com. Bishop's best-kept secret is a funky roadside joint committed to "fresh and locally grown." They deliver a quality burger and other freshly grilled options at a bargain. Their homemade ice cream sandwiched between two oatmeal chocolate-chip cookies hits the sweet-tooth spot. Outside tables with cooling overhead misters let you comfortably dine outdoors with bowser.

Bishop Creek Lodge, 2100 S. Lake Rd., Bishop 93514; (760) 873-4484; info@ bishopcreeklodge.com and on Facebook. There's a store with staples and a cafe with fresh-baked pies. Dine with pooch at the picnic table outside.

Parchers Resort, 5001 S. Lake Rd., Bishop 93514; (760) 873-4177; parchersresort .net. There's a snack shop and cafe with a dog-friendly deck for weekday breakfast and weekend brunches.

Cardinal Village, 321 Cardinal Rd., Bishop 93514; (760) 873-4789; cardinalvillage resort.com (off CA 168/Sabrina Lake Road in Aspendell residential community).

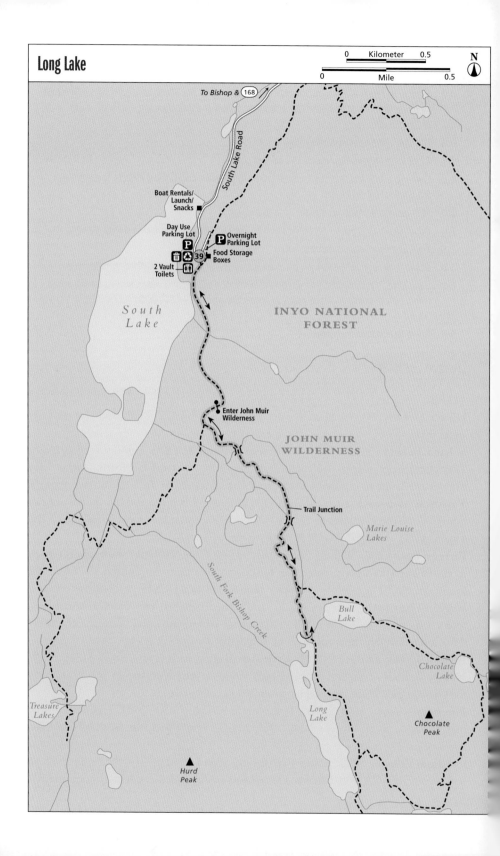

Long Lake

0   Kilometer   0.5

0   Mile   0.5

N

To Bishop & 168

South Lake Road

Boat Rentals/
Launch/
Snacks

Day Use
Parking Lot

Overnight
Parking Lot

39

Food Storage
Boxes

2 Vault
Toilets

South
Lake

INYO NATIONAL
FOREST

Enter John Muir
Wilderness

JOHN MUIR
WILDERNESS

Trail Junction

Marie Louise
Lakes

South Fork Bishop Creek

Bull
Lake

Chocolate
Lake

Treasure
Lakes

Long
Lake

Chocolate
Peak

Hurd
Peak

High country scenery on the shores of Long Lake

Among other grill items, it's the best grilled-cheese sandwich in the Eastern Sierra. Enjoy your meal on the dog-friendly deck.

Farmers' Market, on Church Street off US 395, behind City Hall; Sue Chudy, (760) 937-6768. Saturday 9:00 a.m. to 12:00 noon. Seasonal schedule determined by beginning and end of growing season, weather dependent.

Resting Up

There are several pet-friendly motels in Bishop, including some brand names like Best Western, Holiday Inn Express, Travelodge, and other chains. The pet fee and house rules vary per establishment.

Parcher's Resort, 5001 S. Lake Rd., Bishop 93514; (760) 873-4177; parchersresort .net. Dog-friendly housekeeping cabins.

Bishop Creek Lodge, 2100 S. Lake Rd., Bishop 93514; (760) 873-4484; info@ bishopcreeklodge.com. Dog-friendly housekeeping cabins and hiker cabins with kitchenettes for backpackers wishing to acclimate before setting off to higher elevation.

Campgrounds

Creekside RV, 1949 S. Lake Rd., Bishop 93514; (760) 873-4483; bishopcreeksiderv .com. It's dusty and crowded, but a fallback option if you want hookups for your trailer or RV.

Parchers Resort, 5001 S. Lake Rd., Bishop 93514; (760) 873-4177; parchersresort .net. There are three RV sites with hookups.

There are several **National Forest Service campgrounds** along CA 168 and South Lake Road. Visit fs.usda.gov/inyo and use the "quick link" menu on the right to route to the list of campgrounds in Inyo National Forest by region. Reservations can be made at recreation.gov (877-444-6777) for campgrounds that accept reservations.

Puppy Paws and Golden Years

Bishop Dog Park, at the east end of the Bishop City Park off North Main Street between Yaney and Bruce Streets; bishopdogpark.org, is a good place for some safe off-leash romp time. The dog park has water, benches, a couple of trees for shade, and separate fenced areas for small and large hounds. The dog park was set up as a non-profit corporation and accepts donations.

Approximately 4 miles up South Lake Road from the South Lake turnoff of CA 168/ West Line Road, watch for a parking area on the right shoulder with a picnic table set in the meadow, where the **South Fork Bishop Creek** makes a gentle run on its course downhill. South Fork Bishop Creek is popular with anglers, and this pocket is perfect for a leisurely stroll with less-youthful dogs or pups too young for the high country.

Your best bets for pups and seniors to get a whiff of the great outdoors at their pace (on leash) when traveling along US 395 in the Eastern Sierra are in the town of **Mammoth Lakes.** The recreational trail along gurgling Mammoth Creek begins in the community park on Old Mammoth Road with parking on both the east and west sides of the road. Flat Snowcreek Meadow Trail on the west side of Median Boulevard behind Snowcreek condominiums is a delight for dogs of all ages.

40 First and Second Lakes

Like most hikes on the eastern side of the Sierra, the drive from the high desert valley floor gives little hint of the alpine paradise that waits at the trailhead. This classic Eastern Sierra trail, complete with glacier views, a rushing creek, waterfalls, a historic cabin, and two stunning turquoise lakes is best suited to fit dogs in their prime. Having said that, less-athletic dogs with their less-ambitious two-legged hiking companions can choose to tailor the hike to their stamina level with a shorter distance at four naturally rewarding spots along the trail described below.

Start: From Big Pine Creek Trailhead
Distance: 10 miles out and back
Hiking time: About 5.5 hours
Difficulty: Strenuous
Trailhead elevation: 7,784 feet
Highest point: 10,106 feet
Best season: Summer to fall
Trail surface: Dirt, crushed granite, and rock
Other trail users: Horses
Canine compatibility: Voice control
Land status: National forest; wilderness
Fees and permits: Permits for overnight camping in the wilderness (Wilderness Permit Office, 760-873-2483, recreation.gov). Check with ranger station about the status of campfire permits and restrictions, which vary by season, trail, and elevation.
Maps: USGS Coyote Flat, Split Mountain; USFS Inyo National Forest; John Muir Wilderness; National Geographic Sequoia Kings/Canyon National Parks Trail Map

Trail contacts: Inyo National Forest, White Mountain Ranger District, 798 N. Main St., Bishop 93914; (760) 873-2500 (this number has an excellent menu of information options); fs.usda.gov/inyo; Inyo Wilderness Permit Office, (760) 873-2483
Nearest town: Big Pine
Trail tips: There are 2 vault toilets at the trailhead, a bear-proof food storage locker, picnic tables, and fire grills. This trailhead has the added convenience of the Big Pine USFS campground and Glacier Lodge dog-friendly housekeeping cabins just a stone's throw away on the south side of Big Pine Creek. Funky Glacier Lodge has a small store for supplies and snacks as well as a limited menu for breakfast, lunch, and dinner. There are a few campsites with water and electric hookups for trailers and RVs on site.

If your dog prefers more solitude on the trail, consider starting the hike from the backpacker parking lot described below.

Finding the trailhead: From Big Pine at the intersection of US 395 and Crocker Street, turn west onto Crocker Street for the Big Pine Recreation Area. You are heading toward the Sierra mountain range. At 0.5 mile, Crocker Street becomes Glacier Lodge Road. Continue up the road 10 miles to the day-use parking area at the end of Glacier Lodge for the most convenient trailhead just past the sign for the entrance to Glacier Lodge and Big Pine campground on the left. **GPS:** N37 07.52' / W118 26.26'

If the day-use lot is full you have the option of driving back down Glacier Lodge Road about 0.5 mile to the backpacker parking lot, which will be on north side of the road going down. There is a trailhead to First and Second Lakes that will merge into the main trail from that parking lot.

The Hike

The trail to First and Second Lakes treats you to a majestic and unique view from the start as you look up to the glaciated cirque of the Middle Palisades Glacier, part of the larger Palisades Glacier, hidden from view and the southernmost permanent glacier in North America.

Walk around the closed gate signed Private Residences at the far end of the day-use parking lot. The trail begins left of the information board along an eroded paved road. Big Pine Creek is on your left and a cluster of summer cabins are perched on your right.

The trail leaves the eroded road at a wooden trail sign on the left around the bend and away from the summer cabins' driveway.

The trail climbs for a brief shady stretch and at about 0.3 mile you reach a wooden footbridge at First Falls, often the turnaround for elderly dogs that still enjoy a taste of the wild, while rewarding their human companions with a picturesque, albeit brief, jaunt.

Approximately 50 yards past the footbridge at First Falls, you come to a trail junction for South Fork Big Pine Creek straight ahead up the broad sage canyon, and North Fork Big Pine Creek to the right. Turn right for the North Fork. The North Fork of Big Pine Creek will be on your right as you start uphill on granite steps and switchbacks rewarding you with unobstructed views of the Middle Palisades glacier at the bends in the trail. In the summer, take time to stop and smell the delicate pink California wild roses and keep an eye out for swallowtail butterflies.

At about 0.8 mile, the trail levels off and rejoins the dirt road just ahead. Bear right and continue walking about 50 yards to a second wooden footbridge across the North Fork Big Pine Creek. Just across the bridge you come to a trail intersection with a sign for North Fork Big Pine and two unmarked spurs coming into the trail from the right. Bear left on the trail. North Fork Big Pine Creek will be on your left for the rest of the way to Second Lake.

At about 1.2 miles, Second Falls comes into view in the crease of the canyon ahead as you continue along rushing North Fork. The sprinkle of pine trees lining the bank offers minimal shade. At 1.8 miles you come to a T-junction with a trail sign for Baker Creek uphill to the right and one unmarked spur trail merging in. Bear left to continue along the North Fork Big Pine Creek toward Second Falls. For the next 0.5 mile the trail climbs into the more exposed sage and red-bark manzanita hillside out of the canyon, with North Fork Big Pine Creek still in view on the left below. You rejoin Big Pine Creek at Second Falls and enter the John Muir Wilderness at the posted sign. Second Falls is another popular scenic destination for hikers with dogs who want to call it a day, with a picnic topping off a 5-mile round-trip excursion.

Just above Second Falls, the creek flows alongside the narrower trail with several cool-off opportunities for your canine hiking pal. Be aware that even in the fourth year of drought, North Fork Big Pine Creek had a very robust flow around slippery

Looking across Second Lake toward Temple Crag

rocks and boulders. This is an example of a potentially hazardous trail condition for an exuberant water-loving dog. A harness and leash will keep your dog safer if he goes in for a splash on this section of the trail. At 2.7 miles the trail enters an enchanting cooler aspen grove highlighted by brilliant asparagus ferns and red fire weed.

A little farther up the trail on the left, tucked on the bank of the North Fork Big Pine Creek and in the shadow of Mount Alice, you come to a stone cabin with a small wooden sign nailed to a tree for the Big Pine Creek Wilderness Ranger Camp. Hollywood history buffs will be delighted to hear actor Lon Chaney Sr. originally owned this cabin. The character actor is best remembered for the 1920s *Hunchback of Notre-Dame* and *Phantom of the Opera*. The cabin is yet another idyllic destination for hikers with dogs who are too puffed to climb the remaining 2 miles to First and Second Lakes. From this point on the trail remains forested with a gradual ascent.

At 4.5 miles you come to a trail junction for Lakes 1–7 straight and Black Lake to the right. Continue straight for another 0.1 mile for the startling sight of brilliant turquoise First Lake downhill on the left of the trail. First Lake is a fourth very scenically satisfying destination for a well-deserved picnic break and dog treats.

The last 0.2-mile uphill push to Second Lake will reward you with a perfect granite perch and the turquoise glacial lake's stellar scenery at the foot of the towering serrated Temple Crag. Take time to sit around and bask in this phenomenal setting.

Back on the main trail going down for about 0.1 mile, keep your eye out for the unmarked spur trail you passed on the left on your way up after passing First Lake. Take this short side trail, which will bring you to a metal footbridge across the first outflow of Second Lake to a rock stacked dam, where you can enjoy another photographic perspective of this high-country gem before heading back down to the trailhead.

Miles and Directions

0.0 Start at the Big Pine Creek Trailhead sign and information board behind the closed gate just beyond the day-use parking lot at the end of Glacier Lodge Road.

0.2 Come to a wooden trail sign on the left of eroded road and summer cabins' driveway. Turn left onto trail.

0.3 Arrive at unmarked First Falls and walk across a wooden footbridge. Walk about 50 yards to the trail junction for South Fork Big Pine Creek and North Fork Big Pine Creek. Turn right onto the North Fork Big Pine Creek trail. The North Fork of Big Pine Creek is on your right.

0.9 Come to a trail junction where the trail joins the dirt road. Turn right onto the dirt road and walk about 50 yards to a wooden footbridge and trail junction for North Fork Big Pine Creek and two unmarked spur trails. Bear left on the North Fork Big Pine Creek Trail. North Fork Big Pine Creek will be on your left all the way to Second Lake.

1.2 You get your first peek of Second Falls plunging into the canyon.

1.8 Come to a T-junction for Baker Creek on the right and an unmarked spur trail merging in downhill from the right. Bear left to North Fork Big Pine Creek.

2.3 Enter John Muir Wilderness at the posted sign. Unmarked Second Falls is on the left.

3.0 Come to the Big Pine Creek Wilderness Ranger Camp on the left, aka the Lon Chaney cabin.

4.5 Come to a trail junction for Lakes 1–7 and Black Lake. Continue walking straight toward Lakes 1–7.

4.6 First Lake's turquoise patch comes into view at the bottom of the hill on the left.

4.7 Come to unmarked trail junction. Left spur leads to outflow at stacked rock dam of unmarked Second Lake. Continue walking uphill to scenic vista point on boulders above Second Lake.

4.8 Arrive at vista point overlooking Second Lake and enjoy the view and the idyllic picnic spot. Elevation: 10,106 feet. **GPS:** N37 07.56' / W118 29.23'

4.9 On the way back down to the trailhead, turn right at the unmarked spur trail that you passed earlier about 0.1 mile down. The spur is above First Lake.

5.0 Come to metal footbridge and cross first outflow of Second Lake on the spur.

5.1 Come to stacked rock dam and outflow #2 of Second Lake. Enjoy this other perspective of Second Lake before retracing your steps to the main trail and going back to the trailhead the way you came. Elevation 10,052 feet. **GPS:** N37 07.48' / W118 29.11'

10.0 Arrive back at the trailhead.

First and Second Lakes

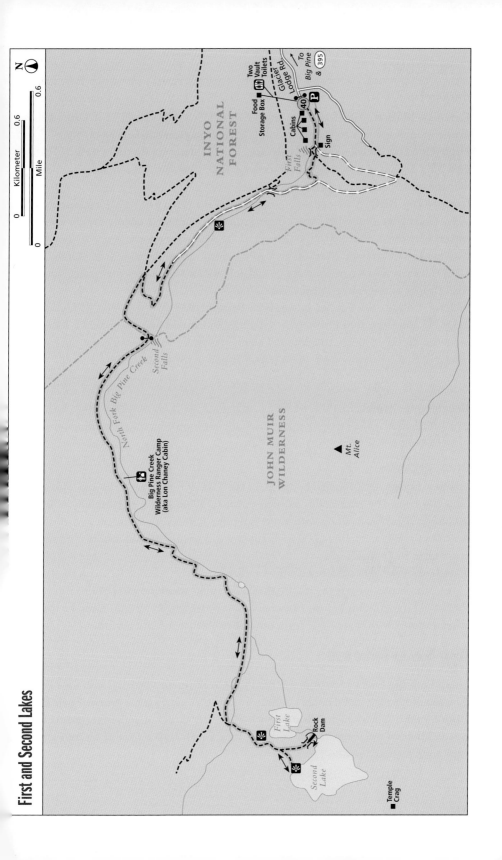

INYO NATIONAL FOREST

Two Vault Toilets

Food Storage Box

Glacier Lodge Rd

To Big Pine
& 395

40

Cabins

Sign

First Falls

North Fork Big Pine Creek

Second Falls

Big Pine Creek
Wilderness Ranger Camp
(aka Lon Chaney Cabin)

JOHN MUIR WILDERNESS

Mt. Alice

First Lake

Rock Dam

Second Lake

Temple Crag

N

Kilometer

0   0.6   0.6

0   0.6
Mile

Creature Comforts

Fueling Up

Carroll's Market, 136 Main St., Big Pine 93513; (760) 938-2718. Clean, well-stocked, family-owned and -operated little grocery store and deli. Friendly staff.

High Country Market and Hardware, 101 N. Main St., Big Pine 93513; (760) 938-2067. It's a one-stop shop for groceries, a little hardware, last minute gear, filling the tank with gas, and the Bristlecone Motel.

Copper Top BBQ, 310 N. Main St., Big Pine 93513; (760) 970-5577; coppertopbbq .com. Great little joint where you can sit at the outdoor picnic tables or order online and pick up to go. You just might have to share with your pooch.

Nawanaki-ti Farmers' Market, in Big Pine north of the Big Pine Tribal Office on US 395. Friday 5 to 8 p.m. from about mid-July to third week in September. Contact Alan Bacock at the Paiute Tribal Office, (760) 938-2003.

Glacier Lodge, 100 Glacier Lodge Rd., Big Pine 93513; (760) 938-2837; glacier lodge395.com. The funky store sells essentials and snacks and also offers a limited menu for breakfast, lunch, and dinner. The setup is funky but you can't beat the spectacular setting for having a bite with pooch at one of the picnic tables.

Resting Up

Bristlecone Motel, 101 N. Main St., Big Pine 93513; (760) 938-2067; bristle conemotel.com. It's not fancy but it's a friendly, one-stop convenient location for gas, groceries, and a warm bed for you and Fido.

Campgrounds

Glacier Lodge, 100 Glacier Lodge Rd., Big Pine 93513; (760) 938-2837; glacier lodge395.com. The main lodge burned down in 1998. But 8 dog-friendly housekeeping cabins remain along with a few campsites, some with full water and electric hookups for RVs and trailers. Glacier Lodge is rustic to funky in a spectacular location convenient to the trailhead.

There are several national forest campgrounds along Glacier Lodge Road on Big Pine Creek. Visit fs.usda.gov/inyo and use the "quick link" menu on the right to route to the list of campgrounds in Inyo National Forest by region. Reservations can be made at recreation.gov (877-444-6777) for campgrounds that accept reservations.

Puppy Paws and Golden Years

South Fork Big Pine Creek from the Big Pine Creek Trailhead takes you to First Falls wooden footbridge, and the trail continues to the trail junction for **North Fork Big Pine Creek** to the right and **South Fork Big Pine Creek** straight. The mostly flat first 0.5 mile of the scenic South Fork Big Pine Creek Trail is suitable for a pleasant stroll with pups and seniors.

41 Gilbert Lake

The good news is that you're in a postcard the moment you step on the trail, with Independence Creek on your left and a couple of cascades to dress up the granite cirque backdrop. The bad news is that you still have to hike up 2 miles of switchbacks on an exposed high-desert slope to claim your prize—pretty little Gilbert Lake with the perfect shoreline for pooch to saunter, sniff, and swim. The scenic playground is well worth the effort for moderately fit dogs and their humans. It helps to have had a couple of days to acclimate to the altitude.

Start: Kearsarge Pass Trail at the Onion Valley Trailhead
Distance: 4.6 miles out and back
Hiking time: About 3 hours
Difficulty: Strenuous due to elevation
Trailhead elevation: 9,205 feet
Highest point: 10,397 feet
Best season: Summer to fall
Trail surface: Crushed granite, dirt, and rock
Other trail users: Horses
Canine compatibility: Voice control
Land status: National forest; wilderness
Fees and permits: Permits for overnight camping in the wilderness (Wilderness Permit Office, 760-873-2483, recreation.gov). Check with ranger station about the status of campfire permits and restrictions, which vary by season, trail, and elevation.
Maps: USGS Kearsarge Peak; USFS Inyo National Forest; John Muir Wilderness; National

Geographic Sequoia/Kings Canyon National Parks Trail Map; Tom Harrison Kearsarge Pass
Trail contacts: Inyo National Forest, Mount Whitney Ranger Station, P.O. Box 8, Lone Pine 93914; (760) 876-6200. Eastern Sierra Interagency Visitor Center, 798 N. Main St., Lone Pine 93914; (760) 873-2500; fs.usda.gov/inyo.
Nearest town: Independence
Trail tips: There are 2 vault toilets, water, trash and recycle bins, and a bear-proof food storage locker. There is a small campground, very popular with backpackers, left of the trailhead (Onion Valley Campground). Gilbert Lake is a great day hike and overnight to introduce your dog to backpacking. You will share the trail with many backpackers on their way over Kearsarge Pass into Kings Canyon National Park. Make sure to take plenty of water for the climb up the dry, exposed slope.

Finding the trailhead: From Independence, at the intersection of US 395 and Market Street, turn west on Market Street for Onion Valley. You are heading toward the Sierra mountain range. Drive 13 miles up to the Onion Valley Trailhead and Kearsarge Pass Trail. The road ends in the Onion Valley Trailhead parking lot. **GPS:** N36 46.35' / W118 20.48'

The Hike

Being able to drive from the Owens Valley floor on US 395 up to 9,000 feet on a paved road to access alpine magic is what makes hiking in the Eastern Sierra so unique and attractive. Onion Valley is no exception. The mountains seem to almost come and meet you as you turn off US 395 onto Market Street/Onion Valley Road.

Boulders provide a panoramic perch for picnics at Gilbert Lake.

The road quickly leaves the high-desert sage-covered flats to trace Independence Creek and wind around the mountains with granite peaks and crests looming closer at every turn. That's the prelude to the hike to Gilbert Lake.

The hike begins with an immediate uphill on Kearsarge Pass Trail, which is a popular 5-mile route for backpackers heading over the pass into the backcountry of Kings Canyon National Park. The trail is basically a series of gradual switchbacks traversing mostly dry and exposed sage and red-bark manzanita slopes. But the sight and sound of Independence Creek gives the mountainside vibrant life with brilliant wildflowers as the several cascades soften the trail's spectacular starkness.

At 0.4 mile you come to a trail junction for Golden Trout Lakes to the right. Continue walking up Kearsarge Pass Trail. You enter the John Muir Wilderness at the posted sign at 0.7 mile. At about 1 mile into the hike, you get a fabulous view of a frothy fall tumbling down the canyon wall. Little Pothole Lake comes into view on your left at 1.6 miles. This is a good spot to step off the trail to offer your dog water while you soak up the view of the jagged peaks around you and back down across the Owens Valley eastward to the Inyo Mountain range.

At 2.1 miles the trail levels off where it crosses a boulder field. Scenic Gilbert Lake sits just ahead at 2.3 miles where the trail skirts the shore, inviting your dog in for a cool-off plunge. The perfect panoramic perch for a picnic before you go back to the trailhead is just ahead on the huge, flat granite slab dominating the shoreline.

Gilbert Lake

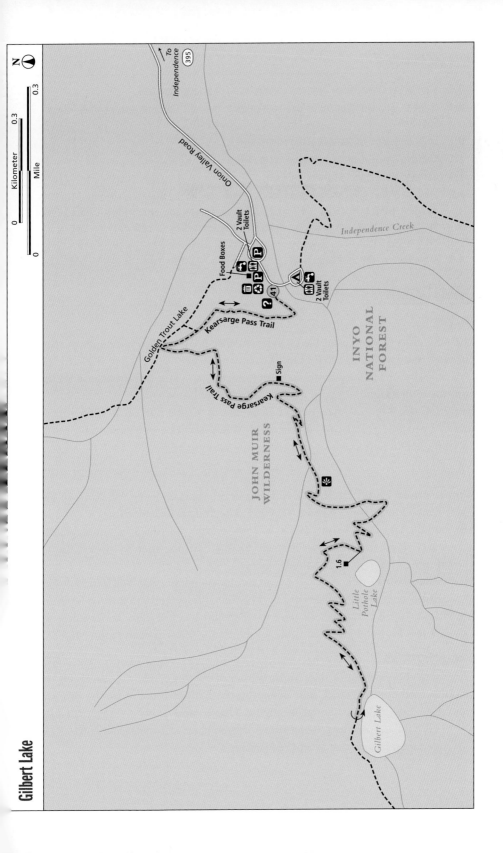

To Independence

395

Onion Valley Road

2 Vault Toilets

Food Boxes

Kearsarge Pass Trail

Golden Trout Lake

Independence Creek

2 Vault Toilets

41

Kearsarge Pass Trail

Sign

JOHN MUIR WILDERNESS

INYO NATIONAL FOREST

1.6

Little Pothole Lake

Gilbert Lake

N

0   0.3   Kilometer
0   0.3   Mile

Miles and Directions

0.0 Start at the Onion Valley Trailhead parking lot on Kearsarge Pass Trail.

0.4 Come to a trail junction for Golden Trout Lakes to the right. Continue straight on Kearsarge Pass Trail.

0.7 Enter John Muir Wilderness at the posted sign.

1.1 Come to a viewpoint for a waterfall on the left.

1.6 Come to Little Pothole Lake on your left.

2.3 Arrive at Gilbert Lake and a perfect pooch plunge spot on the shoreline. Elevation: 10, 397 feet. **GPS:** N36 46.21' / W118 21.35'. Enjoy snacks and water while you bask in the scenic beauty and your canine pal sniffs and saunters before going back to the trailhead the way you came.

4.6 Arrive back at the trailhead.

Creature Comforts

Fueling Up

The only grocery items available in Independence are in the gas station mini-marts. **Subway Sandwich,** 130 S. Edwards St., Independence 93526; (760) 878-2618. It's a quick and relatively healthy take-out option you can share with pooch on the trail or in the campground.

Jenny's Café, 246 N. Edwards St., Independence 93526; (760) 878-2266. Open 7 a.m. to 2 p.m. for breakfast and lunch; closed Wednesday. There's a picnic table outside for take-out and dining with pooch.

Resting Up

Winnedumah Hotel B&B, 211 N. Edwards St., Independence 93526; (760) 878-2040; winnedumah.com. Named after a Paiute Indian legend, this is a cozy, no-frills hotel dating back to the 1920s, and an unexpected touch of country charm in this very sleepy community. There are a couple of dog-friendly rooms. Call for reservations.

Mt. Williamson Hotel, 515 S. Edwards St., Independence 93526; (760) 878-2121. It's a great base camp for hikers and backpackers. Fridge and microwaves in rooms. Breakfast included between mid–June and September 30. Backpacker resupply service packages for hotel guests available for the Pacific Crest Trail and John Muir Trail.

Campgrounds

There are a couple of national forest campgrounds on Onion Valley Road. Visit fs.usda .gov/inyo and use the "quick link" menu on the right to route to the list of campgrounds in Inyo National Forest by region. **Upper and Lower Gray's Meadow** is very pleasant at 6,200 feet. Reservations can be made at recreation.gov (877-444-6777) for campgrounds that accept reservations.

42 Lone Pine Lake

This is a moderately challenging hike with phenomenally scenic rewards. This hike does not hold back. It starts delivering on the drive to the trailhead. No delayed gratification here. The hike to Lone Pine Lake is your chance to experience a short but special section of the Mount Whitney Trail, the route up the iconic mountain to the highest summit (14,505 feet) in the contiguous states. A few refreshing creek crossings, panoramic views of the granite kingdom, and a cornucopia of wildflowers highlight the 3 miles of mostly exposed switchbacks to the shores of this idyllic lake. Mount Whitney Trail to Lone Pine Lake is a portal into one of nature's most sublime settings.

Start: From Mount Whitney Trailhead

Distance: 6.2 miles out and back

Hiking time: About 4 hours

Difficulty: Strenuous

Trailhead elevation: 8,406 feet

Highest point: 10,000 feet

Best season: Summer to fall

Trail surface: Dirt and crushed granite

Other trail users: Hikers only

Canine compatibility: Voice control

Land status: National forest; wilderness

Fees and permits: No permit is required for day hikers going as far as Lone Pine Lake. But a special permit is necessary for even day hiking beyond Lone Pine Lake. Dogs are only allowed as far as Whitney Portal Crest at 13,600 feet. Rangers check for permits randomly. The fine can be as severe as $5,000 and six months in jail for hiking without a permit into the Mount Whitney Zone. Permits are also required for overnight camping in the wilderness, which includes Lone Pine Lake, and that permit can only be obtained at the Eastern Sierra Interagency Visitor Center (contact info below). If you plan on overnighting at Lone Pine Lake, you must apply for the lottery beginning February 1. If you do not obtain a permit through the lottery, you may go to recreation .gov to reserve any remaining permits on a first-come, first-served basis. Permits may become available after 11 a.m. daily directly

at the Interagency Visitor Center from cancelations and no-shows. You should also check with the ranger station about the status of campfire permits and restrictions, which vary by season, trail, and elevation.

Hikers traveling beyond Lone Pine Lake must pack out their human waste. WAG (Waste Alleviation and Gelling) bags are provided with the hiking permits. Hikers overnighting at Lone Pine Lake are also required to pack out their human waste, and a WAG bag can be obtained when you pick up your overnight permit. Dog waste should always be picked up and packed out regardless of official rules.

Maps: USGS Mount Langley, Mount Whitney; USFS Inyo National Forest; John Muir Wilderness; National Geographic Mount Whitney Trail Map; Tom Harrison Mount Whitney

Trail contacts: Inyo National Forest, Mount Whitney Ranger Station; P.O. Box 8, Lone Pine 93545; (760) 876-6200. Eastern Sierra Interagency Visitor Center, Lone Pine, intersection of US 395 and CA 136 1 mile south of town; (760) 876-6200; fs.usda.gov/inyo. Wilderness Permit Office can also answer questions regarding overnight permit for Lone Pine Lake, (760) 873-2483.

Nearest town: Lone Pine

Trail tips: Make time to stop at the Interagency Visitor Center south of Lone Pine, preferably before your hike. Aside from issuing permits, the center is a valuable resource for informa-tion and is well stocked with books, maps, and interesting nature-themed gift-shop items. There are water bowls for hot pooches outside the building.

There are 2 vault toilets, water, trash and recycling bins, and bear-proof food storage lockers at the trailhead. There is also a human-waste disposal bin next to the vault toilets. Hik-ers who travel beyond Lone Pine Lake must not only obtain a permit from the Eastern Sierra

Interagency Visitor Center in Lone Pine, but must pack out their human waste. WAG (Waste Alleviation and Gelling) bags are provided with the permits.

The Whitney Portal Store sells supplies and serves snacks and some meals.

The Mount Whitney trailhead area also has a picnic site with vault toilets, water, grills, trash and recycling bins, and bear-proof food storage lockers. There is a walk-in campground near the trailhead.

Finding the trailhead: From Lone Pine at the intersection of US 395 and Whitney Portal Road, turn west onto Whitney Portal Road and the sign for the Whitney Portal Recreation Area. You are heading toward the Sierra mountain range crowned by Mount Whitney's serrated summit. Drive 12 miles on Whitney Portal Road to the Mount Whitney Trailhead at the large wooden sign for Mount Whitney Trail on the right across from 2 vault toilets. Locating the trailhead is the easy part. Parking can be more complicated depending on how many backpackers with permits are heading to the summit, especially during favorable weather days in the summer. Just past the trailhead and the Whitney Portal Store, follow the signs for the Mount Whitney Picnic Area. This is one parking lot where day hikers can park between the hours of 8 a.m. and 8 p.m. only. The local sheriff issues citations for vehicles left in this parking lot between 8 p.m. and 8 a.m. The official hiker parking area for day use and overnight is the next parking lot below the picnic area. There is also an over-flow parking lot. If all the parking lots are full, then you must park on Whitney Portal Road and walk back to the trailhead. **GPS:** N36 35.21' / W118 14.42'

The Hike

If the altitude does not take your breath away at 8,000 feet, the scenery in the shadow of this granite cathedral surely will. The trail starts with a brief, stiff uphill with the most shade you'll experience until you reach the trail junction for Lone Pine Lake in 2.9 miles. The trail quickly mellows into moderate switchbacks. As you climb higher, the Owens Valley floor becomes more distant and you feel minuscule against the granite walls soaring up the canyon. The seasonal streams and the two tumbling creeks create enough moisture for lush ferns and myriad wildflower blooms, includ-ing purple lupine, white ranger buttons, and flaming Indian paintbrush.

At 0.5 mile your dog will enjoy cooling his paws as you cross Garillon Creek. The next opportunity for a refreshing splash is at 0.8 mile, where you cross North Fork Lone Pine Creek. Watch your footing, as the wet rocks tend to be slippery. Another 0.1 mile ahead, you enter the John Muir Wilderness at the posted sign. Just ahead is a Hiker Notice board about the use of the WAG (Waste Alleviation and Gelling) bags. Interestingly, NASA developed the gel referred to as "poo powder" used in the WAG bags. Hikers and backpackers traveling above Lone Pine Lake are required to have a

The whole pack is ready to hike from the trailhead.

permit issued by the Whitney Ranger District and pack out their human waste. The WAG bags are provided at the time the hiking permit is issued at the Interagency Visitor Center in Lone Pine. As a day hiker only going as far as Lone Pine Lake, you are not required to obtain a permit nor do you have to pack your waste or your dog's waste out. If you were overnighting at Lone Pine Lake, you would not be required to get a permit but you would be required to pack out human waste.

At about 2.1 miles you walk through a willow corridor on a long level switchback. Take advantage of this interlude to offer your dog water and relax your stride. The next best rest spot is at 2.5 miles, where there are large boulders and some shade for sitting and soaking up the view. At 2.8 miles, Lone Pine Creek's flow flares out and you cross the shallow, clear, gurgling water on a cleverly designed footbridge with a string of 11 single logs. Some dogs think of the logs as a fun agility course while others can't wait to trot their way through the cool, wet patch. Dogs who lack coordination when their four paws are not in contact with terra firma, or who lack confidence around water, should be on harness and leash for their safety and your peace of mind as you give them cheerful encouragement across the creek.

The trail junction for Lone Pine Lake appears on the trail at 2.9 miles. Turn left to Lone Pine Lake. You arrive on the beach-like bank of surreal Lone Pine Lake at 3.1 miles. The small lake seems to float on this High Sierra shelf cradled by lofty granite walls on one side and infinity dropping beyond the boulders and pines at the far edge. On a calm day, the reflections on the dark waters are nothing short of mesmerizing. But to your dog, this is yet another awesome playground. Find a cozy spot to share snacks with your dog. If you're curious about the Mount Whitney Trail that continued right at the junction where you turned left to the lake, you can explore the Mount Whitney Trail for about 0.1 mile up to the flats. The sign at the head of the gorge reminds hikers that permits are required beyond that point. When you're done nosing around, go back down to the trailhead the way you came.

Miles and Directions

0.0 Start at the trailhead for the Mount Whitney Trail across from the vault toilets.

0.5 Walk across Garillon Creek.

0.8 Walk across North Fork Lone Pine Creek.

0.9 Enter John Muir Wilderness at the posted sign.

2.8 Walk across Lone Pine Creek on log footbridge.

2.9 Come to trail junction for Lone Pine Lake to the left.

3.1 Arrive at Lone Pine Lake. Enjoy snacks, water, and exploring with your dog before going back to the trailhead the way you came. Elevation: 9,913 feet. **GPS:** N36 34.58' / W118 14.93'

6.2 Arrive back at the trailhead.

Creature Comforts

Lone Pine, lonepinechamber.org, is a busy gateway to Mount Whitney and a vibrant little Eastern Sierra outpost with the most services of any community south of Bishop, including a gas station, a couple of fast-food chains, a small grocery store, a few restaurants, an outdoor-supply store, motels, local museums, and a small airport.

Fueling Up

Alabama Hills Café and Bakery, 111 Post St., Lone Pine 93945; (760) 876-4675. Hearty cooking 7 a.m. to 2 p.m. Takeout available. Fresh baked goods sell out fast, but you can call and order a whole pie to go ahead of time.

Whitney Portal Store, at the trailhead for the Mount Whitney Trail that leads to Lone Pine Lake; whitneyportalstore.com. For seasonal hours of operation, visit the website and click on "contact." The store is stocked with last-minute hiking and camping supplies, snacks, and Mount Whitney memorabilia. The outdoor deck is a good place to sit with pooch for a serving of pancakes or a burger.

Resting Up

Best Western Plus Frontier Motel, 1008 S. Main St., Lone Pine 93545; (760) 876-5571; bestwestern.com. Limited number of pet-friendly rooms.

Lone Pine Lake

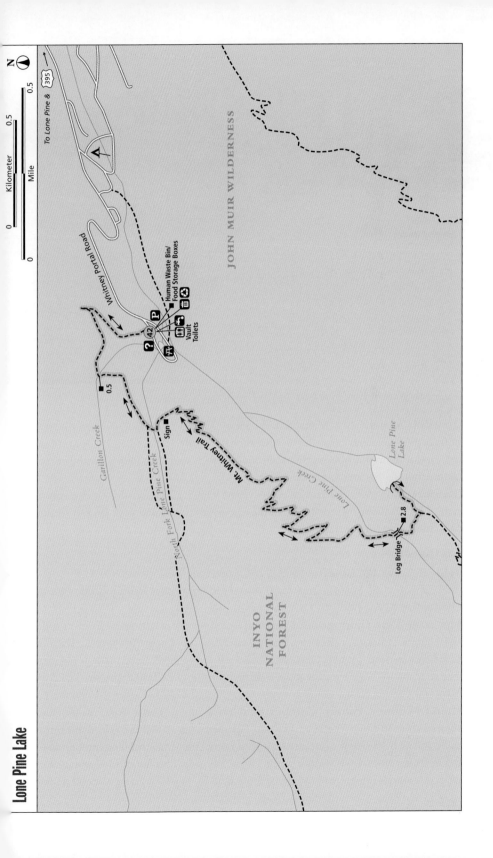

Cooling the paws in Lone Pine Lake

Dow Villa Motel, 310 S. Main St., Lone Pine 93545; (760) 876-5521; dowvillamotel .com. A property with classic history dating back to the 1920s when Hollywood stars and producers found housing while filming movies, and later television shows, with the precipitous Eastern Sierra backdrop.

Comfort Inn, 1920 S. Main St., Lone Pine 93545; (760) 876-8700; choicehotels .com. Hot breakfast included. The outdoor pool is a welcome perk on hot summer days after being on the trail.

Campgrounds

Boulder Creek RV Resort, 2550 US 395, Lone Pine 93545; (760) 876-4243; boulder creekrvresort.com. Full hookups for RVs and trailers 4 miles south of Lone Pine and a bonus fenced dog-walk area. Open year-round.

The Lone Pine Campground at 6,000 feet has a great setting, clean vault toilets, water, fire rings with a grill top, and picnic tables on Lone Pine Creek. Trash and recycling bins, bear-proof food storage lockers. Reservations can be made at recreation .gov (877-444-6777). There is also a trailhead for the USA Trail mentioned in Puppy Paws and Golden Years.

Mount Whitney Family Campground on Whitney Portal Road is sometimes referred to as Whitney Portal and Group Campground. It is about 0.5 mile from the trailhead and by far has the sweetest spot with Lone Pine Creek running through it. Tent and RV sites, water, no hookups, picnic tables, fire grills, bear-proof food storage lockers. Reservations can be made at recreation.gov (877-444-6777). The east end trailhead for the historic 4-mile Whitney Portal Recreational Trail is at the southwest end of the campground with 0.5-mile portion described below in Puppy Paws and Golden Years.

Puppy Paws and Golden Years

Whitney Portal Recreational Trail

The historic 4-mile **Whitney Portal Recreational Trail** is part of the original route to the top of Mount Whitney. You and pooch can access the lower portion of this trail at the west end of the Lone Pine Campground. This trailhead with parking allows you to sample a piece of history while enjoying up to about a mile of gentle ascent to almost flat stretches on a high desert plain with a loose dirt surface. Lone Pine Creek flows in the canyon below on the right against a backdrop of Sierra sentinels.

The other option is to park at the top of the trail in the Mount Whitney Picnic Area just past the trailhead for the Mount Whitney Trail to Lone Pine Lake. From here you can explore the shady upper section of trail as it traces the creek and weaves downhill for about 0.5 mile around boulders and down wooden steps into the Mount Whitney Family Campground, aka Whitney Portal Campground, which is on the north side of the creek between Whitney Portal Road and the trail. What goes down must come up, unless someone is picking you and your four-legged pal up at the campground trailhead, so make sure you don't walk farther than your dog can walk back uphill.

If you are looking for a shorter strolling area, you can meander around the flat picnic area by the picturesque fishing pond.

Alabama Hills Recreation Area

In 2014 the Bureau of Land Management (BLM) dedicated almost 30,000 acres of this maze of rounded stone hills, weathered arches, eroded obelisks, and unique geologic formations as the **Alabama Hills Recreation Area.** To dogs, this swath of public lands means mostly flat loose-dirt terrain to romp around while friskier canines boulder hop. Miners named the hills after the confederate warship C.S.S. *Alabama* during the Civil War. But the Alabama Hills are most famous for the more than 400 movies that have been filmed here since the 1920s, along with shots in several television series. The hills are easily recognized in numerous television commercials.

Hikers and pooches can wander around "movie flats," where a roster of iconic films and TV series has been shot. From *Gunga-Din* and *Lone Ranger* to *Star Trek* and *Ironman*, Hollywood has left its mark in the shadow of the glacier-chiseled Eastern Sierra crest. Drive 2.5 miles west on Whitney Portal Road from US 395 in Lone Pine to Movie Road and turn right at the information panels with the "movie location" map. There are several dirt roads where you can park and make your staging area for a hike. The area is open year-round, but early mornings and early evenings are best in the summer to avoid heat exertion from the very hot daytime temperatures at this lower altitude.

Film buffs and Hollywood fans can obtain more information at the **Lone Pine Film History Museum,** 701 S. Main St., Lone Pine 93545; (760) 876-9909. Download the Self-Guided Tour Booklet at lonepinefilmhistorymuseum.org.

43 Cottonwood Lakes

The 20-mile paved zigzag road up the side of the mountain to the trailhead looks intimidating from the valley floor, but don't let that deter you from this hike. It's everything that makes a dog happy—shade, meadows for frolicking, seasonal streams, and lakes. If it weren't for the high altitude, this mostly level to gently climbing trail to the lakes basin would be rated "easy to moderate." It's not just about your dog. This hike throws you a couple of bones as well. Even if you are not a fisher, this hike is a rare opportunity to access the Golden Trout Wilderness, home of the native and rare California golden trout. You'll be wowed by the granite backdrop cradling Cottonwood Lake 2's stunning setting.

Start: From Cottonwood Lakes Trailhead
Distance: 11 miles out and back
Hiking time: About 6.5 hours
Difficulty: Strenuous
Trailhead elevation: 10,054 feet
Highest point: 11,008 feet
Best season: Summer to fall
Trail surface: Dirt, crushed granite, and rock
Other trail users: Horses
Canine compatibility: Voice control
Land status: National forest; wilderness
Fees and permits: Permits for overnight camping in the wilderness (Wilderness Permit Office, 760-873-2483, recreation.gov). Check with ranger station about the status of campfire permits and restrictions, which vary by season, trail, and elevation.
Maps: USGS Cirque Peak; USFS Inyo National Forest; John Muir Wilderness; Golden Trout Wilderness; National Geographic Mount Whitney Trail Map; Tom Harrison Golden Trout Wilderness

Trail contacts: Inyo National Forest, Mount Whitney Ranger Station, P.O. Box 8, Lone Pine 93545; (760) 876-6200. Eastern Sierra Interagency Visitor Center, Lone Pine; Intersection of US 395 and CA 136, 1 mile south of town; (760) 876-6200; fs.usda.gov/inyo.
Nearest town: Lone Pine
Trail tips: Make time to stop at the Interagency Visitor Center south of Lone Pine, preferably before your hike. Aside from issuing permits, the center is a valuable resource for information and is well stocked with books, maps, and interesting nature-themed gift-shop items. There are water bowls for hot pooches outside the building.

At the trailhead, there are 2 vault toilets, water, bear-proof food storage lockers, and trash bins. Pack booties to protect your dog's paws on the rough trail surface. There are a lot of marmots in this area. However cute, they can injure a nosy dog, so if your dog is a marmot hunter, best to keep him on leash.

Finding the trailhead: From Lone Pine at the intersection of US 395 and Whitney Portal Road, turn west onto Whitney Portal Road and the sign for the Whitney Portal Recreation Area. You are heading toward the Sierra mountain range. Feast your eyes on 14,505-foot-high Mount Whitney, the highest summit in the contiguous states. Drive 3 miles and turn left on Horseshoe Meadow Road. Drive 19 miles on Horseshoe Meadow Road and turn right at the sign for Cottonwood Lakes Trailhead. Drive 0.6 mile to the hiker parking lot. The trailhead is left of the vault toilets. **GPS:** N36 27.19' / W118 10.20'

The Hike

This hike is sure to rate among your dog's favorite mountain jaunts with you. This is the southernmost Eastern Sierra hike in this book and probably the most unique. Rarely do you get to drive to a 10,000-foot trailhead on a paved road, let alone enjoy negligible elevation gain through sub-alpine meadows before being dropped off in an alpine lake's basin at the foot of dramatic granite palisades. This hike takes you into two wilderness areas, including the Golden Trout Wilderness, known for being the home of the state fish, the rare native coveted golden trout. The hike begins at the Cottonwood Lakes trailhead along the New Army Pass Trail. Take the time to read the interpretive panels at the trailhead about the fascinating history of the golden trout.

Most of the journey to Cottonwood Lakes 1 and 2, a surprisingly level to gently rising trail, cuts through a pine-scattered landscape with Cottonwood Creek within earshot or eyesight as it rushes behind curtains of willows or quietly meanders across meadows. The landscape in this pocket of the Eastern Sierra is more characteristic of the western side of the range, where granite crags and caps peer above the pine-covered slopes on undulating high plateaus.

You enter the Golden Trout Wilderness at 0.2 mile and will cross the South Fork Creek on a single log footbridge about a mile farther up the trail. At 2.8 miles you come to your first trail junction with a wooden trail sign directing you to the left. The unmarked spur trail to the right leads to the Golden Trout Camp, a non-profit environmental educational compound of rustic cabins and tent cabins. You may see or hear some of their stock donkeys in the meadow to the right just before reaching the unnamed junction.

Keeping a safe distance from horses at the trailhead

At 3.1 miles you leave the Golden Trout Wilderness and enter the John Muir Wilderness at the posted sign. Just ahead you will cross Cottonwood Creek on a single log footbridge. The trail parallels meadows. The willow-lined creek is on your left. The landscape now becomes more boulder-strewn.

At 3.7 miles you come to a significant trail junction with New Army Pass and South Fork Lakes to the left, and Cottonwood Lakes to the right. Turn left to follow New Army Pass Trail. This trail is the most direct route to Cottonwood Lakes 1 and 2. Cottonwood Lake 2 is this hike's destination.

Just ahead at 3.8 miles cross Cottonwood Creek on the large rocks. You will continue to hear Cottonwood Creek on your right. Thus far the trail has been fairly level with slight inclines, with an elevation gain of about 400 feet. The next 1.3 miles up to the plateau at Cottonwood Lakes will get moderately steeper as you gain about another 500 feet of elevation. Stop to rest and offer your dog water and a fueling-up treat before continuing uphill. At 4.6 miles stop to enjoy the view of a cascade above on the right as you catch your breath and give your dog a rest.

At 4.9 miles you will come to a trail junction for South Fork Lakes to the left and New Army Pass to the right. Continue toward New Army Pass.

At 5.1 miles you reach the broad spread of Cottonwood Lake 1 on a barren plateau with pines on the northwest shore in the shadow of the granite and scree backdrop. There's a fork in the trail with an unmarked trail to the right and New Army Pass to the left. Continue toward New Army Pass with Cottonwood Lake 1 on your right.

Lovely Cottonwood Lake 2 is just 0.4 mile ahead at the base of more granite palisades and is partially obscured by a gentle boulder-dotted knoll. This is your destination, with ample opportunities for exploring the meadows and lakeshore and picking your perfect picnic and photo spots. Cottonwood Lakes 3, 4, and 5 are strung beyond the north end of Cottonwood Lake 2 over about another mile. Cottonwood Lake 2 is the most pleasing. Cottonwood Lakes 3, 4, and 5 have more dramatic but far less hospitable and nourishing settings for hikers with dogs. After you and your dog have had your fill of fun, go back to the trailhead the way you came.

Miles and Directions

0.0   Start at the Cottonwood Lakes Trailhead toward New Army Pass.

0.2   Enter Golden Trout Wilderness at the posted sign.

1.4   Walk across South Fork Creek on the single log footbridge.

2.8   Come to a trail junction with an unmarked spur to the right (Golden Trout Camp 100 yards ahead to the left) and a wooden trail sign with arrow pointing left. Continue on the trail to the left.

3.1   Enter John Muir Wilderness at the posted sign.

3.2   Walk across Cottonwood Creek on a single log footbridge.

Cottonwood Lakes

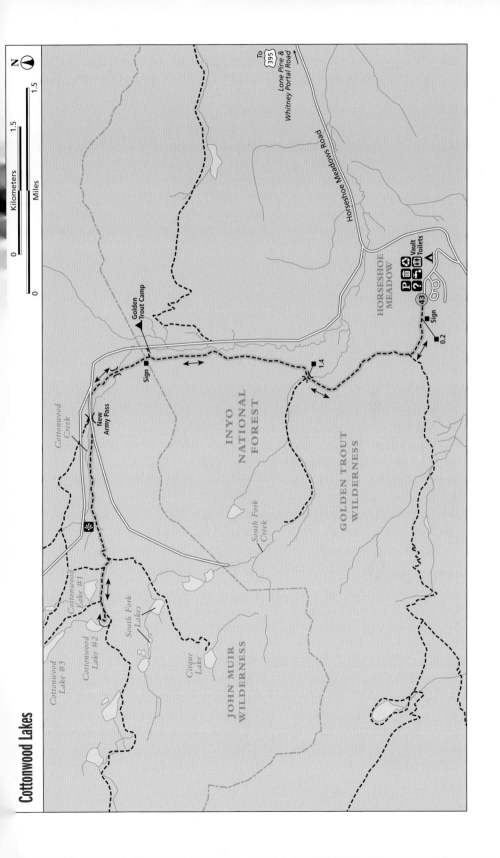

3.7 Come to a trail junction for New Army Pass left, South Fork Lakes left, and Cottonwood Lakes right. Turn left toward New Army Pass for the most direct route to Cottonwood Lakes 1 and 2.

3.8 Walk across Cottonwood Creek on row of rocks.

4.6 Come to a clearing on the right for a view of the cascading fall above.

4.9 Come to a trail junction for South Fork Lakes left and New Army Pass right. Continue walking toward New Army Pass.

5.1 Come to Cottonwood Lake 1 and an unmarked fork to the right on the trail. Bear left and continue toward New Army Pass. Cottonwood Lake 1 is now on your right.

5.5 Arrive at Cottonwood Lake 2 on your right. Enjoy the views and exploring for a snack and photo spots with your four-legged pal. Go back to the trailhead the way you came. Elevation: 11,005 feet. **GPS:** N36 29.30' / W118 12.88'

11.0 Arrive back at the trailhead.

Creature Comforts

Fueling Up

Alabama Hills Café, 111 W. Post St., Lone Pine 93545; (760) 876-4675. Pick up some fresh-baked pie and other goodies.

Resting Up

Best Western Plus Frontier Motel, 1008 S. Main St., Lone Pine 93545; (760) 876-5571; bestwestern.com. Limited number of pet-friendly rooms.

Dow Villa Motel, 310 S. Main St., Lone Pine 93545; (760) 876-5521; dowvillamotel .com. A property with classic history dating back to the 1920s when Hollywood stars and producers found housing while filming movies, and later television shows, with the precipitous Eastern Sierra backdrop.

Comfort Inn, 1920 S. Main St., Lone Pine 93545; (760) 876-8700; choicehotels .com. Hot breakfast included. The outdoor pool is a welcome perk on hot summer days after being on the trail.

Campgrounds

Boulder Creek RV Resort, 2550 US 395, Lone Pine 93545; (760) 876-4243; boulder creekrvresort.com. Full hookups for RVs and trailers 4 miles south of Lone Pine and a bonus fenced dog-walk area. Open year-round.

There are a few Forest Service site options on the way to the **Cottonwood Lakes Trailhead.** Visit fs.usda.gov/inyo and use the "quick link" menu on the right to route to the list of campgrounds in Inyo National Forest. Reservations can be made at recreation.gov (877-444-6777) for campgrounds that accept reservations.

The Lone Pine Campground, 3.5 miles past Horseshoe Meadow Road, has a great setting at 6,000 feet, clean vault toilets, water, fire rings with a grill top, and picnic tables on Lone Pine Creek. There are also trash and recycling bins and bear-proof food storage lockers. Reservations can be made at recreation.gov (877-444-6777).

Capturing the moment in a snapshot at Cottonwood Lake 1

There is also a trailhead for the Whitney Portal Recreational Trail in this campground. See Puppy Paws and Golden Years.

Horseshoe Meadow Walk-in and Equestrian Campground is actually three campgrounds conveniently set near the Cottonwood Lakes Trailhead. Cottonwood Pass and Cottonwood Lakes are the two walk-in campgrounds and Horseshoe Meadow is one of the best drive-in equestrian campgrounds. Each of the ten sites has a corral and hitch rail. Reservations can be made at recreation.gov (877-444-6777).

Puppy Paws and Golden Years

Whitney Portal Recreational Trail

The historic 4-mile **Whitney Portal Recreational Trail** is part of the original route to the top of Mount Whitney. You and pooch can access the lower portion of this trail at the west end of the Lone Pine Campground. This trailhead with parking allows you to sample a piece of history while enjoying up to about a mile of gentle ascent to almost flat stretches on a high-desert plain with a loose-dirt surface. Lone Pine Creek flows in the canyon below on the right against a backdrop of Sierra sentinels.

Alabama Hills Recreation Area

In 2014 the Bureau of Land Management (BLM) dedicated almost 30,000 acres of this maze of rounded stone hills, weathered arches, eroded obelisks, and unique geologic formations as the **Alabama Hills Recreation Area.** To dogs, this swath of public lands means mostly flat, loose-dirt terrain to romp around while friskier canines boulder hop. Miners named the hills after the confederate warship C.S.S. *Alabama* during the Civil War. But the Alabama Hills are most famous for the more than 400 movies that have been filmed here since the 1920s, along with shots in several television series. The hills are easily recognized in numerous television commercials.

Hikers and pooches can wander around "movie flats," where a roster of iconic films and TV series has been shot. From *Gunga-Din* and *Lone Ranger* to *Star Trek* and *Ironman*, Hollywood has left its mark in the shadow of the glacier-chiseled Eastern Sierra crest. Drive 2.5 miles west on Whitney Portal Road from US 395 in Lone Pine to Movie Road and turn right at the information panels with the "movie location" map. There are several dirt roads where you can park and make your staging area for a hike. The area is open year-round, but early mornings and early evenings are best in the summer to avoid heat exertion during the very hot daytime temperatures at this lower altitude.

Film buffs and Hollywood fans can obtain more information at the **Lone Pine Film History Museum,** 701 S. Main Street, Lone Pine 93545; (760) 876-9909. Download the Self-Guided Tour Booklet at lonepinefilmhistorymuseum.org.

White Mountains

The White Mountains brace the east side of the Owens Valley above the Inyo Mountain Range across the Sierra Nevada. The Paiute Indians were the first to roam the high country of the Whites from their summer hunting camps. White Mountain Peak (14,252 feet) is the highest point in the range and third-highest peak in California after Mount Whitney (14,505 feet) and Mount Williamson (14,379 feet).

The White Mountains are home to the ancient Great Basin bristlecone pines and a couple herds of bighorn sheep, as well as some wild horses. The native sheep are slowly recovering from disease carried by the domestic sheep first brought to graze the land by early Europeans.

44 Methuselah Walk

This is a unique opportunity to share a natural history treat with your dog. The drive from the Owens Valley up into the White Mountains east of the Sierra boasts an exceptional and seldom-seen bird's eye view of the Sierra crest. The hike itself is a veritable vista fest of sweeping views down canyons and across the Great Basin toward Death Valley among the oldest trees on earth. Maybe your four-legged pal will be the one to sniff out the unidentified unmarked famous 4,000-year-old "Methuselah" among all the other ancient trees on the trail.

Start: Left of the Bristlecone Pine Forest Visitor Center at the Methuselah Walk trailhead
Distance: 4.5-mile loop
Hiking time: About 2.5 hours
Difficulty: Strenuous due to altitude
Trailhead elevation: 10,085 feet
Highest point: 10,211 feet
Best season: Early summer to avoid the heat and early fall before snowfall. Road to visitor center is closed during the winter months due to snow at this higher elevation.
Trail surface: Dirt and rocks
Other trail users: None
Canine compatibility: On leash
Land status: National forest
Fees and permits: Parking fee
Maps: USGS Blanco Mountain; Inyo National Forest; Methuselah Walk brochure and map from visitor center
Trail contacts: Ancient Bristlecone Pine Forest Visitor Center, (760) 873-2500. Inyo National Forest, White Mountain Ranger District, 798 N. Main St., Bishop 93914; (760) 873-2500 (this number has an excellent menu of information options); fs.usda.gov/inyo.
Nearest town: Big Pine; Bishop for more services
Trail tips: There are 2 vault toilets, picnic tables, trash and recycling containers, and interpretive panels. There are brochures at the trailhead and in the visitor center with information about the 24 bristlecone pine points of interest along the trail. A $1 donation is requested if you want to keep the brochure. There is no drinking water at the trailhead, but bottled water can be purchased in the visitor center. Dogs are not allowed in the visitor center, but on a cool day when your dog can safely wait for you in the car, the 20-minute film on the history of the bristlecone pine forest is a great introduction to the hike.

Finding the trailhead: From the north end of Big Pine on US 395 turn east on CA 168 at the sign for the Ancient Bristlecone Pine Forest and Inyo National Forest. The unattended information kiosk at the southeast corner of US 395 and CA 168 is worth a stop for some background about the bristlecone pine forest and the Big Pine Recreation Area. The giant sequoia next to the kiosk is the "Teddy Roosevelt Tree," planted in 1913 to commemorate the opening of the Westgard Pass to vehicles.

Drive 13 serpentine miles up CA 168 to the sign for the Ancient Bristlecone Pine Forest and University of California Research Stations. Turn left at the sign onto the paved but unsigned White Mountain Road/Ancient Bristlecone Pine Forest National Scenic Byway and drive 10 winding stupendously scenic miles to the Schulman Grove Visitor Center. The trailhead is to the left of the visitor center at the sign for the Methuselah Walk. **GPS:** N37 23.15' / W118 10.72'

The Hike

Bristlecone pines are considered the oldest trees in the world. At the top of the Inyo National Forest's White Mountain Range, these ancient sentinels have adapted to the inhospitable, harsh, arid climate of hot summers and freezing-cold, wind-battered winters by clinging to the white dolomite limestone rock that gave this mountain range its name. Bristlecone pines are fascinating and beautiful examples of nature's ability to adapt. The Schulman Grove was named after Edmund Schulman, who came to the White Mountains in the 1950s in search of trees with the longest lifespans to further his research of modern dendrochronology (study of tree rings to learn about past climate conditions). In 1953 the Forest Service declared 2,330 acres of bristlecone forest a protected area. Edmund Schulman came upon the tree that would become known as Methuselah, the more than 4,000-year-old tree, in the late 1950s.

Schulman died of a heart attack at age 49, just two months before *National Geographic* published the 1958 article about his findings, which put the spotlight on the Great Basin's bristlecone pines. The White Mountains Natural Area was soon expanded to almost 28,000 acres and named the Ancient Bristlecone Pine Forest.

Thousands-of-years-old bristlecone pines are works of art in progress.

The examination of dead bristlecone pines and their rings revealed a timeline reaching back more than 7,000 years. In order to protect it from vandalism, Methuselah is not identified on the trail. But that does not diminish the thrill of knowing that the minute you and pooch step on the Methuselah trail, you have entered through the portal flipping back the pages of natural history.

Take a moment to get oriented at the visitor center with the outdoor interpretive panels and glance inside this fairly newly constructed building (September 2012) following an arson fire in 2008. Although the artifacts and artwork destroyed in the fire can never be replaced, the new building's innovative rustic architectural style is a very welcoming home for the educational exhibits and well-stocked gift shop. The rangers are very knowledgeable and eager to answer questions.

As you leave the parking area at the trailhead, the narrow trail takes you on a meandering loop with some undulating along a steep slope sprinkled with young, old, tall, shaggy, and stalky bristlecone pines along with piñon pines and Utah juniper trees. Even the smooth, dry, twisted trunks, roots, and bare limbs of the dead bristlecone trees add a graceful beauty to the stark landscape. There are several benches sprinkled along the way, strategically placed to invite hikers to sit and soak up the serene setting and dramatic views. Take advantage of the comfort of the benches to share a snack and have a drink of water with your furry companion.

The brochure describing the bristlecone life cycle and other vegetation sharing the eco-community of the scantly forested slopes marked by twenty-four numbered wooden posts enhances the hike, while making the excursion a scentual experience for pup.

You will come to only two well-marked trail junctions along the way until the close of the loop at 4.3 miles, where you go back to the trailhead the way you came.

Miles and Directions

0.0 Start at the trailhead for the Methuselah Walk to the left of the visitor center.
0.2 Come to a trail junction. To the left is the close of the loop. Bear right on the trail.
0.9 Come to a trail junction for the Bristlecone Cabin Trail, Mine Site, and Visitor Center to the right. Continue walking straight.
2.5 Enter Methuselah Grove at the sign.
4.3 Arrive at the close of the loop and continue walking straight back to the trailhead.
4.5 Arrive back at the trailhead.

Creature Comforts

Fueling Up

Carroll's Market, 136 Main St., Big Pine 93513; (760) 938-2718. Clean, well-stocked, family-owned and -operated little grocery store and deli. Friendly staff.
High Country Market and Hardware, 101 N. Main St., 93513; (760) 938-2067. It's a one-stop shop for groceries, a little hardware, last-minute gear, filling the tank with gas, and the Bristlecone Motel.

Methuselah Walk

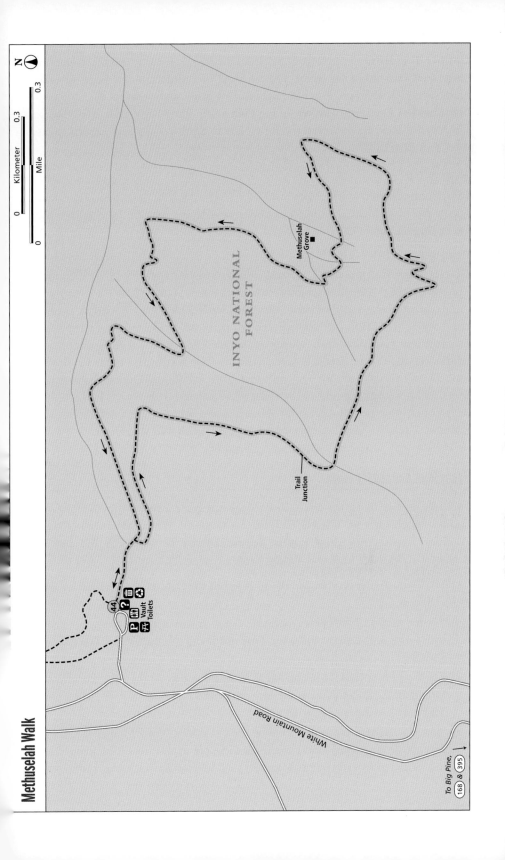

INYO NATIONAL FOREST

Methuselah Grove

Trail Junction

Vault Toilets

White Mountain Road

To Big Pine, 168 & 395

N

Kilometer 0 0.3

Mile 0 0.3

Copper Top BBQ, 310 N. Main St., Big Pine 93513; (760) 970-5577; coppertop bbq.com. Great little joint where you can sit at the outdoor picnic tables or order online and pick up to go. You just might have to share with your pooch.

Nawanaki-ti Farmers' Market, in Big Pine north of the Big Pine Tribal Office on US 395. Friday 5 to 8 p.m. from about mid July to third week in September. Contact Alan Bacock at the Paiute Tribal Office, (760) 938-2003.

Resting Up

Bristlecone Motel, 101 N. Main St., 93513; (760) 938-2067; bristleconemotel.com. Hot breakfast included. The outdoor pool is a welcome perk on hot summer days after being on the trail.

Campgrounds

Glacier View Campground, 0.5 mile north of Big Pine off US 395 at the southeast corner of CA 168; Inyo County Parks Department, (760) 872-6911; inyocounty camping.com. Tents and RVs (some sites with water and electric hookups). Brown's campgrounds concessionaire manages the campground. No reservations accepted.

Grand View Campground, 5 miles up unsigned White Mountain Road/Ancient Bristlecone Pine Forest Scenic Byway, on the west side as you drive to the Bristlecone Pine Forest Visitor Center from US 395; Inyo National White Mountain Ranger District, 798 N. Main St., Bishop 93914; (760) 873-2500; fs.usda.gov/inyo. This primitive high-desert campground offers solitude and closest access to the Methuselah Walk trailhead. There are vault toilets, picnic tables, and grills. No water, and it's "Pack it in–Pack it out" garbage and recycling.

Puppy Paws and Golden Years

Even young and older, less-adventurous dogs can get a scent of the ancient Great Basin sentinels on four different trails off the unsigned **White Mountain Road/ Ancient Bristlecone Pine Forest Scenic Byway** between CA 168 and the Ancient Bristlecone Pine Forest Visitor Center.

- The 1-mile Discovery Trail trailhead is just to the right of the Methuselah Walk trailhead.

- The old mine Cabin Trail is a moderate 1-mile round-trip hike to the cabin ruins with views of the Sierra and toward the north end of Death Valley. The trailhead is on the right of the visitor center.

- The Vista Point Trail is a panoramic 0.25-mile lollipop on the west side of White Mountain Road going up to the Ancient Bristlecone Pine Forest Visitor Center. There are benches and a picnic table.

- Piñon Picnic Area and Nature Trail on the east side of White Mountain Road is a 0.5-mile gentle, sloping loop. The trail identifies piñon pine trees, Utah juniper trees, and various grasses and bushes. There is a vault toilet and picnic tables, but no water.

San Bernardino Mountains

The rugged San Bernardino Mountain range was designated a national forest more than 100 years ago in 1907. Most recently (February 12, 2016) President Obama gave Southern California nature lovers an early Valentine's Day present by designating a new national monument. The Sands to Snow National Monument encompasses 71,000 acres of the San Bernardino National Forest and 83,000 acres of Bureau of Land Management lands.

The San Bernardino Mountains are one of Southern California's most visited year-round outdoor playgrounds for hiking and skiing, as well as a crucially protected watershed.

San Gorgonio Mountain is the highest peak in the range. The mountain is the headwaters of several rivers, and the range continues to rise as a result of the ongoing tectonic plate grinding along the San Andreas Fault.

45 North Shore National Recreation Trail to PCT Bridge

This easily accessible trail unconventionally takes you downhill, saving the uphill climb for the return trek. The trail meanders down a new-growth forested canyon with views eastward across the rugged San Bernardino Mountains. The trail parallels and crosses a seasonal stream before leveling off at the site of the old Splinter cabin just before pooch gets to cool off at Deep Creek and paw the iconic Pacific Crest Trail (PCT).

Start: From the paved parking spaces at the entrance to the North Shore Campground behind the campground sign off Hospital Road

Distance: 6.4 miles out and back

Hiking time: About 3.5 hours

Difficulty: Moderate

Trailhead elevation: 5,307 feet

Highest point: 5,362 feet

Best season: Spring, summer, and fall (summers can be hot)

Trail surface: Dirt, rock, roots

Other trail users: Horses (off-highway vehicles on some sections)

Canine compatibility: On leash

Land status: National forest

Fees and permits: Adventure Pass fee for day use (passes available at ranger stations, visitor centers, and some local businesses, or online at fs.usda.gov/adventurepass)

Maps: USGS Lake Arrowhead; San Bernardino National Forest

Trail contacts: Mountaintop Ranger District Big Bear Discovery Center, P.O. Box 69, 40971 N. Shore Dr./Hwy. 38, Fawnskin 92333; (909) 382-2790. San Bernardino, fs.usda.gov/sbnf.

Nearest town: Lake Arrowhead Village

Trail tips: The trailhead sign warns hikers about rattlesnakes, which are more common in the late spring to early fall. Keeping your dog on leash will keep him safer from getting too nosy with the wrong critter.

Finding the trailhead: From SH 18 at SH 173, turn north onto SH 173 toward Lake Arrowhead (north). Drive 1.5 miles on SH 173 to the stop sign just before the entrance to Lake Arrowhead Village and turn right to continue on SH 173 North Shore. Drive 2.8 miles and turn right on Hospital Road. Drive 0.1 mile on Hospital Road to North Shore Campground on your left across from the Lake Arrowhead Medical Center. If you hike this trail from October to end of April, the campground is closed and you must park at the entrance behind the campground sign just off Hospital Road and walk 0.3 mile to the east end of the campground to the North Shore National Recreation Trailhead sign. We hiked this trail when the campground was closed. **GPS:** N34 16.00' / W117 10.08'

The Hike

As is the case for most of the wild lands of California, the San Bernardino National Forest was first home to Native Americans before the arrival of European, Spanish, and Mexican settlers. California was part of Mexico from 1822 until 1848 and became a state in 1850.

Little paws take a rest at Deep Creek.

The Gold Rush hit the San Bernardino Mountains in 1855, and the next thirty years saw the land abused by mining, logging, and overgrazing, which also began to take its toll on water quality.

The Forest Reserve Act of 1891 was the beginning of the turnaround toward better resource management and more preservation. The San Bernardino Forest Reserve became the San Bernardino National Forest in 1907. Today the forest spans almost 680,000 acres of biodiversity, from desert at 1,000 feet to evergreen forest and alpine tundra above 11,000 feet, creating a wide range of wildlife habitat.

It is an almost unimaginable contrast to be crawling in traffic gridlock on freeways lacing through the spread of Greater Los Angeles urban communities within an hour of walking among pines toward a wild, untamed horizon. Such is what the San Bernardino National Forest offers Southern California residents and visitors.

Lake Arrowhead, named for a rock formation on the face of the San Bernardino Mountain, sits on what was once Little Bear Valley. From the early 1890s to early 1900s, the area was a hornet's nest of litigation over proposed reservoir and water diversion dam projects. A real estate development company finally bought Lake Arrowhead, formerly known as Little Bear Lake, and the surrounding almost 5,000 acres in 1920. A dam was completed in 1923 and the seed was planted for Lake Arrowhead Village residential/resort community. Since then, the area has passed through the hands of different investors and the newer village's European alpine style boasts services and amenities enjoyed by locals as well as visitors, including hikers and campers in the surrounding national forest.

The hike begins in the lovely mountaintop North Shore Campground. Although the trail traces Little Bear Creek down a canyon ravaged by the Old Fire of 2003, the new growth of oak woodland dotted with fledgling pines is healing the scarred land. Willows and ferns are bountiful along the creek, and the slopes are covered with manzanita, buckwheat, and rock outcrops. The views reach across the rugged mountainous horizon as you continue the descent to the creek bed. Even after four years of severe drought, there was water nourishing the riparian habitat closer to the bottom.

At 1.3 miles, the narrow trail becomes more primitive with denser vegetation in the creek bed. At 1.5 miles the trail emerges onto more exposed ground. At 2.0 miles the trail drops back into the creek bed and you cross Little Bear Creek just before the trail meets the unmarked dirt road where you turn left toward the San Bernardino National Forest sign and map of the Deep Creek off-highway vehicle (OHV) forest service roads and hiking trails. You will share this dirt road with OHVs for only about 0.2 mile before bearing left onto Forest Road 3N34 and crossing Little Bear Creek before reaching the sign for Splinter's Trailhead Parking 0.25 mile ahead.

Continue walking on Forest Road 3N34C toward Splinter's Trailhead parking. You reach the trailhead parking at 3.0 miles, where there are two vault toilets, garbage and recycling cans, and a picnic gazebo at the historic Splinter's cabin site. The cabin was built in 1922, but only the rock wall and fireplace remain. In 1992 a picnic gazebo was built on the site of the original cabin, showcasing the rock wall and fireplace. There is no drinking water at this trailhead parking.

The PCT sign is to the left of the picnic gazebo. Follow the sign and cross Little Bear Creek. There is a sandy beach to the right on Deep Creek. Bear left away from Deep Creek sandy beach and continue walking 0.1 mile to the PCT and turn right to walk on the bridge spanning over Deep Creek to enjoy the view up and down the lush canyon. This is your turnaround point. Go back the way you came and take time to savor the creekside beach and Splinter's picnic area on the way back to the trailhead.

Miles and Directions

0.0 Start at the North Shore Campground entrance.

0.3 Come to the sign for the North Shore National Recreation Trail and walk downhill, following the signs for the 3W12 trail. Elevation 5,350 feet. **GPS:** N34 16.02' / W117 09.77'

0.5 Come to a dirt road and walk across the road to continue on trail 3W12 downhill.

1.2 Walk across Little Bear Creek.

1.3 Come to a T-junction and bear left at the trail sign and arrow.

2.25 Follow the trail sign and walk across Little Bear Creek.

2.3 Come to a dirt road and turn left on the dirt road.

North Shore National Recreation Trail to PCT Bridge

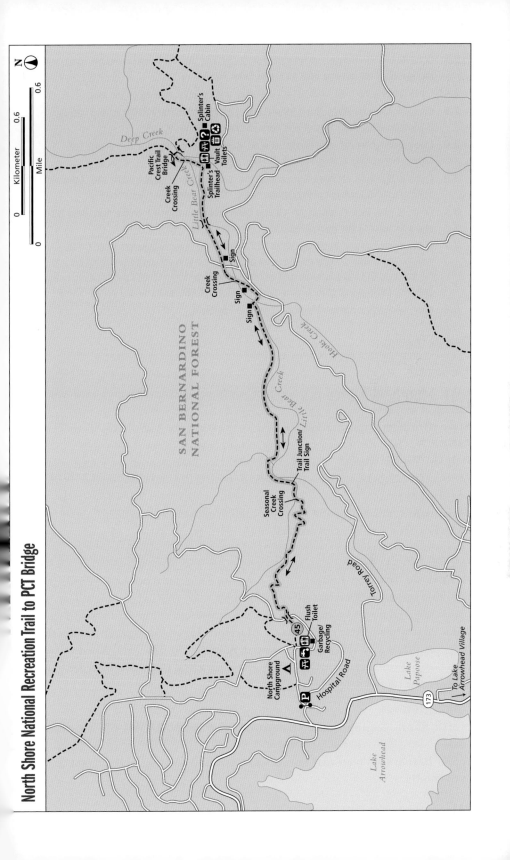

2.4   Come to the San Bernardino National Forest sign and map for Deep Creek OHV roads and hiking trails. Bear left and walk on Forest Road 3N34.

2.45   Creek crosses the road. Walk across the creek and continue walking on the road.

2.5   Come to a sign for Forest Road 3N34C and the sign for Splinter's Trailhead and Parking 0.25 mile ahead. Walk toward Splinter's Trailhead and parking.

2.8   Creek flows under concrete section of road. Continue walking on the road across the creek.

3.0   Come to Splinter's Trailhead and parking. The rock wall picnic gazebo is the site of the old Splinter's cabin. Bear left of the gazebo to the PCT sign and walk toward the PCT.

3.1   Come to Little Bear Creek on the left and Deep Creek sandy beach on the right. Bear left and walk across Little Bear Creek.

3.2   Come to the PCT and turn right on the PCT to the bridge spanning across Deep Creek. Walk on the bridge to enjoy the views up and down the lush canyon before going back to the trailhead the way you came and enjoying a snack by Deep Creek's sandy beach or the Splinter's cabin picnic gazebo. Elevation: 4,600 feet. **GPS:** N34 16.44' / W117 07.68'

6.4   Arrive back at the trailhead in North Shore Campground.

Creature Comforts

Fueling Up

Lake Arrowhead Village is a compact lakefront outdoor shopping mall with a variety of services.

Stater Brothers Supermarket, 28200 CA 189 #M, Lake Arrowhead Village 92352; (909) 337-5854. Provisions for camping and snacking.

Belgian Waffle Works, 28200 CA 189 #E-150, Lake Arrowhead Village 92352; (909) 337-5222; belgianwaffle.com. Waffles served all day, and more, on the lakefront dog-friendly patio.

McDonald's, 28200 CA 189 #D-100, Lake Arrowhead Village 92352; (909) 693-3413. Fast-food standby with outdoor tables.

Resting Up

Arrowhead Tree Top Lodge, 27992 Rainbow Dr., Lake Arrowhead 92352; (909) 337-2311; arrowheadtreetop.com. Pooches love their rise-and-shine stroll on the nature trail, and it's a 10-minute walk to Lake Arrowhead Village for the social scene.

Lake Arrowhead Resort & Spa, a Marriott Hotel Autograph Collection property, 27984 CA 189, Lake Arrowhead 92352; (909) 336-1511; lakearrowhead resort.com. If your pal appreciates luxury, this is the place. Leashed four-legged guests are welcome on the resort's beach.

Campgrounds

North Shore Campground, Lake Arrowhead 92352; (877) 444-6777; recreation .gov.

A **San Bernardino National Forest Campground** on Hospital Road off CA 173 at the northeast side of Lake Arrowhead.

Reaching the Pacific Crest Trail (PCT) bridge above Deep Creek

Dogwood Campground, in San Bernardino National Forest off Daley Canyon Road in Rim Forest 92378; (877) 444-6777; recreation.gov. Forest setting with showers and electric hookups. There are two hiking trailheads in the campground (Dogwood Trail and the Nature Trail).

Puppy Paws and Golden Years

Heaps Peak Arboretum, from San Bernardino on CA 18, 2 miles past CA 173 turnoff. The arboretum is on the left. There's a small Forest Service sign for Hiking Opportunity ¼ Mile Ahead on the shoulder of CA 18. Enjoy a 1-mile loop.
Arrowhead Queen tour boat, 28200 CA 189, Suite C100, Lake Arrowhead 92352; (909) 336-6992; lakearrowheadqueen.com. Narrated boat tour of the lake for pooches that want to sample the area without paws on the trail.

46 Children's Forest Exploration Trail

This lovely uphill hike on a multi-use trail with mellow switchbacks rewards hikers and dogs with fresh forest scents of pine, oak canopies, and inspiring views across boulder canyons and mountaintops. The trail's unique trademark is that it was "designed by children and built by a community."

Start: From trailhead at parking area 0.2 mile up Keller Peak Road on the right side

Distance: 9 miles out and back or shuttle

Hiking time: About 4 hours

Difficulty: Strenuous due to distance and elevation

Trailhead elevation: 6,024 feet

Highest point: 7,316 feet

Best season: Year-round (summer, fall, and spring are best; weather-depending in winter)

Trail surface: Dirt and rock

Other trail users: Horses and mountain bikes

Canine compatibility: On leash

Land status: National forest

Fees and permits: Adventure Pass for day use (passes available at ranger stations, visitor centers, and some local businesses or online at fs.usda.gov/adventurepass). Adventure Pass required for lower and upper trailhead parking.

Maps: USGS Keller Peak; San Bernardino National Forest; Children's Forest Exploration Trail Map from the Visitor Center

Trail contacts: Mountaintop Ranger District Big Bear Discovery Center, P.O. Box 69, 40971 N. Shore Dr./Hwy. 38, Fawnskin 92333; (909) 382-2790. San Bernardino fs.usda.gov/sbnf. National Children's Forest Information Visitor Center 32573 SH-18, Running Springs 93285; (909) 867-5996; mountainsfoundation.org. The Children's Forest Visitor Center is open weekends from Memorial to Labor Day. Youth Volunteers provide information and maps for hiking, biking, and camping.

Nearest town: Springville; Bear Lake Village has the most services

Trail tips: There are no services at the trailheads at either end of the Exploration Trail. Water, flush toilet, and 1 picnic table at the Children's Forest Information Visitor Center. Water, 2 vault toilets, and picnic tables at the trailhead for the Children's Forest Interpretive Trail, 0.25 mile beyond the end of the trail at the top of Keller Peak Road. No water along the trail. Bring plenty of water during the warmer summer months.

Finding the trailhead: From Big Bear Village on SH-18 at Big Bear Boulevard, drive 15 miles west to Keller Peak Road (Deerlick Fire Station is on the southwest corner next to the Children's Forest Visitor Information Center). Turn south on Keller Peak Road and drive 0.2 mile up the road to the first curve. The 2-vehicle paved parking area is on the right side of the road, and you will see the interpretive panel and a wooden bench in the forest marking the trailhead to the right of the parking area. **GPS:** N34 12.14' / W117 05.19'

From Running Springs on SH-18, drive 0.5 mile east to Keller Peak Road (Deerlick Fire Station is on the southwest corner next to the Children's Forest Visitor Information Center). Turn south on Keller Peak Road and drive 0.2 mile up the road to the first curve. The 2-vehicle paved parking area is on the right side of the road and you will see the interpretive panel and a wooden bench in the forest, marking the trailhead to the right of the parking area. **GPS:** N34 12.14' / W117 05.19'

The Hike

The San Bernardino National Forest is an incredible nature oasis of front country recreation and backcountry adventure. Southern California's notoriously congested freeway sprawl quickly recedes as visitors climb the forested slopes on the paved highway into a world where trees, canyons, creeks, and wildlife habitat dominate the horizon. Geologically speaking, it's also fascinating to picture how the seismic action between the Pacific and North American plates in the San Bernardino Mountains is raising the range by 2 inches a year.

Climate change and drought have made California's forests more vulnerable, and in Southern California, fall's warm and often vigorous Santa Ana desert winds have always raised fire danger in the wild lands. In November 1970 the Butler Peak fire-lookout staff member spotted what became the Bear Fire, fueled by warm winds of 70 mph, destroying 70,000 acres of the San Bernardino National Forest and 49 homes. The tragedy planted the seed for an ambitious visionary cooperative project between the Children's Forest Association, youth groups, Forest Service staff, and community organizations.

The National Children's Forest comprises 3,400 acres of newly planted trees bearing children's names. In 1993, children from around the country contributed to creating a mile-long interpretive trail at the top of Keller Peak Road. The display panels showcase nature through artwork and vignettes from a child's perspective.

The vision evolved to create the Children's Forest Exploration Trail with youth and adult teams training and working on grading, mapping, and interpretive design. The visitor center opened in 2001, and the 4.5-mile multi-use trail (hikers, dogs, bikes, and horses) opened to the public in September 2005.

It is well worth the time to stop in at the Children's Forest Visitor Center on the corner of Keller Peak Road and SH 18 to learn more about the ecology of the trail and nature's post-fire resilience.

The trail begins off Keller Peak Road at an interpretive panel illustrating the cooperative process that created the gem you are about to enjoy with pooch at your side. The trail is narrow but well worn and maintained as it climbs up the slope through a mix of manzanita, pine, and oak woodland dotted with magnificent stacks of granite boulders. There is only one dry creek-bed crossing near the bottom of the trail and two locations where the trail crosses an old dirt road winding up through the forest.

As you hike up the first 0.5 mile, notice the wooden posts sprinkled on the side of the trail with small metal markers depicting some of the wildlife whose home you are visiting and invited to respect.

At 1.2 miles, views open up to the stadium of mountainous wilderness. The trail undulates upward in and out of the forest onto exposed, level stretches overlooking canyons and dry, boulder-strewn gullies. The open plateau at 2.8 miles is a perfect spot for a rest stop to share a snack and water break with your furry pal.

Fog drapes the slopes above 6,000 feet.

At 4.5 miles you come to the interpretive panel and parking area marking the top terminus to the Exploration Trail and your turnaround point. The huge, dry fallen tree paralleling the trail at this end makes a great bench to lay out your picnic snacks to refuel before going back down to the trailhead the way you came.

If you have time and pooch is up for it, you can walk along Keller Peak Road up to the Children's Interpretive Trail. You can see the fork in the road at the directional sign on paved Keller Peak Road just beyond the parking area. Children's Forest Interpretive Trail is to the left, 0.25 mile. The trail is a 1-mile circuit loop and there are two vault toilets, two drinking fountains, trash and recycling bins, picnic tables, and dog-waste bags in the upper parking lot at the interpretive trailhead. The paved road going right takes you to the Keller Peak fire lookout 1.2 miles farther up. The fire lookout is open to the public seven days a week from 8 a.m. to 4 p.m. It's a unique opportunity for panoramic views and to learn about the history of fire lookouts from the volunteer on duty. Pooch will have to be leashed at the bottom of the stairs.

Miles and Directions

0.0   Start at the interpretive panel to the right of the two-vehicle paved parking area on Keller Peak Road.

0.2   Walk across seasonal Dry Creek.

Children's Forest Exploration Trail

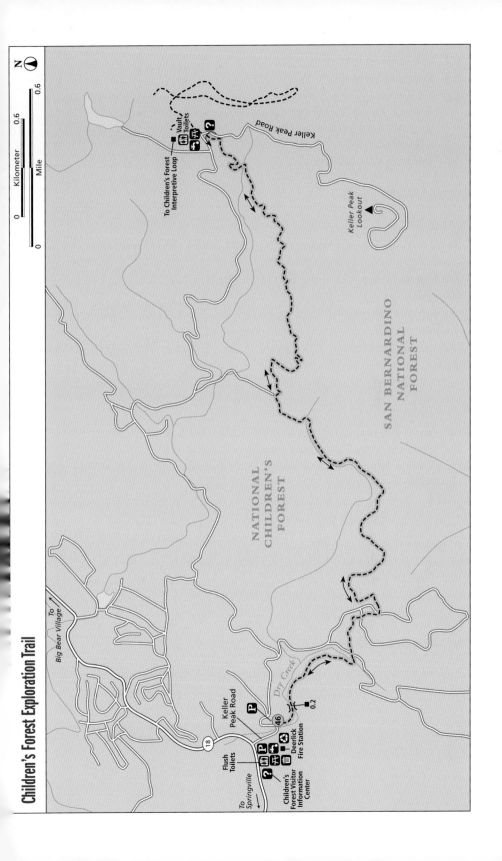

0.7   Walk across dirt road.

0.9   Walk across dirt road.

4.5   Arrive at parking area and interpretive panel marking the end of the trail. Sit and enjoy the view while you and your four-legged hiking companion refuel with snacks and water before going back to the trailhead the way you came. Elevation: 7,316 feet. **GPS:** N34 12.37' / W117 02.63'

9.0   Arrive back at the trailhead.

Creature Comforts

Fueling Up

Gifford's Market and Deli, 35637 CA 190, Springville 93265; (559) 539-2637. Convenient stop for snacks in rural area.

Vons Supermarket, 42170 Big Bear Blvd., Big Bear Lake 92315. Best selection for food supplies.

Nottinghams Tavern, 40797 Lakeview Dr., Big Bear Lake 92315; (909) 866-4644; nottinghamstavern.com. Dog-friendly courtyard.

Teddy Bear Restaurant, 583 Pine Knot Ave., Big Bear 92315; (909) 866-5415; teddybearrestaurant.com. Breakfast, lunch, and dinner served on dog-friendly patio in good weather. To-go menu available.

Resting Up

Robinhood Resort, 40797 Big Bear Blvd., Big Bear Lake 92315; (909) 866-4643; robinhoodresorts.com. Pet-friendly rooms.

Best Western Big Bear Chateau, 42200 Moonridge Rd., Big Bear Lake 92315; (909) 866-6666; bestwestern.com. Pet-friendly rooms.

Motel 6, 42899 Big Bear Blvd., Big Bear Lake 92315; (909) 585-6666; motel6.com. Pet-friendly rooms (strict policy and no fee).

Campgrounds

There are several primitive **Yellow Post Sites** campsites as you climb up Keller Peak Road. Fires are permitted in the designated fire rings. First-come, first-served basis, and pack out what you pack in. You must obtain a free California Campfire Permit, available from any ranger station.

Puppy Paws and Golden Years

Children's Forest Interpretive Trail at the top of Keller Peak Road is a 1-mile flat loop with views, benches, dog-waste bag dispenser, and vault toilet.

47 Alpine Pedal Path

Yes, it's paved and flat, but loved by young and not-so-young canines for its forest setting and multiple opportunities to set paws on the sandy beach and in the cool waters of Big Bear Lake. Dog owners happily tag along to enjoy the surrounding mountain and lake vistas.

Start: From the entrance to the Carol Morrison East Boat Ramp across from the Woodland Interpretive Trail parking lot
Distance: 5.2 miles out and back
Hiking time: About 2.5 hours
Difficulty: Easy
Trailhead elevation: 6,776 feet
Highest point: 6,822 feet
Best season: Spring, summer, and fall (fall colors are a treat)
Trail surface: Pavement
Other trail users: Bicycles
Canine compatibility: On leash
Land status: National forest

Fees and permits: Adventure Pass fee for day use (passes available at ranger stations, visitor centers, and some local businesses or online at fs.usda.gov/adventurepass)
Maps: USGS Fawnskin; San Bernardino National Forest; Big Bear Valley Trails Foundation map
Trail contacts: Mountaintop Ranger District Big Bear Discovery Center, P.O. Box 69, 40971 N. Shore Dr./Hwy. 38, Fawnskin 92333; (909) 382-2790. San Bernardino fs.usda.gov/sbnf
Nearest town: City of Big Bear Lake
Trail tips: Drinking water available at Carol Morisson East Boat Ramp (summer season only)

Finding the trailhead: From City of Big Bear Lake on SH 18 at Stanfield Cut-off, turn north onto Stanfield Cut-off to SH 38/North Shore Drive and drive 0.2 mile west to the Woodland Interpretive Trail parking lot. Walk across SH 38/North Shore Drive to the entrance of Carol Morrison East Boat Ramp and begin walking east on the paved Alpine Pedal Path. **GPS:** N34 15.75' / W116 53.34'

The Hike

Long before Big Bear Lake was developed into the year-round "tourist central" mountain community it is now, Serrano Indians (people of the mountains) and grizzly bears roamed the lush meadows of Yahaviat (Pine Place). A small lake referred to as Lower Bear Lake sat in the valley, which nearby ranchers called Big Bear Valley.

In 1884 a narrow gorge at the west end of Big Bear Valley became the site of a rock dam that created Big Bear Lake, a 5-mile-long reservoir hailed as the "largest man-made lake in the world." Citrus growers in the lowlands now had the water they craved. A new dam was constructed in 1912 and the lake is now almost 8 miles long with 23 miles of shoreline.

Hunted to eradication, grizzlies have not been part of the ecosystem in this picturesque pocket of the San Bernardino Mountains since 1906. Fortunately the Forest

Sharing the Pedal Path

Reserve Act of 1891 turned the tide toward preservation in the San Bernardino Forest Reserve, which became the San Bernardino National Forest in 1907. This nature playground boasts rich habitat for wildlife, including mountain lions, coyotes, and various reptiles. Between November and April some lakeside recreation sites are closed to protect roosting eagles.

Although there are numerous trails in the surrounding mountains for the most gung ho of hikers and dogs, the north shore Alpine Pedal Path is a favorite of local dogs and unique in combining forest, beach, and views on a jaunt suitable for dogs of all ages and fitness levels.

This excursion begins at the Carol Morrison East Boat Ramp entrance across from the Woodland Interpretive Trail parking lot. The paved path runs east-west between the lakeshore and SH 38/North Shore Drive, and you will begin walking east (left as you face the lake). This stretch is a short 0.2 mile to the end of the trail sign for the Alpine Pedal Path. There is a trash and recycling container and a dog-waste bag dispenser. The short, narrow, dirt trail on the right is your dog's first opportunity to dip a paw in the lake. The dirt trail almost directly behind the trail sign will take you back to the Carol Morrison East Boat Ramp parking area if you want to vary your experience and rejoin the Pedal Path at the entrance of the boat ramp to continue your hike to the west end of the path. Otherwise just go back to the boat ramp entrance the way you came and continue walking west from there.

The path wanders above the shore past benches weaving through corridors of pine trees and past a couple of day-use picnic areas where you can access the lake and stretches of sandy beach along the way.

The boardwalk across the wetland at 1.2 miles is an especially scenic photo spot at sunset looking west toward the mountains. You come to a wooden footbridge 0.1 mile ahead, over lusher wetland with similar open vistas.

The path continues meandering and lacing through a more-forested landscape as you approach North Shore Lane just past the National Forest information board, trash and recycling containers, and a dog-waste bag dispenser. Carefully walk across the road to continue on the path. At the trail junction and sign for Cougar Crest Trail, Big Bear Discovery Center, and the PCT on a paved path going right, continue walking straight.

Depending on how ambitious you and pooch feel, you can add more mileage by walking the 0.8 mile of path up to the Discovery Center (1.6-mile total extension to the hike). It's a gentle grade along a sweet stretch of forested path with benches for rest stops. The Discovery Center is a worthwhile stop for information and interesting exhibits, whether you include it as part of your wanderings or drive up to it just off SH 38/North Shore Drive. There is also a 0.5-mile dog-friendly dirt Nature Trail at the Discovery Center.

As you continue on the Pedal Path past the trail junction, you come to the Serrano Campground entrance. Walk across the entrance road. The Meadow's Edge Picnic Area across from the campground entrance on the lake side of North Shore Lane is a pleasant side jaunt to the water's edge along the way or on the return.

As you continue walking on the Pedal Path heading west, the pine-studded Serrano Campground sites are on your right. The trail continues for almost 1 more mile to the Alpine Pedal Path sign at North Shore Lane.

You can complete your excursion here and go back to the Woodland Interpretive Trail parking lot the way you came, or walk across North Shore Lane to the No Overnight Camping sign, where a short dirt trail leads you and pooch for a stroll along the beach and a view to your left of the Big Bear Solar Observatory on a jetty that projects out into the lake.

Miles and Directions

0.0 Start at the entrance of the Carol Morrison East Boat Ramp entrance across from the Woodland Interpretive Trail parking lot.

0.2 Come to the east end of the Alpine Pedal Path and turn around to walk west. Elevation: 6,781feet. **GPS:** N34 15.67' / W116 53.11'

1.1 Come to the trail junction for Juniper Point. Continue walking straight.

1.2 Walk on boardwalk across wetland.

1.3 Walk on wooden footbridge across wetland.

Alpine Pedal Path

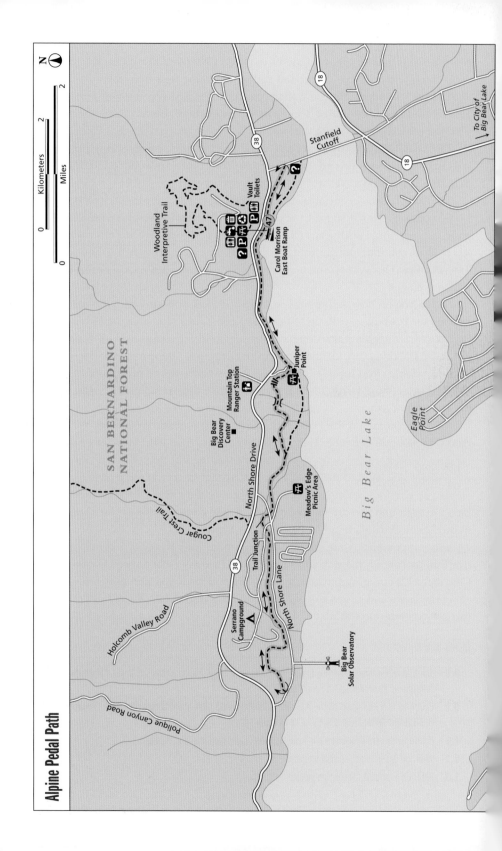

Boardwalk crosses the wetland above Big Bear Lake.

1.85 Come to North Shore Lane and walk across the road to continue on Pedal Path.

1.9 Come to the trail junction for Big Bear Discovery Center on the right. Continue walking straight.

1.95 Come to the trail junction for Serrano Campground on the right and Meadow's Edge Picnic Area on the left. Continue walking straight across Serrano Campground entrance.

2.6 Come to the end of the trail and sign for Alpine Pedal Path. Go back the way you came. Elevation 6,775 feet. **GPS:** N34 15.68' / W116 55.40'

5.2 Arrive back at Carol Morrison East Boat Ramp.

Creature Comforts

Fueling Up

Vons Supermarket, 42170 Big Bear Blvd., Big Bear Lake 92315. Largest grocery store for biggest selection.

Nottinghams Tavern, 40797 Lakeview Dr., Big Bear Lake 92315; (909) 866-4644; nottinghamstavern.com. Dog-friendly courtyard.

Teddy Bear Restaurant, 583 Pine Knot Ave., Big Bear 92315; (909) 866-5415; teddybearrestaurant.com. Breakfast, lunch, and dinner served on dog-friendly patio in good weather. To-go menu available.

General Store at Lighthouse Resort and Marina, 40445 N. Shore Ln., Big Bear 92314; (909) 866-9464. Supplies across the road from the Serrano Campground.

Resting Up

Robinhood Resort, 40797 Big Bear Blvd., Big Bear Lake 92315; (909) 866-4643; robinhoodresorts.com. Pet-friendly rooms.

Best Western Big Bear Chateau, 42200 Moonridge Rd., Big Bear Lake 92315; (909) 866-6666; bestwestern.com. Pet-friendly rooms.

Motel 6, 42899 Big Bear Blvd., Big Bear Lake 92315; (909) 585-6666; motel6.com. Pet-friendly rooms (strict policy and no fee).

Campgrounds

Serrano Campground, North Shore Lane, Big Bear Lake 92314; (877) 444-6777; recreation.gov. This national forest campground is exceptional in that it has RV sites with hookups as well as tent sites. It also has showers.

Big Bear Lighthouse Trailer Resort and Marina, 40545 N. Shore Ln., Big Bear 92314; (909) 866-9464; bigbearlighthouseresort.com. There are breed restrictions at this RV resort. Open May to October.

Things to Do with Pooch

Paddles to Pedals at the Lighthouse Resort and Marina, 40545 N. Shore Ln., Big Bear 92314; (909) 936-2907; paddlesandpedals.com. Rent a kayak with pooch May through October.

Puppy Paws and Golden Years

Nature Trail at Discovery Center, 40971 N. Shore Dr./Hwy. 38 Fawnskin; 92333. This is a 0.5-mile trail.

Woodland Self-Guided Interpretive Trail is on North Shore Drive across from the Carol Morrison East Boat Ramp entrance 1 mile east of the Discovery Center. Free maps are located at the trailhead of the 1.5-mile loop. Pooch will sniff and saunter on leash while you learn all sorts of fun nature facts. The trail also offers a view of "old grayback" Mount San Gorgonio, the highest peak in the San Bernardino Mountain Range.

Riverside County

This county's geography displays a wide swing from forested ridges and oak valleys to desert sands and stream-fed palm canyons as well as a saline rift lake on the San Andreas Fault.

Most of the eastern portion of the county is desert, which includes the popular and dog-friendly winter resort regions of Palm Springs and Palm Desert in the Coachella Valley.

48 Devil's Slide Trail

This hike on the pine slopes hugging the community that touts itself as the "most dog-friendly town in America" offers dazzling views of granite outcrops soaring above the valley floor. This trail takes you up to a saddle at the Pacific Crest Trail (PCT) and up to the threshold of the pristine Mount San Jacinto State Park Wilderness, where dog-friendliness ends.

Start: From the Devil's Slide Trailhead in Humber Park
Distance: 5.0 miles out and back
Hiking time: About 2.5 hours
Difficulty: Moderate
Trailhead elevation: 6,499 feet
Highest point: 8,105 feet
Best season: Spring, summer, and fall (spring and early summer for seasonal streams; early mornings for shade in the summer)
Trail surface: Dirt and rock
Other trail users: Horses
Canine compatibility: On leash
Land status: National Forest Wilderness
Fees and permits: Adventure Pass fee for parking (passes available at ranger stations, visitor centers, and some local businesses or online at fs.usda.gov/adventurepass). There's a 30-hiker quota on Devil's Slide Trail on Saturday and Sunday from Memorial Day weekend to Labor Day weekend. The free Wilderness Permit during that quota season can only be obtained from the ranger during business hours at the San Bernardino National Forest Ranger Station in Idyllwild.

Free self-service Wilderness Permits are required for day hiking in the San Jacinto Wilderness, including Devil's Slide Trail, the rest of the year. These permits are available at both the national forest and state park ranger stations (there are permit boxes outside when stations are closed).
Maps: USGS San Jacinto Peak; San Bernardino National Forest; Mount San Jacinto State Park map; Tom Harrison Maps San Jacinto Wilderness
Trail contacts: San Jacinto Ranger District, 54270 Pine Crest Ave., P.O. Box 518, Idyllwild 92549; (909) 382-2921; fs.usda.gov/sbnf
Nearest town: Idyllwild
Trail tips: There are 2 vault toilets and picnic tables at the trailhead parking lot in Humber Park, but no water. The trail is very popular with hikers and climbers on weekends even outside of peak season (Memorial Day to Labor Day) since this is the gateway to the PCT as well as other trails continuing into the Mount Jacinto State Park and State Wilderness.

Finding the trailhead: From Idyllwild at CA 243 and North Circle Drive, turn north on North Circle Drive, drive 0.6 mile to South Circle Drive, and turn right on South Circle Drive. Make an almost immediate left onto Fern Valley Road. Drive 1.6 miles on Fern Valley Road to Humber Park. Follow the signs to Humber Park. There are several groups of parking spaces as you climb up the hill. Devil's Slide Trailhead is 0.2 mile up the road on the right after you enter the park. **GPS:** N33 45.87' / W116 41.15'

The Hike

The trailhead has a very interesting interpretive panel about the history of Tahquitz Rock dating back to Indian legends, Shaman lore, and the beginning of technical rock climbing in the United States in the 1930s. The granite colossus looms over Humber Park on the right as you start up the trail.

The trail climbs 1,600 feet over 2.5 miles of moderate switchbacks spiked by a few steeper stretches. This enchanting trail of granite and pines on the east side of the canyon rewards hikers with several stunning views of Suicide Rock across the canyon. The trail weaves upward through the forest, frequently showing off Mother Nature's whimsy with unusual rock formations and trees sculpted into organic forms by wind and time. Give your dog water breaks as you admire this natural art gallery.

You will cross two seasonal streams at 1.0 and 1.3 miles, but at the time we hiked this trail in the fall of 2015, California was still in drought conditions and the trail was completely dry.

Devil's Slide Trail ends at Saddle Junction and the intersection of the Pacific Crest Trail (PCT) and several other trails. This is a lovely, flat patch of forest perfect for resting and snacks before going back down the way you came.

Super-fit dogs and their ambitious acclimated owners carrying lots of water can continue right on the PCT an additional 1.4 miles towards Tahquitz Peak and turn right at the next junction onto South Ridge Trail and walk approximately 0.4 mile more to Tahquitz Peak and fire lookout. Keep in mind that you would be adding almost 4 miles and at least two hours to the excursion.

Reviewing the map at the trailhead

Devil's Slide Trail

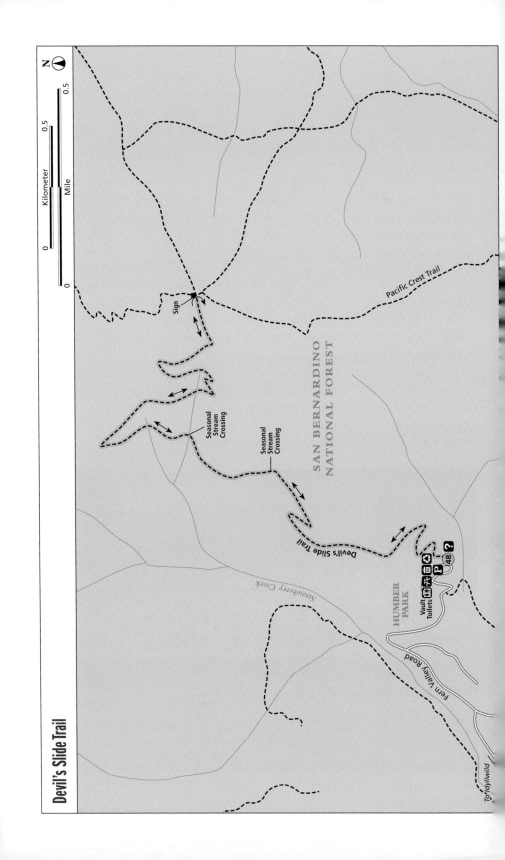

N

0   0.5
Kilometer
0   0.5
Mile

Sign

Seasonal
Stream
Crossing

Seasonal
Stream
Crossing

Devil's Slide Trail

SAN BERNARDINO
NATIONAL FOREST

Pacific Crest Trail

Strawberry Creek

HUMBER
PARK

Vault
Toilets

48

Fern Valley Road

To Idylwild

Dogs are also permitted on the PCT to the left from Saddle Junction for almost another 2 miles until you reach the San Jacinto State Park Wilderness boundary. San Jacinto State Park and State Wilderness are off-limits to pooches. Truthfully, the Devil's Slide Trail is the sweetest section of trail for views, topography, and tail-wagging smells.

Miles and Directions

0.0 Start at the Devil's Slide Trailhead in Humber Park.

1.0 Walk across a seasonal stream.

1.3 Walk across a seasonal stream.

2.5 Come to the Pacific Crest Trail at Saddle Junction and your turnaround point. Go back down the trail the way you came after serving up water and snacks to your dog. Elevation: 8,105 feet. **GPS:** N33 46.46' / W116 40.39'

5.0 Arrive back at the trailhead.

Creature Comforts

Fueling Up

Idyllwild Bake Shop and Brew, 54200 N. Circle Dr., Idyllwild 92549; (951) 659-4145. Hole-in-the-wall shop with mouthwatering fresh-baked morning goodies.
Idyllwild Village Market, Deli and Pizzeria, 26000 CA 243, Idyllwild 92549; (951) 659-3800. Provisions to go and Grand-Ma's Pies are a real treat.
Gastrognome, 54381 Ridgeview, Idyllwild 92549; (951) 659-5055; gastrognome .com. Dog-friendly patio.

Resting Up

Silver Pines Lodge, 25955 Cedar St., Idyllwild 92549; (951) 659-4335; silverpines lodge.com. A cozy rustic spot with 50's charm tucked in the pines and on a creek steps away from town.

Campgrounds

Mount San Jacinto State Park Idyllwild Campground, 25905 CA 243, Idyll-wild; (951) 659-2607, (800) 444-7275; parks.ca.gov, reserveamerica.com. This is a state park campground with a few sites with hookups for RVs. The park has very clean showers and you can't beat the location 1 block from town.

Things to Do with Pooch

Mountain Paws, 54380 North Circle, Idyllwild 92549; (951) 468-4086; mtnpaws .com. Visit the well-stocked pet store for supplies, products, and accessories.
Meet **Idyllwild's canine mayor**, Max, (951) 659-0283; mayormax.com.

Puppy Paws and Golden Years

Nature Trail in Idyllwild Campground of Mount San Jacinto State Park. The day-use parking lot is on the left at the entrance.

49 Canyon View Loop

At the right time of year, this hike, in one of the Wildlands Conservancy preserves, delivers a unique facet of the Southern California desert landscape. Hikers and their dogs cross a ribbon of the Whitewater River before climbing to an exposed ridge along the Pacific Crest Trail for panoramic views of green slopes against snow-dusted peaks cradling the Coachella Valley.

Start: From the Whitewater Preserve Ranger Station parking lot
Distance: 3.7-mile loop
Hiking time: About 2 hours
Difficulty: Easy
Trailhead elevation: 2,210 feet
Highest point: 2,766 feet
Best season: Late fall to early spring (summers are extremely hot)
Trail surface: Dirt and loose rock
Other trail users: None
Canine compatibility: On leash
Land status: Conservancy
Fees and permits: None (walk-in permits on first-come, first-served basis with permits from the ranger station during open hours, 8 a.m. to 5 p.m.)
Maps: USGS Whitewater and Whitewater Preserve map from ranger station
Trail contacts: Whitewater Preserve, 9160 Whitewater Canyon Rd., Whitewater 92282; (760) 325-7222; wildlandsconservancy.org
Nearest town: Palm Springs
Trail tips: There is a pleasant picnic area with stone tables and some tables under a shelter, restrooms, and water next to the ranger station. The trailhead has a map and brochures. No fires. Gas stoves and grills only. No smoking or alcohol permitted. Carry water on the trail.

Finding the trailhead: From the north end of Palm Springs on I-10, take exit 114 to Whitewater. Drive 0.1 mile east and turn left onto Whitewater Canyon Road and follow the signs for Whitewater Preserve. Drive 4.7 miles to the ranger station parking lot at the end of the road. The trailhead is on the north side of the parking lot across from the ranger station and the picnic area. **GPS:** N33 59.36' / W116 39.38'

The Hike

This hike is the centerpiece to the Whitewater Preserve's almost 3,000 acres of protected habitat within the 60,000-acre Sands to Snow Preserve system. The preserve was established by the Wildlands Conservancy and is one of the fifteen preserves in the 147,000-acre nature preserve system, the "largest nonprofit nature preserve system in California." The portal to the preserve is a former 291-acre trout farm at the end of the canyon road, where the historic trout farm building now houses the ranger station/visitor center. The canyon is a key wildlife corridor between the San Bernardino and San Jacinto Mountains.

The conservancy's long-standing campaign and dream came true in February 2016, when President Obama officially designated the Sands to Snow National

Crossing Whitewater River after a winter storm

Monument. The Wildlands Conservancy's Whitewater Preserve is now officially the "Gateway to the Sands to Snow National Monument."

We had the good fortune of hiking this trail the day after a cold front blew a Pacific storm across the desert, dousing the valley with water and dusting the mountains with snow. The Whitewater River had a fresh ribbon of water fed by the snows of Mount San Gorgonio (11,503 feet) in the Transverse Range and the highest peak in Southern California as it flows toward the Salton Sea. Whitewater Preserve is surrounded by public land managed by the Bureau of Land Management, which is also dog-friendly territory. In addition to the scenic qualities of the Canyon View Trail, there's always a special sense of adventure and privilege to putting boots and paws on the Pacific Crest Trail (PCT).

The hike begins on the desert canyon floor on a rock-lined path past a pond, some cottonwood trees, and a couple of large boulders with interesting inscriptions. The most inspiring of these is a quote by John Muir that reads, "I only went out for a walk and finally concluded to stay out till sundown, for going out I found was really going in." Sign in the register box just beyond the trout pond.

You pass two trail junctions within the first 0.5 mile as you follow the signs for the PCT. At 0.5 mile you cross Whitewater River on two wooden footbridges. The river is more of a permanent stream than the typical image that comes to mind when thinking of a river.

You enter the Bureau of Land Management Wilderness Area just ahead and another sign for the PCT at 0.7 mile. Turn left on the PCT South and begin climbing out of the canyon along the gradual switchbacks with views of the surrounding mountains and the ribbon of water on the canyon floor.

At 1.5 miles the trail levels off on a chamise-dotted mesa. Turn left off the PCT South trail to continue the hike on the Canyon View Trail. The best viewpoint looking toward the mountains at the north end of the canyon is just ahead. The trail veers southward, undulating on the plateau. Following some winter rain, the greening slopes on the right of the plateau are a sharp contrast to the otherwise arid landscape and the sandstone bluff across the canyon on the left.

The trail begins a mellow set of long switchbacks back down to the canyon floor. Chamise gives way to some beavertail cacti. At 3.0 miles you come to unmarked Whitewater Canyon Road. Walk across the road and turn left. You will pass the Whitewater Preserve sign on the right and Whitewater River crosses the road just ahead. Continue walking up the road for about 0.1 mile and turn left at the wooden trail sign for the ranger station shortly after crossing Whitewater River. The path is rock-lined and parallels Whitewater River, which is on your left, and the sandstone bluff is on your right. The trail rises on a narrow berm as you traverse a lovely riparian zone with willows and grasses highlighted by the croaking of nearby frogs.

At 3.5 miles you come to a trail junction for the ranger station to the right. Continue walking along the trail to the unmarked trail junction. You will see the picnic area, restrooms, and parking ahead. Bear left and walk between the picnic grounds on your right and the parking lot on the left. Arrive back at the trailhead after crossing to the north end of the parking lot. The picnic area and trout ponds make a superb stopover for sharing a snack with your pooch at the end of the hike.

Miles and Directions

0.0 Start at The Wildlands Conservancy's Whitewater Preserve—Gateway to the Proposed Sands to Snow National Monument sign and map board.

0.1 Come to a trail junction and turn right for the PCT Access.

0.2 Turn left at the sign for the PCT Access.

0.5 Walk across the Whitewater River on two wooden footbridges.

0.6 Walk past the sign for the Bureau of Land Management Wilderness Area.

0.7 Come to a trail junction and turn left onto the PCT South. Begin switchbacks uphill.

1.5 Come to a trail junction on a plateau. Leave the PCT and turn left for the Canyon View Loop.

1.6 Come to a panoramic viewpoint overlooking the canyon floor.

3.0 Arrive down at the Whitewater Canyon Road. Walk across the road and turn left.

3.1 Walk across Whitewater River on the road and continue to the trail sign for the Ranger Station ahead and a rock-lined path on the left side of the road.

3.5 Come to a trail junction and a sign for the ranger station to the right.

3.6 Come to a trail junction. Bear left with the picnic area on your right and parking lot on your left.

3.7 Arrive back at the trailhead on the north side of the parking lot.

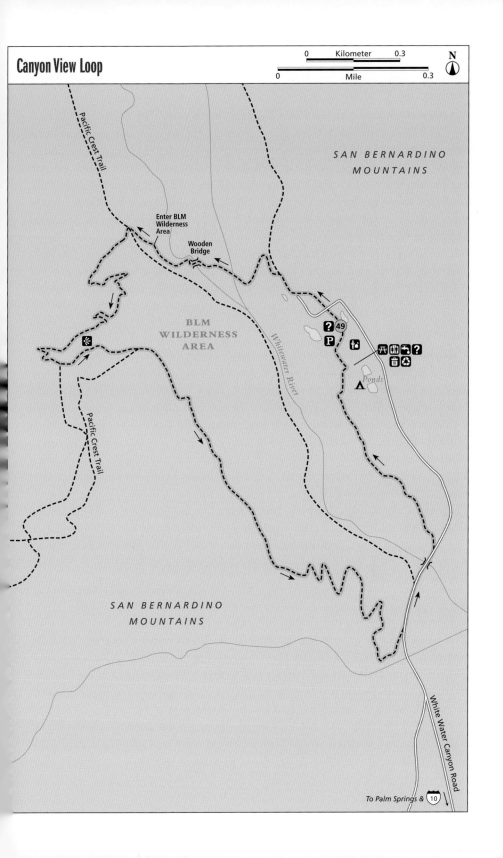

Canyon View Loop

0 Kilometer 0.3

0 Mile 0.3

N

SAN BERNARDINO
MOUNTAINS

Pacific Crest Trail

Enter BLM
Wilderness
Area

Wooden
Bridge

BLM
WILDERNESS
AREA

Whitewater River

Pacific Crest Trail

? 49

P

Ponds

SAN BERNARDINO
MOUNTAINS

White Water Canyon Road

To Palm Springs & 10

Creature Comforts

Fueling Up

Spencer's Restaurant at the Palm Springs Tennis Club, 701 W. Baristo Rd., Palm Springs 92262; (760) 327-3446; spencersrestaurant.com. The restaurant was named after Spencer Matzner, the owner's regal husky. Although Spencer has since gone over Rainbow Bridge, the Matzner pack's cavalier spaniels (Buster boys) and Alex, their golden retriever big brother, love to dine under the stars on the one-of-a-kind glassed-in patio. Well-mannered canine guests are welcome for breakfast, lunch, and dinner. Your bowser might even be lucky enough to be at the restaurant when the Buster boys have their traditional birthday party at Spencers every spring. Be sure to order the giant, and I mean *giant*, prawn cocktail to start, and end with the chef's signature ice cream and sorbet flavors of the day.

Sherman's Deli and Bakery, 401 E. Taquitz Canyon Way, Palm Springs 92262; (760) 325-1199; shermansdeli.com. The New York–style deli is famous for its all-day Kosher fare. Dogs welcome on the patio.

Resting Up

Caliente Tropics Resort Hotel, 411 E. Palm Canyon Dr., Palm Springs 92264; (760) 327-1391; calientetropics.com. This retro resort has a tiki atmosphere. Pet fee.

A Place in the Sun, 754 San Lorenzo Rd., Palm Springs 92264; (760) 325-0254; aplaceinthesunhotel.com. A dog-friendly retreat with gardens and a touch of old Palm Springs and Hollywood history. Some rooms have kitchens. Pet fee.

Villa Rosa Inn, 1577 Indian Trail, Palm Springs 92264; (760) 327-5915; villarosainn .com. It's an intimate, classic property. Pooches love the cool tile floors. Be advised that the rate will be double if your dog is the sneaky kind who doesn't register at check-in. The suites have kitchens. Pet fee.

Historic Casa Cody Country Inn B&B, 175 S. Cahuilla Rd., Palm Springs 92262; (760) 320-9346; casacody.com. Dogs are welcome at the oldest operating hotel in Palm Springs, founded by none other than "Buffalo Bill's" cousin Harriet Cody in the 1920s. The hacienda-style architecture comes with tile floors that keep bow-wows cool. Some rooms have kitchens. Pet fee.

Puppy Paws and Golden Years

The paver walkway along the trout ponds at the **Whitewater Preserve** on the left side of the picnic area is an idyllic stroll for four-legged pals with limited energy.

Palm Canyon Drive in the heart of Palm Springs is a happening place on Thursday evenings with its pedestrian-friendly Village Fest of crafts, music, and farmers' market between Tahquitz Canyon Drive and Baristo Road.

If Fido is a Hollywood film fan, he'll enjoy sniffing out his favorite celebrities' gold stars in downtown **Palm Springs Walk of Stars** on the west sidewalk of Palm Canyon Drive. Visit palmspringswalkofstars.com for a list of celebrities.

50 Araby Trail

This is a pleasant jaunt of switchbacks to the boundary of the Santa Rosa and San Jacinto Mountains National Monument. The trail heads into the Santa Rosa Mountains and overlooks Palm Springs and the Coachella Valley with the San Jacinto Mountains to the west.

Start: From Araby Trailhead parking lot
Distance: 2.4 miles out and back
Hiking time: About 1.5 hours
Difficulty: Moderate
Trailhead elevation: 403 feet
Highest point: 877 feet
Best season: Late fall to early spring (summers can be dangerously hot)
Trail surface: Dirt and rock
Other trail users: Horses
Canine compatibility: Off leash
Land status: National Monument and City
Fees and permits: None

Maps: USGS Palm Springs
Trail contacts: Santa Rosa and San Jacinto National Monument Visitor Center, 51-500 CA 74, Palm Desert 92260; (760) 862-9984; fs.fed.us. City of Palm Springs; 401 S. Pavilion Way, Palm Springs 92262; (760) 323-8272; ci.palm-springs.ca.us.
Nearest town: Palm Springs
Trail tips: There is a dog-waste bag dispenser at the trailhead parking lot. There are no amenities or services at the trailhead. There is no water on the trail. Bring plenty of water on sunny days, even in the winter.

Finding the trailhead: From the south end of Palm Springs at CA 111/Palm Canyon Drive and Southridge Drive, turn south onto Southridge Drive and turn immediately right into the Araby Trailhead parking lot at the corner of Rim Road. **GPS:** N33 47.84' / W116 30.63'

The Hike

Palm Springs is set against the foothills of the westernmost extension of the Sonoran desert, and therefore most of the hikes in this area take you uphill on exposed slopes. Araby Trail is no exception. The trailhead right off CA 111 is one of the most convenient, and although the trail climbs up a canyon, the hike is a gradual ascent up sweeping switchbacks interrupted by mellow, undulating stretches. The narrow and sometimes rocky trail quickly rewards hikers with expansive views across the flatlands of the Coachella Valley and the rugged outline of the San Jacinto Mountain Range to the west with San Jacinto's 10,834-foot peak peering above the range.

Although the Araby Trail extends into the phenomenal Santa Rosa and San Jacinto Mountains National Monument and on Bureau of Land Management public land, the bad news is that dogs are only allowed as far as the boundary of the monument. The posted sign explains that dogs are prohibited in the national monument to protect bighorn sheep.

The consolation prize at the turnaround point is a view of an unusual futuristic house resembling a circular spacecraft across the canyon. This 23,000-square-foot

Palms and snow-dusted mountains provide a scenic backdrop.

architectural landmark was built in the 1970s as the Palm Springs home for legendary actor and comedian Bob Hope and his wife Dolores.

The trailhead and parking is right off CA 111 and the marked trail begins just a few steps up the paved road on the left. There is a sign for the Araby Trail on the right with an arrow pointing left. The narrow trail traces the base of the slopes paralleling a mobile home development on the left and some residences on the right. Respect the Private Property signs posted along the way reminding hikers to stay on the trail. Grasses and cacti cover the lower slopes as you begin the hike, but the landscape transitions to a rockier topography as you begin the switchbacks at 0.3 mile. The trail levels for a short stretch before it descends into a canyon at 0.8 mile before winding back up on the other side for another 0.4 mile to the national monument and Dogs Prohibited sign across the ravine from Bob Hope's UFO home.

There are a couple of spur trails leading to knolls off the main trail, which make good picnic and photo perches before going back down to the trailhead the way you came.

Miles and Directions

0.0 Start at the Araby Trailhead parking lot.

1.2 Arrive at the Santa Rosa and San Jacinto Mountains National Monument boundary and posted sign prohibiting dogs beyond that point. Go back down the trail the way you came. Elevation: 877 feet. **GPS:** N 33 47.21' / W116 30.67'

2.4 Arrive back at the trailhead.

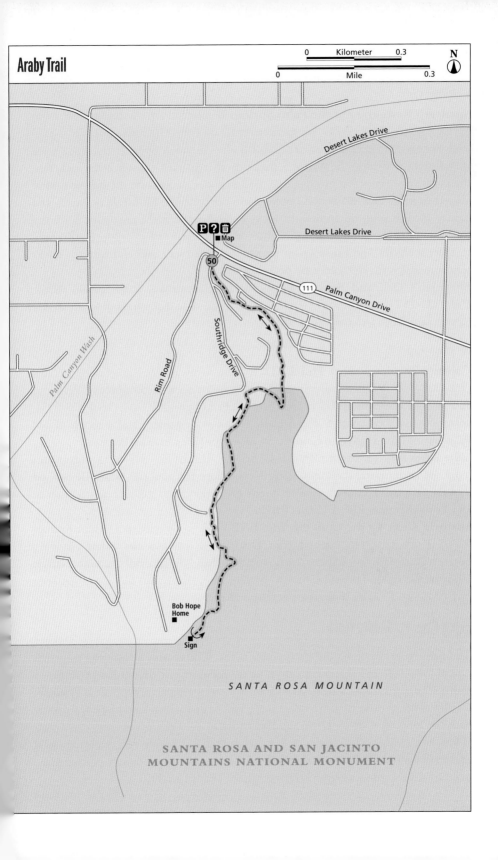

0   Kilometer   0.3

0   Mile   0.3

N

Desert Lakes Drive

Desert Lakes Drive

■ Map

50

111   Palm Canyon Drive

Southridge Drive

Rim Road

Palm Canyon Wash

Bob Hope
Home
■

■
Sign

SANTA ROSA MOUNTAIN

SANTA ROSA AND SAN JACINTO
MOUNTAINS NATIONAL MONUMENT

Creature Comforts

Fueling Up

Spencer's Restaurant at the Palm Springs Tennis Club, 701 W. Baristo Rd., Palm Springs 92262; (760) 327-3446; spencersrestaurant.com. The restaurant was named after Spencer Matzner, the owner's regal husky. Although Spencer has since gone over Rainbow Bridge, the Matzner pack's cavalier spaniels (Buster boys) and Alex, their golden retriever big brother, love to dine under the stars on the one-of-a-kind glassed-in patio. Well-mannered canine guests are welcome for breakfast, lunch, and dinner. Your bowser might even be lucky enough to be at the restaurant when the Buster boys have their traditional birthday party at Spencer's every spring. Be sure to order the giant, and I mean *giant*, prawn cocktail to start, and end with the chef's signature ice cream and sorbet flavors of the day.

Sherman's Deli and Bakery, 401 E. Taquitz Canyon Way, Palm Springs 92262; (760) 325-1199; shermansdeli.com. The New York–style deli is famous for its all-day Kosher fare. Dogs welcome on the patio.

Resting Up

Caliente Tropics Resort Hotel, 411 E. Palm Canyon Dr., Palm Springs 92264; (760) 327-1391; calientetropics.com. This retro resort has a tiki atmosphere. Pet fee.

A Place in the Sun, 754 San Lorenzo Rd., Palm Springs 92264; (760) 325-0254; aplaceinthesunhotel.com. A dog-friendly retreat with gardens and a touch of old Palm Springs and Hollywood history. Some rooms have kitchens. Pet fee.

Villa Rosa Inn, 1577 Indian Trail, Palm Springs 92264; (760) 327-5915; villarosainn .com. It's an intimate, classic property. Pooches love the cool tile floors. Be advised that the rate will be double if your dog is the sneaky kind who doesn't register at check-in. The suites have kitchens. Pet fee.

Historic Casa Cody Country Inn B&B, 175 S. Cahuilla Rd., Palm Springs 92262; (760) 320-9346; casacody.com. Dogs are welcome at the oldest operating hotel in Palm Springs, founded by none other than "Buffalo Bill's" cousin Harriet Cody in the 1920s. The hacienda-style architecture comes with tile floors that keep bow-wows cool. Some rooms have kitchens. Pet fee.

Puppy Paws and Golden Years

The paver walkway along the trout ponds at the **Whitewater Preserve** on the left side of the picnic area is an idyllic stroll for four-legged pals with limited energy.

Palm Canyon Drive in the heart of Palm Springs is a happening place on Thursday evening with its pedestrian-friendly Village Fest of crafts, music, and farmers' market between Tahquitz Canyon Drive and Baristo Road.

If Fido is a Hollywood film fan, he'll enjoy sniffing out his favorite celebrities' gold stars in downtown **Palm Springs Walk of Stars** on the west sidewalk of Palm Canyon Drive. Visit palmspringswalkofstars.com for a list of celebrities.

51 Homme-Adams Park to Cahuilla Hills Park

What's not to love about a hike that begins with a designated off-leash patch of desert sand in the Santa Rosa and San Jacinto National Monument to sniff and romp, before snapping on the leash for an up-and-down-and-around-the-mountain panoramic jaunt overlooking the Coachella Valley?

Start: From Homestead Trailhead in Homme-Adams Park
Distance: 3.6 miles out and back
Hiking time: About 2 hours
Difficulty: Moderate
Trailhead elevation: 410 feet
Highest point: 752 feet
Best season: Late fall to early spring
Trail surface: Loose dirt and rock
Other trail users: Horses and mountain bikes
Canine compatibility: Voice control on the flats and on leash on the trail
Land status: National Monument and City
Fees and permits: None
Maps: USGS Palm Desert; San Bernardino National Forest; City of Palm Desert Hiking Trails Map
Trail contacts: Santa Rosa and San Jacinto National Monument Visitor Center, 51-500 CA 74, Palm Desert 92260; (760) 862-9984; fs .fed.us. Palm Desert Visitor Center, 73470 El Paseo Suite F7, Palm Desert 92260; (760) 568-1441.
Nearest town: Palm Desert
Trail tips: There is a sheltered picnic table, water, trash, and recycling at the trailhead. There are no restrooms at Homme-Adams Park. There are vault toilets at Cahuilla Hills Park along with water and picnic tables. Even when temperatures are cool to chilly in the morning between late fall to early spring, do not let that fool you. Temperatures rise quickly in this desert, and the exposed trail with the sun beating down on you and pooch can get dangerously hot, especially on the uphill. It is easy to become dehydrated. Offer your dog water frequently and plan to complete your hike before midday.

Finding the trailhead: From Palm Desert at CA 111 and CA 74, Drive 1 mile south on CA 74 to Thrush Road. Turn right on Thrush Road and follow the signs for Homme-Adams Park. Drive across the bridge over the wash and turn right at the T-intersection to follow the Trailhead sign. Park along the road and walk to the north end of the gravel road to the Homestead Trail sign and the walk-in opening to the wooden split-rail fence. **GPS:** N33 42.54' / W116 23.92'

The Hike

This trail is an interesting example of land management and cooperation between local, state, federal, and Native American agencies to determine policy and blend habitat protection with recreation. Most of the 280,000-acre Santa Rosa and San Jacinto Mountains National Monument is off-limits to dogs, and protection of bighorn sheep is the primary reason. But the city of Palm Desert has designated a few select trails within the base of the monument for multi-use recreation, including hikers with dogs, equestrians, and mountain bikers.

Sweeping switchbacks across the arid landscape

Homestead Trail and the unmarked Hopalong Cassidy and Gabby Hayes Trail make up the continuous thread that links Homme-Adams Park to Cahuilla Hills Park on this out-and-back hike across a canyon.

A split-rail fence at the foot of Homestead Trail in Homme-Adams Park defines the flat off-leash area (voice control) of Sonoran sand sprinkled with creosote and burrow bush along with desert lavender. For older dogs not keen on uphill treks or rugged terrain, this patch of desert scents is enough adventure to replay in their dreams. The sheltered picnic area at the north end complete with water to keep pooches hydrated is another thoughtful touch for dogs playing on the flats while their more energetic bow-wow buddies take to the hills.

The hike to Cahuilla Hills Park begins with a cardio crank up Homestead Trail next to the information kiosk just beyond the palm grove and picnic shelter. At 0.3 mile you come to Engstrom Point and another sheltered picnic table, water, and trashcan. This is a pleasant viewpoint overlooking the valley. On a cool day, even older dogs and not-so-fit Fidos might enjoy the short sprint to the viewpoint to share a midday collation with their human. The remainder of the hike is across an arid, sparsely vegetated landscape interrupted by veins of seasonal runoff. In spite of the less-than-hospitable environment, there is a Spartan, rugged beauty to this hike and there's a sense of freedom that comes with such vast openness.

At 0.6 mile you come to an unmarked trail junction. The left trail winds up to a bridge with a cross. Although there are no signs stating that dogs are prohibited and it is not uncommon to see dogs hoofing it up that trail, this is not one of the designated "dog-friendly" trails. Turn right to continue the hike to Cahuilla Hills Park.

The narrow trail bends around to the left and undulates along the canyon hillside with a winding, gradual descent. The tennis courts and a parking lot in the distance beyond the large water tank are the landmarks at Cahuilla Hills Park. Mornings can be busy, with hikers, joggers, and dogs of all sizes in both directions. This narrow trail provides a good opportunity for you and your four-legged pal to practice trail etiquette and stepping aside to yield to the uphill traffic.

At 1.5 miles you come to an unmarked trail junction. Bear right on the trail and continue in the direction of the tennis courts.

You arrive at Cahuilla Hills Park at 1.8 miles. Vault toilets, water, and picnic tables provide a comfortable rest stop before going back to the trailhead the way you came.

Miles and Directions

0.0 Start from the north end of Homme-Adams Park parking area and walk toward the palm grove to Homestead Trailhead.

0.3 Arrive at Engstrom Point.

0.6 Come to an unmarked trail junction. Turn right on the trail.

1.5 Come to an unmarked trail junction. Bear right to continue toward the tennis courts ahead at Cahuilla Hills Park.

1.8 Arrive at Cahuilla Hills Park. Take time to share a snack with your dog and offer your dog water before going back to the trailhead the way you came. Elevation: 332 feet. **GPS:** N33 42.86' / W116 24.03'

3.6 Arrive back at the trailhead.

Creature Comforts

Fueling Up

Café des Beaux Arts, 76-640 El Paseo, Palm Desert 92260; (760) 346-0669; cafedesbeauxarts.com. The corner French bistro where palms meet Paris in Palm Desert's highbrow shopping district.

BB's at the River restaurant at River Mall, 71-800 CA 111, Rancho Mirage 92270; (760) 62-9800; bbsattheriver.com. Dog-friendly patio for breakfast, lunch, dinner, and happy hour. Fresh California cuisine favorites including burgers named after iconic California characters.

Resting Up

Best Western Plus Palm Desert, 74695 CA 111, Palm Desert 92260; (760) 340-4441; bestwestern.com. Pet fee.

Homme-Adams Park to Cahuilla Hills Park

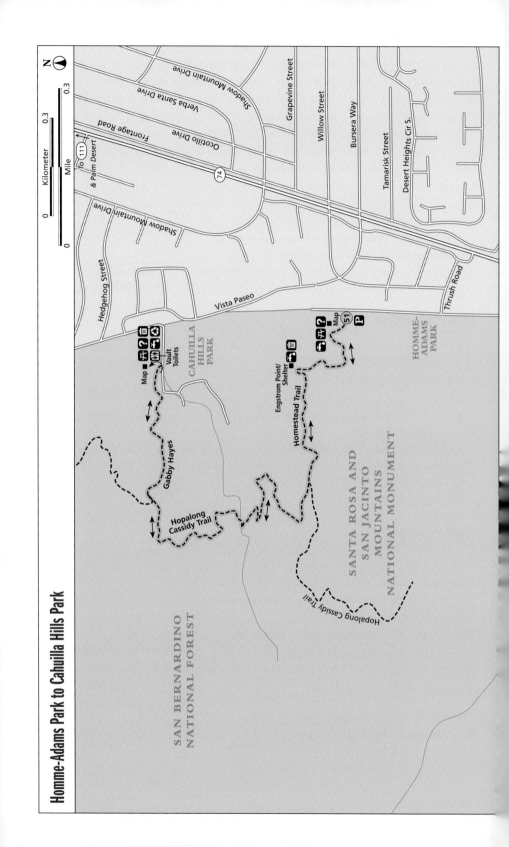

N

0   Kilometer   0.3
0   Mile   0.3

To 111
& Palm Desert

Shadow Mountain Drive
Frontage Road
Ocotillo Drive
Verba Santa Drive
Shadow Mountain Drive

74

Grapevine Street
Willow Street
Bursera Way
Tamarisk Street
Desert Heights Cir S.

Thrush Road

Hedgehog Street
Vista Paseo

CAHUILLA HILLS PARK

Map
Vault Toilets

Gabby Hayes

Hopalong Cassidy Trail

Engstrom Point/ Shelter

Homestead Trail

Map
51
P

HOMME-ADAMS PARK

SAN BERNARDINO NATIONAL FOREST

SANTA ROSA AND SAN JACINTO MOUNTAINS NATIONAL MONUMENT

Hopalong Cassidy Trail

Omni Rancho Las Palmas Resort, 41000 Bob Hope Dr., Rancho Mirage 92270; (760) 568-2727; omnirancholaspalmas.com. If your dog is less than 50 pounds, he'll think the $100 pet fee per stay is worth the Spanish villa ambiance for resting and dining after his hike.

Campgrounds

Emerald Desert RV Resort, 76000 Frank Sinatra Dr., Palm Desert 92211; (877) 624-4140; emeralddesert.com. This is luxury if you have a trailer or an RV. Pooch's favorite amenity is the two grassy dog runs where well-mannered canine snowbirds love to play and socialize off leash.

Puppy Paws and Golden Years

Santa Rosa and San Jacinto National Monument Visitor Center, 51-500 CA 74, Palm Desert 92260; (760) 862-9984. The ADA-accessible Ed Hastey Desert Garden Trail is an enchanting 0.25-mile-long stroll. The brick path meanders among identified native plants. This is the only dog-friendly trail at the visitor center. The small, round wood table and chairs by the palm trees make an idyllic spot for a picnic. The visitor center is an excellent resource for learning about the local ecology and the national monument trails.

Ramadas *(arbors) provide shady respite along the trail.*

Appendix A: Day Hike and Campout Checklists

Day Hike Checklist

- Collar, harness, bandanna, leash, permanent I.D. tag with home/cell number and temporary tag
- Health and vaccination certificate
- Collapsible water bowl and water supply in metal or plastic (32-ounce bottle for half-day hike (under 4 hours) and 2-quart bottle for longer hikes. Bring 8 ounces of water per dog per hour or 3 miles of hiking, in addition to water for you.
- Water purifier for full-day hike
- Kibbles for him and snacks for you at meal times on the trail and extra protein snacks for energy boost for both. Yummiest treats for "recalls."
- Plastic resealable bags for carrying food, treats, medication, first-aid essentials. They can be converted into food and water bowls as well as poop-scoop bags to carry waste out if necessary.
- Biodegradable poop-scoop bags
- Booties for him; sturdy waterproof hiking footwear for you
- Dog packs (optional)
- Reflective vest (if hiking during hunting season)
- Life vest (if planning to be on water)
- Flyers for a lost dog
- Flea and tick application prior to hike
- Bug repellent in sealed plastic bag
- Sunscreen for you and your dog (dog's tips of ears)
- Sunhat and glasses for you
- Wire grooming brush to help remove stickers and foxtails from your pet's coat
- Extra clothing: sweater or coat/raincoat for a thin-coated dog; breathable long-sleeved sweater, rain-repelling windbreaker for you
- Extra-large, heavy-duty plastic garbage bags (good to sit on and make a handy poncho in the rain or line inside of your backpack)
- Pocketknife (Swiss Army–type knife that includes additional tools)
- Flashlight
- Matches or cigarette lighter and emergency fire starter
- Space blanket
- Whistle
- USGS map, compass, GPS (extra batteries for electronic devices and flashlight)

- Camera
- First-aid kit (including phone numbers for National Animal Poison Control Center and your veterinarian)

Backpacking Checklist

Dog Necessities

All items on day hike checklist, plus the following:

- Extra leash or rope
- Dog pack (optional)
- Doggie bedroll (foam sleeping pad or inflatable pad with waterproof side)
- Dog's favorite chew toy
- Dog food (number of days on the trail times 3 meals a day)
- Additional water in a 2-quart bottle
- Dog snacks (enough for 6 rest stops per hiking day)
- Nylon tie-out line in camp (expandable leash can be extra leash and tie-out rope)

Human Necessities

- Tent with rain fly (large enough for you and your dog to sleep inside)
- Clothing (moisture-wicking socks, wind/raingear, gloves, fleece or knit hat, long pants, wicking top, fleece top)
- Camp stove and fuel bottle
- Iodine tablets (backup water purifier)
- Food: lightweight, nutritious carbs and proteins—instant oatmeal, energy bars, granola cereal, almond or peanut butter, dried fruits and nuts, dark chocolate for energy boosts, pasta, rice, canned tuna, dehydrated backpacking meals, tea bags or cocoa packets.
- Extra garbage bags (use one in your backpack as a liner to keep contents dry in case of rain)
- Bear-proof food canisters
- Pepper spray (if hiking in bear country)

Note: Always let someone at home know where you are going and when you plan to return.

Appendix B: Trail Emergencies and First Aid

Planning, a common-sense approach, and a leash will help prevent most mishaps on the trail. Keep your dog on leash when:

- Hiking in territory known for its higher concentration of specific hazards (bears, mountain lions, snakes, skunks)
- Crossing fast-moving streams
- Negotiating narrow mountainside trails
- Hiking in wind and snow (dogs can become disoriented and lose their way)

If your dog gets into trouble, here are some basic first-aid treatments you can administer until you can get him to a vet.

Bleeding from Cuts or Wounds

1. Remove any obvious foreign object.
2. Rinse the area with warm water or 3 percent hydrogen peroxide.
3. Cover the wound with clean gauze or cloth and apply firm, direct pressure over the wound for about 10 minutes to allow clotting to occur and bleeding to stop.
4. Place a nonstick pad or gauze over the wound and bandage with gauze wraps (the stretchy, clingy type). For a paw wound, cover the bandaging with a bootie. (An old sock with duct tape on the bottom is a good bootie substitute. Use adhesive tape around the sock to prevent it from slipping off. Be careful not to strangle circulation.)

Frostbite

Frostbite is the freezing of a body part exposed to extreme cold. Tips of ears and pads are the most vulnerable.

1. Remove your dog from the cold.
2. Apply a warm compress to the affected area without friction or pressure.

Heatstroke

Heatstroke occurs when a dog's body temperature is rising rapidly above 104 degrees F and panting is ineffective to regulate temperature.

Don't put your dog at risk during hot weather.

1. Get your dog out of the sun and begin reducing body temperature (no lower than 103 degrees F) by applying water-soaked towels on the head (to cool the brain), chest, abdomen, and feet.

2. Let your dog stand in a pond, lake, or stream while you gently pour water on her. Avoid icy water—it can chill her. Swabbing the footpads with alcohol will help.

3. Carrying an Instant Cold Pack can save your dog's life if caught on a trail without water to cool your dog.

Hypothermia

Hypothermia occurs when a dog's body temperature drops below 95 degrees F because of overexposure to cold weather.

1. Take the dog indoors or into a sheltered area where you can make a fire.

2. Wrap him in a blanket, towel, sleeping bag, your clothing, or whatever you have available.

3. Wrap him in warm towels or place warm water bottles in a towel next to him.

4. Hold him close to you for body heat.

Insect Bites

Bee stings and spider bites may cause itching, swelling, and hives. If the stinger is still present, scrape it off with your nail or tweezers at the base away from the point of entry. (Pressing the stinger or trying to pick it from the top can release more toxin.) Apply a cold compress to the area and spray it with a topical analgesic like Benadryl spray to relieve the itch and pain. As a precaution, carry an over-the-counter antihistamine (such as Benadryl) and ask your vet about the appropriate dosage before you leave, in case your dog has an extreme allergic reaction with excessive swelling.

Skunked

When your dog gets skunked, a potent, smelly cloud of spray burns his eyes and makes his mouth foam. The smell can make you gag, and contact with the spray on your dog's coat can give your skin a tingling, burning sensation. Apply de-skunking shampoo as soon as possible.

De-Skunking Shampoo Mix

1 quart hydrogen peroxide

¼ cup baking soda

1 tablespoon dishwashing detergent

Put on rubber gloves and thoroughly wet your dog, apply mixture, and let stand for 15 minutes; rinse and repeat as needed.

FIRST-AID KIT CHECKLIST FOR FIDO

- First-aid book
- Alcohols swaps for dog's footpads and Instant Cold Pack to cool head, neck, chest, and abdomen (dog or human) if caught in an emergency heatstroke situation on a dry trail.
- Muzzle—the most loving dogs can snap and bite when in pain. Muzzles come in different styles and sizes to fit all dog nose shapes.
- Ascriptin (buffered aspirin)—older dogs in particular may be stiff and sore at the end of a hike or a backpacking excursion. Consult your vet on the appropriate dosage.
- Antidiarrheal agents and GI protectants: Pepto-Bismol, 1–3 ml/kg/day; Kaopectate, 1–2 ml/kg every 2–6 hours
- Indigestion and stomach upset: Pepcid (famotidine) decreases gastric acid secretions, 0.1–2 mg/kg every 12–24 hours
- Scissors (rounded tips) to trim hair around a wound
- Hydrogen peroxide (3%) to disinfect surface abrasions and wounds
- Antiseptic ointment
- Gauze pads and gauze
- Clingy and elastic bandages
- Sock or bootie to protect a wounded foot
- Duct tape to wrap around the sole of sock used as a bootie
- Tweezers to remove ticks, needles, or foreign objects in a wound
- Styptic powder for bleeding
- Rectal thermometer
- Hydrocortisone spray to relieve plant rashes and stings
- Diphenhydramine (Benadryl) dosed at 1mg/lb 2–3 times daily can relieve some allergy reactions exasperated by the heat
- Lemon juice for quick rinse (recipe for skunking shampoo mix)
- Tape your veterinarian's telephone number and the ASPCA National Animal Poison Control Center, (888) 426-4435, inside the kit.

Sore Muscles

1. Rest your dog.
2. Apply cold-water compresses to tight muscle areas to reduce inflammation.
3. Administer Ascriptin-buffered aspirin (check with your vet on dosage for your dog's breed and weight).

Venomous Bites

1. Keep your dog calm (activity stimulates the absorption of venom).
2. Rinse the area with water, and transport your dog to the nearest vet.

Cardiopulmonary Resuscitation

Check with your veterinarian or local humane society for pet CPR classes.

Appendix C: Wildlife Conflicts

On the trail, you and your dog are in someone else's home. Be the kind of guest you would want in your house. Be considerate of those who live there, disturb nothing as you pass through, and take only the memory of the experience and photographs of the beauty that moved you.

Protecting Wildlife and Your Dog

The surest way to avoid wildlife conflicts is to keep your dog on a leash. Dogs chasing deer deplete the animal of survival energy and can cause debilitating injury to both the pursued and the pursuer.

Curious dogs nosing around off leash risk incurring the pungent wrath of a skunk, the painful quills of a porcupine, or a bite from an ill-tempered rattlesnake. All are responding defensively to a perceived threat and are not lurking to attack you or your dog.

Birds nesting in meadows and low brush are vulnerable to roaming dogs in the spring, and fawns can fall prey to your dog's primal instincts. These animals are not hosting you and your dog in their home by choice, so be respectful guests.

Some trails cross cattle- and sheep-grazing land. Know that a dog harassing stock can be shot.

Keep your dog on leash for the first 30 minutes of a hike to give him a chance to absorb some of the new sights, smells, and sounds that might make him go berserk with excitement fresh out of the starting gate and make him more likely to burn off excess energy chasing wildlife or trying to entice cattle in a game of tag.

Preventing Encounters

With regard to predators, the potential for being attacked by a wild animal in Southern California is extremely low compared to many other natural hazards. Wildlife sightings are a privilege. Mountain lions and bears, when given the option, generally prefer avoidance to confrontation with humans unless you are a threat to them or their young.

Coyotes and bobcats are just as elusive and usually find rodents satisfying enough. But small dogs could be considered tender morsels and should be kept on leash especially at dawn and dusk when predators are most likely to shop for food.

Development and human intrusion are at the core of the encounter problems. Encroachment on habitat and more hikers in the backcountry have exposed bears and coyotes to human food and garbage. Animals accustomed to easy meals become brazen and can pose a threat to human safety. Sadly, humans create these "problem" animals. Destruction, not relocation, is their fate. There's a good reason for the "Don't feed wildlife" campaign.

This is not to say that a dog responsive to voice control should not enjoy tagging along and bounding with joy off leash, but be informed about the area where you plan to hike, and when in doubt make your presence known with a small bell attached to your pack, dog harness, or walking stick. Stay on the trail and talk or hum to avoid surprising a bear in the berry bushes or startling a big cat from his nap.

Bear Safety

When it comes to odor, in bear country the motto is "less is safer." Pack all food items (human and dog) and any other odorous items in airtight resealable bags. Dispose of all items with food smells in airtight bags, in bear-proof storage containers. Clean your dishes and pet bowls as quickly as possible so food smells do not float through the forest as a dinner invitation to the local bears. Some national forests and wilderness areas require that campers use plastic, portable bear-resistant food canisters. These canisters (some collapsible) are available for sale and rent at sporting goods stores and some ranger stations.

If you see a bear in the distance, stop, stay calm, and don't run. Keep your dog close to your side on leash. You should feel awe rather than panic. Walk a wide upwind detour so the animal can get your scent, and make loud banging or clanging noises as you leave the area. If the bear is at closer range, the same principles apply while you keep your eye on the bear and back down the trail slowly if the terrain doesn't allow you to negotiate a detour.

Avoid sudden movements that could spook or provoke the bear. Be cool, slow, but deliberate as you make your retreat.

BEAR FACTS

- Bears can run, swim, and climb trees.
- Bears have good vision, excellent hearing, and a superior sense of smell.
- Bears are curious and attracted to food smells.
- Bears can be out at any time of day but are most active in the coolness of dawn and dusk and after dark.
- Bears and wild animals in general prefer anonymity. If they know you are out there, they will avoid your path.

Mountain Lions

Trailheads on public land in Southern California typically have signs to make you aware if you are hiking in mountain-lion country.

- Keep your dog on leash on the trail.
- Keep your dog in the tent at night.
- Seeing doesn't mean attacking. If you come across a mountain lion, stay far enough away to give it the opportunity to avoid you.
- Do not approach or provoke the lion.

- Walk away slowly and maintain eye contact. Running will stimulate the lion's predatory instinct to chase and hunt.
- Make yourself big by putting your arms above your head and waving them. Use your jacket or walking stick above your head to appear bigger. Do not bend down or make any motion that will make you look or sound like easy prey.
- Shout and make noise.
- If necessary, walking sticks can be weapons, as can rocks or anything you can get your hands on to fight back. (For more information on hiking in mountain lion country, refer to Mountain Lion Alert by Steven Torres [Falcon Publishing, 1997].)

Mountain Lion Facts

- Mountain lions are elusive, and preying on humans is uncharacteristic.
- Mountain lions are most active at dawn and dusk and usually hunt at night.
- They are solitary and secretive and require a vegetated habitat for camouflage while they stalk prey.
- Their meal of choice is big game (deer, bighorn sheep, and elk). In the absence of game, however, they can make a meal of domestic livestock and small mammals including small pets.
- They feed on what they kill. An unattended dog in camp is far more appetizing than his kibble.

Snakes

Southern California's warm climate, chaparral vegetation, and desert landscape make good rattlesnake habitat. It is common to see signs posted at the trailheads reminding hikers that they are entering rattlesnake habitat.

Most dogs have an instinctive aversion to anything that slithers and will jump away at first sight, sound, or touch. Snakebites are usually the result of stepping on a snake unknowingly rather than conscious provocation. Most snakebites occur on the nose or front legs and can be lethal to a small or young dog. If taken to the vet quickly, larger adult dogs will survive the majority of bites. Ask your veterinarian about the snake vaccine. It can help in response to snakebite treatment. Ask your veterinarian or local dog club about snake avoidance classes in your area. (See Appendix B for treatment of venomous bites.) A leash is the best tool to keep your dog safe.

Appendix D:
Sources for Pooch Gear, Useful Websites, and Books

Visit petfoodexpress.com to locate store locations in Southern California. Find quality food, treats, gear, accessories, and toys. Some locations have vaccination clinics and affordable wellness centers. The self-wash pet stations are clean and well appointed.

Hiking Gear and Accessories for Your Dog

- wolfpacks.com
- ruffwear.com
- thedogoutdoors.com
- hotdogcollars.com
- petmountain.com
- whitepineoutfitters.com

Travel Information

- naturedogs.com: source for dog-friendly hiking trails
- bringfido.com: source for dog-friendly lodging and dining
- dogtrekker.com: source for dog-friendly lodging, dining, and activities

Campground Reservations

- reserveamerica.com: campground reservations including state parks
- recreation.gov: public land campground reservations including national parks and national forests

Maps and Guides

- natgeomaps.com
- store.usgs.gov
- wilderness.net: source for purchasing topographic maps and links to wilderness information

Companies that Deliver Rental Trailers to Campgrounds:

- adventureincamping.com
- sierravacationtrailerrentals.net
- 101rvrentals.com
- luv2camp.com

- campnstyle.com
- rvrentalssandiego.com
- camperrentalsusa.com
- sierra-teardrops.com

Helpful Reads

On the Trail and Road

Backpacker Trailside Navigation: Map and Compass by Backpacker magazine, Guilford, CT: Globe Pequot Press, 2010.

Using a GPS by *Backpacker* magazine, Guilford, CT: Globe Pequot Press, 2010.

Traveling with Your Pet: The AAA PetBook, 17th ed. Heathrow, FL: AAA Publishing. (**Note:** Membership in the American Automobile Association [AAA] gives you free access to United States and Canada tour books and public land campground maps. The Southern California book includes a list and map of national, state, and other recreational areas, including a chart indicating which have hiking trails that allow pets on leash. Contact 800-JOIN-AAA; aaa.com/petbook.)

The Dog Lover's Companion to California, 7th ed., by Maria Goodavage, Avalon Travel Publishing, 2011.

First Aid

Field Guide: Dog First Aid—Emergency Care of the Outdoor Dog, Randy Acker, DVM, Belgrade, MT: Wilderness Adventure Press; 2009 (note: pocket-size for your first-aid kit).

Training Tips

The Focused Puppy, Deborah Jones and Judy Keller, South Hadley, MA: Clean Run Productions, 2010.

The Wolf Within, David Alderson, Hoboken, NJ: Howell Book House, 1998.

Nutrition

Not Fit for a Dog, Dr. Michael W. Fox, Fresno, CA: Quill Driver Books, 2009.

Hike Index

About the Authors

David Mullally, a native Californian, and Quebec-born Linda Mullally have been a husband-and-wife team adventuring around the globe and co-creating with her writing and his photography for more than thirty years. He, an attorney/photographer, and she, a travel columnist/author and "doggie nanny," share their passion for travel, hiking, and dogs through articles, books, and multi-media presentations. Linda's *Monterey Herald* travel column "Away We Go" inspires readers to go explore the world's bounty of natural and cultural treasures on bike and on foot. David and Linda share life at their California basecamps in Carmel on the Central Coast and Mammoth Lakes in the Eastern Sierra with Gypsy, a perky, trail-happy fourteen-year-old Queensland/Chihuahua mix, and Gem, a year-old Siberian husky and newest member of the pack. *Best Dog Hikes Southern California* is their seventh book, with several titles in progress.